Run Britain

www.penguin.co.uk

Also by Nick Butter

Running the World

Run Britain

My World-Record-Breaking Adventure to
Run Every Mile of the British Coastline

Nick Butter

with contributions from Andy Swain

bantam

TRANSWORLD PUBLISHERS
Penguin Random House, One Embassy Gardens,
8 Viaduct Gardens, London SW11 7BW
www.penguin.co.uk

Transworld is part of the Penguin Random House group of companies
whose addresses can be found at global.penguinrandomhouse.com

First published in Great Britain in 2023 by Bantam
an imprint of Transworld Publishers

A CIP catalogue record for this book
is available from the British Library.

ISBN 9781787636415

Typeset in 11/14.75pt Times NR MT Std by Jouve (UK), Milton Keynes
Printed and bound in Great Britain by Clays Ltd, Elcograf S.p.A.

The authorized representative in the EEA is Penguin Random House Ireland,
Morrison Chambers, 32 Nassau Street, Dublin D02 YH68.

Penguin Random House is committed to a sustainable future
for our business, our readers and our planet. This book is made
from Forest Stewardship Council® certified paper.

The following pages are dedicated to every person who shared a footstep with me on every long day spent snaking slowly around the coast – days made richer by the smiles and energy of so many. Thank you for bringing warmth on the cold, wet days and refuelling me with your boundless enthusiasm and laughter. The Great British spirit is alive and well . . . and, even better, running!

To Andy, to Nikki, and to the team. My legs moved me, but your dedication, heart and patience carried me, hour after hour, day after day, to the finishing post.

And, finally, to our wonderful country. Great Britain, you truly are great!

Contents

Author's Note

There are two key words that sum up my general philosophy of life.

Time and Kindness.

It's my belief that the most valuable commodity in our lives is time. We all have our own circumstances and our own priorities, but every decision we make is governed by time. No matter your wealth, your background or your opportunities, time and the passing of it is something we all share. When we sleep, when we eat, or when we brush our teeth, time passes. You cannot cheat it. But each of us can individually choose how to spend it.

It is an unavoidable fact of life that our time on this planet is continuously reducing. And rather than shy away from that idea and think of it as morbid, I would encourage you to embrace it. Let it smother you with impatience, let it awaken you. Let it push you towards opportunities and steer you around conformities. Your time credits are yours to spend how you wish. How are you spending yours?

When I do eventually run out of time I would like to know that I used it well. That I didn't frivolously and mindlessly fumble through the hours and days without asking more of myself, discovering more about the people around me and the infinite beauty of the planet on which we live. I want to invest my time, not just spend it.

If each day equals one time credit, then I invested over a hundred credits running around the coastline of Britain. In exchange, I gained memories to treasure, and a fresh perspective; I learnt lessons, and forged deep emotional bonds that are only earned through this particular type of investment.

As for kindness, it is the greatest gift we have. Unlike time, each of us can determine the amount of kindness in our lives. Kindness is a multiplier. We can choose to be kind to others, and that kindness spreads like ripples in a pond, and is often returned. In turn, the feelings it generates enhance our time. During this journey I was gifted packets of kindness daily. Others were investing their time and kindness in me.

My hope, as you read these pages, is that you'll see that time, although constant and uniform for us all, if invested wisely, will bring you unparalleled rewards.

Are you spending your credits or investing them?

I invested 128 credits to run Britain. Like all worthwhile investments, it was a risk. But without risk there can be no reward, and the experiences and friendships I gained in return were more than I could ever have dreamed of.

My eternal thanks to all who invested their time and kindness to make this journey and this book possible.

A thousand times, thank you.

Introduction

I couldn't take my eyes off the lion.

She sat totally still and to attention, her hind legs neat, back straight, eyes soft but wide and fixed on mine. She was mid-distance between the toffee-coloured sand in the foreground and the frothy, ink-black waters of the English Channel behind her. It was a beautifully still night. Nothing but sand, ocean, sky, and lion. She sat and stared me down from less than 20 feet away. Her left ear stood tall, cocked to the heavens, sharp and unwavering. She had an air of calm and concentrated elegance. Must have been young, but old enough to hunt, I thought – and, importantly, old enough to spot the weak. And weak I was. Very.

I was limping along the Jurassic Coast of Dorset, approaching Bournemouth Pier. It was 1 a.m., towards the final stages of day 6. It's fair to say that it's rare to see a lion on the beaches of the south coast of Britain – some would say unthinkable – but no, I saw her all right.

'Chris, do you see her?'

'Who?'

'That lion with the one big ear – she's beautiful!'

I pointed to the sand, but she was gone.

Naturally, Chris, my brother, who was running alongside me at the time, raised an eyebrow combined with a frown, along with a slight smile in the corner of his mouth, not sure what to make of what I'd said.

I was deep in the caverns of my own mind. A hallucination, of course, but it felt as real as anything I'd ever seen. I smiled back to him, realizing that I must be in a pretty bad way to have seen a lion on a beach on which I'd spent much of my childhood. My mind felt mushy, my body barely standing. With a shake of my head in an attempt to fling the nonsense from my thoughts, and a squint of confusion as I looked down at my feet again, I stumbled on into the night with Chris by my side to steady me, making outrageously slow progress – so much so in fact that at one point two drunks staggered past us despite leaning backwards and weaving all over the place.

Chris had come to join me for the final few miles of day 6, which started in Portland and finished at Bournemouth Pier. He met me at the short chain ferry that links Studland with Sandbanks. He had his bike with him, having cycled from the hospital after his night shift. He'd obviously received a call from the team and been told that I was struggling. He was planning to come and meet us somewhere, likely near his home in Bournemouth, but neither of us had expected me to be limping with poles, and for him to be pushing his bike, with one eye on my health. He'd just finished twelve hours as a nurse in A&E, and I was on the verge of becoming his next patient.

I was in way over my head, having decided to attempt to run around Britain's mainland coastline – 5,240 miles – in a hundred days.

Running is a solo endeavour, and spending this much time on your own is hard for some. For me, it's utter peace – at least it is when I'm not on the verge of collapse and being haunted by beastly apparitions. Usually, the rhythm of running helps to settle my thoughts and order my head. With my mind at rest, my senses are heightened, sharpening further with every step. The church bells in small villages, the jangle of keys as a commuter walks to their car to begin their day, the distant trudge of a tractor. I treasure running in the early mornings – just birdsong and a rising sun signalling the beginning of a new day, my inner thoughts and regular steps a metronome of peaceful, patient progress. As I write this, I can still hear the sounds and take in the smells of Britain as I traversed its streets and footpaths, morning to night, day after day. The first cry of a seagull above a harbour, the smell of freshly baked bread wafting up a sleeping high street, the tang of cut grass and snatches of passing conversation – all remain as vivid as the day I encountered them, just as the infinite patterns of ruptured and fractured tarmac remain ingrained on the soles of my feet, an indelible imprint of the journey.

Clouds became a daily obsession. Some were fluffy, bright white, light and gentle. Others streaked and smeared across the sky. Long, thin and wispy ones would narrow and tail off to nothing, or curl and swirl with the wind. Others, heavy with shades of grey and black, would loom on the horizon as they brewed a concoction of lightning and thunder. At times, a carpet of cloud would vanish, quite literally into thin air, opening the tarpaulin above to nothing but a palette of pastels, baby blues with flashes of sharp white sun flickering through the gaps in the trees. When you do nothing but run for twelve hours a day, every day, for four months, you become highly attuned to the weather. Mother Nature manipulated my soul and spirit daily, as both my close companion and my feared foe.

As my unwilling and increasingly frail body heaved my bruised and disfigured feet into my socks and then my shoes, morning after morning, my body groaned daily for just a few more minutes of bed. But as Britain slept I began another day that wouldn't end until the miles were covered. One road, one shop, one street, one pub, one path, one roundabout, one wrong turn – one step at a time.

Most mornings my mind remained in a state of slumber as I plodded from crest to combe and combe to crest, again and again. My body defaulted to autopilot, flopping from foot to foot, doing what it knew well, while I was frequently lost in a dozy, melodic haze. The progress was slow – tremendously slow – but slow would do. Forward motion was enough.

This is a story of places, moments and emotions strung together through footsteps. There are so many forms in which I remember this journey. I had battles with the weather, and naturally many with myself. There was physical and mental torment and torture. I had fleeting conversations with temporary new friends every day. Like an old cliff crumbling into the sea, I endured the ravages of time and distance, worn down in mind and body by challenge and circumstance. And of course I formed a new type of bond with Britain and its glorious coastline, its natural beauty and the communities it harbours.

Britain is a magical place in so many ways. Firstly, our little island turns out to be not so little when you run around it. The people, scenery, wildlife and the sense of history surprised me in every way, from the selfless support of strangers to birds and plants that I'd never noticed before, and breathtaking places I'd never thought to visit. It opened my eyes to life in a vastly more profound way than I could have hoped. I had placed Britain in a box of 'just Britain' – familiar, everyday and, if I'm honest, a little unexciting. How wrong I was.

This book serves as a long and winding thank-you note to Britain, to nature, to freedom and opportunity, and to the select few who patiently ushered me towards the finishing post: to Andy, to Nikki, to my team, to the running community, to donors and sponsors, and to everyone whose small acts of support and kindness cheered me on.

Each of the eleven and a half million steps that formed the journey combine to make a patchwork of memories. Each small step was unique; fleeting, yet also permanent. Without every one of those individual steps, the destination would not have been reached. It's these 128 days, meandering painfully around the British coast, that I'd like to share with you. And that is not a typo, as it would have appeared to me at the outset of the journey: I completed the run in 128 days – twenty-eight more than my initial target.

But first, let's rewind exactly ten days before my encounter with that Jurassic Coast lion, before the torture, before the pain . . . I am sitting in my PJs, tucking into a hearty casserole, smiling, laughing, excitement bubbling up through me. I know what lies around the corner, but at this point it is out of sight and out of mind. Mouthful after mouthful of delicious dinner, with family, with friends, a world away from the isolated suffering of what I am about to endure.

1

Final Preparations

CORNWALL

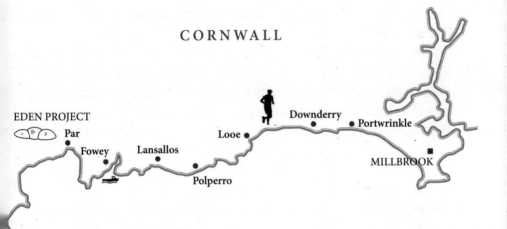

On 15 April 2021 the headlines in all the major newspapers and on TV news channels were about the Covid lockdown finally coming to an end. Masks were still required, and distancing was advised rather than enforced, but restaurants and businesses were open as normal. Britain was free – and I could legally run, with other people, around the country.

A few days earlier, my good friend Andy had arrived at my parents' place in Cranborne, Dorset. Andy has run many marathons with me around the world. We originally met through 'real' work in the banking sector about a decade earlier, and have bonded through a life of running. From what started as an occasional hello in passing, we began to venture out on extended lunch breaks for long runs, and eventually formed a solid friendship. We both then left the corporate world, for anything less mundane, Andy only recently having taken the plunge to turn his hand to business. He's annoyingly talented at making more or less anything, from small robots made of old electrical components to bigger, more conventional things like extensions and theatre sets. I didn't want him for his construction skills, though – I needed Andy for his loyalty, his pragmatism, and his ability to dig deep when the going gets tough. Andy ran nineteen countries with me on my 2018–19 Running the World expedition, and we bonded further. Run Britain would bond us like brothers. We just didn't know it yet.

With only about two weeks until Go Day – Saturday, 17 April – I'd got in touch with Andy and asked if he'd be my right-hand man for the attempt to run around the British coast in a hundred days. I needed someone to drive the van, our portable HQ, which was to be our support vehicle as well as our home during the expedition. I knew I would also need help with both the physical and mental struggles of the trip, as well as with logistics and basic supply concerns like food, water and suitable places to rest and sleep along the way.

My childhood bedroom at my parents' house, as well as somewhere I still occasionally sleep, has become home to my running collection, and there, surrounded by medals and mementos from countless marathons and running events, books by the runners and adventurers who have inspired me, piles of running kit, and souvenirs from all over the world, I sat down to call Andy. He answered, and once he'd removed his dust mask, unmuffling his voice, I could hear that he was in an echoey room – a sign that he was at work in a half-renovated building. Once he'd finished coughing up some of the building dust he likes to inhale to keep his lungs in tip-top running condition, we covered pleasantries, then I got to the real reason for my call. Once I'd finished running through what would be involved, there was a pause while Andy took on board the extent of what I was asking of him. He said he was interested in principle, but would have to think it over before deciding.

If I'm totally honest, I didn't expect Andy to say yes to supporting Run Britain. I could offer him only a pittance for his time, and it meant him giving up his normal duties, turning down work, being away from his partner for over three months and, most foolishly, looking after me. I desperately wanted him to say yes, and if I could have afforded more I would have offered it, but funds were tight. They always are on these kinds of hastily arranged expeditions.

Andy called me back a day later and confirmed he would indeed be there as my right-hand man. I was over the moon. I played it cool on the phone, but I knew what it meant. I had the best person in my corner to see this through. It gave me a huge boost of confidence.

Throughout this book are snippets of Andy's diary, which he wrote daily while on the road. Andy must have a voice in this book – and not just out of some polite sense of inclusion: this journey was truly felt and experienced by both of us. Everything I felt, he felt. The physical side perhaps differed, but this was without a doubt as much of a sufferfest for him as it was for me. Without his heart, soul and dedication, the challenge would have fallen apart within days. That is not an exaggeration. He really did suffer, as you'll read.

Start Line: T Minus 96 Hours

Andy made the short train ride from Bristol to Salisbury, where I met
him at the station. As he walked out through the doors, we exchanged
a familiar look: here we go again. We were some steps away from each
other, but from the curl at the corners of his mouth I could tell he was
smiling. We were excited. So many times I'd met him in far-flung countries and seen on his face the same eager anticipation to share a mini
adventure together, but also knowing that misadventure was inevitable.
It would be joyous, but naturally there would be unavoidable challenges too. This is, of course, what adventure, and indeed life, is all
about. And we knew it. But whatever happened, to be able to embark
on this journey was a privilege.

My crow's-feet wrinkles and weathered face mean that, side by side,
Andy and I look roughly the same age. If anything, I look a few years
his senior. In reality, as frustrating as it is, Andy is forty-six and I'm
only thirty-two. (Needless to say, I've started moisturizing now.) He's a
little shorter than me, just about 6 feet, with a slight build that's kept
in shape through decent running mileage. He has a narrow face and
floppy, nonchalant brown hair. They say the eyes are the windows to
the soul – this is true with Andy. He does a good job at keeping a lid on
his outward-facing mood, but get to know him well and his eyes betray
him, letting slip his true feelings. Andy grew up in Devon, by the sea,
and this is evident in his slow saunter and relaxed dress sense. Jumper,
jeans, shoes with laces undone. Not untidy, but not smart either.

It should also be noted that Andy is a notoriously light packer – he
only ever travels with a small backpack. Whatever size you're thinking,
think smaller – the kind of bag Ryanair would allow you to carry three
of, in an overhead locker, on a standard ticket. Even though this was a
hundred-day challenge, he still only had the one small bag draped over
his shoulder, plus a lightweight waterproof, and old scruffy shoes without laces. Classic Andy.

Once back at the ranch, we sat around my parents' kitchen table,
caught up a little, and began to talk shop. We had a couple of days till
the drive from Dorset to Cornwall, which had become our start/finish

line following a series of phone calls with Sky News and the Eden Project. This was a small piece of the massive puzzle we'd had to assemble in a matter of weeks, having decided to embark on this voyage at the very last minute once we had some confidence that Covid restrictions would be lifted.

In my folks' rustic kitchen, we were gathered around a casserole prepared brilliantly by my mum, who seems to be able to rustle up a feast as if from nowhere. I was averagely grateful at the time, but am so much more so in hindsight: it turned out to be one of my last great meals for months.

At the table, with dogs roaming around under our feet, the doors open to the garden and the gentle breeze swaying distant trees, we were in good spirits, my dad cracking bad jokes, Mum playing referee to control our mutual father–son jibes. The project had kind of started without us noticing – this is how all great journeys begin – but the planning phase for this one was now nearing its end. The running was scarily close. Every so often, as chatter around the table continued without me, my mind would wander to the start line, and imagine what lay beyond it. My hands and fingertips would tingle with an eager nervousness that felt like it had bubbled up from my feet. Nobody noticed – I simply let the butterflies subside and took another mouthful of food. I'd be back in the conversation, my mind gently and slowly prepping me in some subconscious way.

We chatted through all the things Andy would need to know. He now would not see his own bed or his own home for what turned out to be four months: things were starting to get real. Up to this point, there hadn't been much discussion on the matter – I knew Andy could handle anything – but it was probably time to explain roughly how the next hundred days would work, or at least how I thought they'd work. I approached the subject of Everything Andy Needed to Know with some hesitation – after all, he still had time to run away in fear, and I was conscious not to scare him off before the trip had even begun.

However, Nikki, my girlfriend, who was naturally with us at my parents' house, had been in Andy's position before, and she didn't hold back in telling him the realities of life in a van with me running mile after mile, day after day. Of all the people in the world, Nikki knew me totally – and not just regular me, but expedition-mode me too.

Nikki started to list off the various princess-like traits that Andy would become subjected to. Andy laughed some of them off, but I could tell he knew there were hard realities behind Nikki's semi-humorous comments. Andy bravely (or foolishly, perhaps) stayed seated. I was between him and the door anyway, should he have tried to bolt.

Run Britain – The Origin

The evening before Christmas Eve in 2020, I reached the southernmost point of Sicily, having successfully run from the border with Austria – Italy's most northerly point, high in the Italian Alps. That concluded what was a hundred-day journey covering 2,620 miles, zigzagging down the country, taking in all the best bits Italy had to offer. And yes, you guessed it, I was running a marathon a day, every day.

Hitting the self-imposed finish line in the dark at about 10 p.m. on a scrubland-style beach, I was chaperoned diligently by Nikki, driving the van with the side door open up a very bumpy single-track road that led to the beach and rocks, just before the water's edge. She was driving with the side door open because there was a hefty dog aggressively barking and getting ever closer: I could jump into safety at the last moment, should the beast decide to go for me. A bumpy road, in the dark, just before Christmas Eve, after 2,620 miles of running, in the middle of a pandemic . . . and now a dog chasing me right to the finish line.

The last few weeks of Italy had been brutal, and I'd earned that finish line – we both had – so I wasn't about to let a grumpy dog stop me. Once I reached the end of the sandy bit of the beach with the light of my head torch swaying in front of me, I braved the last bit and scooted, on my bum, down the few erosion-stopping boulders, to touch the water. The waterline, at the most southerly point, had to be my finish line, a kind of proof there was no more land to run.

After stumbling into the van, Nikki handed the driving reins back to me. She was done. She'd driven every mile with me, waiting, supporting, and ultimately sacrificing months of her time to dedicate her efforts to me and my goal . . . to run Italy. We called it the Italian Grand Tour. It was grand, it was in Italy, and it was a tour of the country. However, the name hid the realities of what turned out to be an exceptionally hard emotional journey for us both. We did not know it then, but this trip sadly marked the beginning of the end for our relationship.

As positive-thinking humans, we romanticized running Italy. When we discussed the expedition, I blindly ignored the potential conflicts that might arise. I thought of the stunning mirror lakes of the north, the white sandy beaches of the Amalfi coast, the vast jutting peaks of the Dolomite mountain range, the endless pastel-coloured cities, and the food, naturally. We were touring a beautiful country, we were young and in love, we enjoyed living out of a van, and we were on the road with our virtually newborn puppy (Poppy, my Hungarian vizsla). What could go wrong?

And so, once the miles were done and the mission was complete, we could now finally rest, reset and rebuild. We were both elated to be finished. We were proud of each other, we hugged, we cried, and we both sat in relieved silence, taking it in – not just the accomplishment, but the fact that it was now finally over. But just two hours after finishing, the calendar ticked over to 24 December, and our minds mutually wandered to 'What now?' We immediately thought of our planned and long-awaited reward: Christmas in the French Alps. We had arranged to finish a week earlier and then slowly drive north to the mountains for a few weeks, skiing over the festive period. Obviously it was now too late for that. Or was it?

After removing the layers of crusty hundred-day-old clothes and turning the van around in a heavily potholed gravel car park, we chatted for a few minutes. The clock was ticking, so we hastily made a plan. Maybe we could make Christmas happen after all.

For the last few days, Nikki had been driving behind me at running pace. She didn't always do this, but that had become unavoidable towards the end, thanks to a stupid mistake on my part. On day 92, just eight days from the end of the journey, I'd dropped my phone and it was now broken and unusable. This was significant because I used it to navigate while Nikki would usually drive ahead 5 or 10 miles, prep food, take Poppy for toilet breaks, catch up with her business, look for sleeping spots and then wait for me. But with no phone, we devised a terrible plan where I'd look at the map, know roughly where I was going, and she'd drive as close as possible to me to navigate. We also couldn't lose each other because we had no alternative way of keeping in contact. This was all made more stressful by some very sketchy highways and underpass interchange sections that were hard to understand while she drove on the wrong side of the road and I ran into the traffic on the opposite side. Think slipways, motorway speeding traffic, hopping over central reservations, and shouting instructions to one another across traffic, all the while trying to hide our individual and collective frustrations and fatigue.

Taking the last few days into consideration, our new plan was simple; we could, if we drove constantly, still make Christmas happen, but we'd have to take shifts. I'd do my best to get us as far north as possible – up to northern Sicily, back over to mainland Italy on the ferry, and then hopefully between us we'd reach our beloved skiing village, St Martin-de-Belleville, in time for Christmas morning. The journey that had just taken us three and a half months, we were now attempting to retrace in less than twenty-four hours. Easy in a van without any running, right? Think again. We were both totally and utterly devoid of energy. But our thinking was, what's one more day of brutal exhaustion when we've already had a hundred? And so, with the van turned to face north, and after a hundred days of back-to-back marathons, we started to drive.

Google Maps said 1,836 kilometres, a drive time of twenty hours and three minutes with tolls and ferries. Factor in stopping for fuel maybe three times and it was going to be close; and we had no idea of Covid testing rules, red areas of Italy that we couldn't drive through, or if the ferry times were going to work in our favour.

I'd like to say that I heroically drove all the way and made it in time for Christmas. That, however, would be only half true. I lasted about ninety minutes and had to pull over. I reluctantly woke Nikki up and explained that I couldn't drive any longer without falling asleep. All credit to Nikki – who gave me a look of 'Seriously?' – without flinching, she swapped seats and started to drive. I stayed awake for about fifteen minutes and tried to google the new and ever-changing Covid laws regarding Brits travelling from Sicily to the mainland and from Italy into France. I learnt nothing and fell asleep.

Twenty-two hours and fifty minutes later we drove into the sleepy, snowy village of St Martin-de-Belleville. A place I've been coming to all my life, but this time, arriving here was extra sweet.

St M-de-B is the epitome of a French alpine village. Traditional church, small town hall and basic wooden-clad homes. The skiing industry, with all its glamour and glitz, has crept into this valley but St M-de-B has cleverly embraced it without losing its essential identity and character.

While everyone was waiting for Santa, tucked up tight, we drove through the village to a small parking spot next to the ski slopes. It was a dark night, and thick white snowflakes were falling as the tyres crunched through the fresh snow. It was an unbelievable feeling to be there. We'd worked in four-hour shifts, with me taking the wheel for the final ascent up the mountain roads I'd driven many times. I pressed the brake pedal, pulled the handbrake on, turned the key, and the engine shuddered to a halt. Nikki woke up, Poppy woke up, and all three of us almost immediately closed our eyes with smiles on our faces as we slumped into our seats. Nikki held out her hand, squeezed mine, and held it tight. We'd made it. We slept in the front seats as the clock on the dash showed 23:10. When we woke up it would be Christmas morning.

Britain and France went into another lockdown shortly after. This left Nikki, Poppy and me with an unexpected reward for our efforts: we ended up having over three months in the Alps. The mountains were empty, barring a few locals, and we had the place to ourselves for the first and, most likely, the last time in our lives. Everything was shut, but we were still allowed out and about, to ski, to explore, to build igloos. And to make things extra special, our good family friend Colin and his wife Pip offered us their chalet for the entire time we were there.

After all, they couldn't get out to use it, and nor could anyone else. It turned into one of the best periods of my life. A bubble of fourteen weeks with heavy snow and sunny blue skies.

As just the three of us, those weeks passed in mountainous bliss: daily ski touring and 'skinning up' (hiking up hills on skis because the lifts were all closed, thanks to the pandemic), exploring in the snow together, and generally reconnecting with each other over lazy French breakfasts and evenings playing cards. It wasn't long, though, before I began to crave a new challenge. All the turmoil of Italy had faded, for me at least. And so I started to speak of potential ideas for the next running trip. It was here, in post-expedition bliss, surrounded by empty, snowy mountains, in a strange Covid time warp, that running around the coast of Britain was dreamt up.

It was, however, probably a bad idea. Even with all the issues Italy had thrown at us, I went ahead and started planning something twice as difficult just a few months later. In hindsight, project Run Britain was a bloody stupid idea, all things considered.

Pre-Covid, I had dreamt up three other challenges that I felt were possible and would keep me busy in the foreseeable future. But they all involved running abroad, and with travel restrictions and border closures becoming increasingly unpredictable I knew something British-based would have to satisfy my addiction for adventure . . . something fun and hard enough to grab my attention.

There were plenty of options. I thought of Land's End to John O'Groats, but experience told me that running down the middle of an island is far less enjoyable than being by the coast. And so circumnavigating Britain seemed the better option. There was just the minor factor of the distance – over 5,000 miles, even following the most efficient route and sticking to the mainland only. And frankly I didn't want to run for more than a hundred days because I had other things to be doing. So there it was: a double marathon every day would mean I could get the job done and we would be finished in time for our birthdays in August (Nikki's falls within a day of mine). This became our deadline, with enough time built in for a few setbacks along the way.

The rumour was that Britain was unlocking from 15 April. We heard this news around the middle of March. Not long, but maybe long enough to put together a mission.

I ran the idea past Nikki.

'What if . . .' I started tentatively.

'No!' she said with some firm eye contact and an unspoken plea. She knew what was coming. At that point I promised she would have no duties, no responsibilities, no need even to be present. I would find a crew, so she could come and go as she pleased. This seemed to reassure her a little, but Nikki is smart and knows me well – she was dubious. Nikki would never stop me doing expeditions – she knew it was my passion and always supported my crazy ideas – but she had just broken her arm and had had surgery to pin it into place. She couldn't drive the van for the next 3 months whilst she recovered, and knew I would require both a support driver again and our home to be used as a base for the next challenge, which was now due to start in one month's time.

After a few days of discussion, and Nikki laying down some ground rules, my mind was made up. Running around Britain was happening, albeit with a whole heap of planning left to do. Run Britain was just an idea at this point, but Nikki knows that when I work at something I become completely, relentlessly focused on making it happen, even to the point of forgetting to eat. It's complete tunnel vision, which has its pros and cons but mainly makes me rather difficult to reason with.

By about 20 March, the plan was set. I would run a double marathon every day, covering over 5,000 miles around the mainland coast. With a few tweaks to the route, I could bring the total to 5,240 miles, or two lots of 26.2 miles per day for a hundred days. Simple. I had, however, never run 370-mile weeks back to back before, let alone run marathon after marathon on some of the most famously steep coastlines in Europe. I'd run close to 72,000 miles in my life, with nearly seven hundred marathons under my belt, but double marathons back to back for months on end would be a whole different kettle of fish. That, though, at the time, was not the main problem on my mind.

I had less than a month to find some people to help, drum up some media, find some cash to pay for it, and iron out the 'little things' like where I'd start and finish, satisfying Covid rules in Wales and Scotland, deciding on a route (even whether to run clockwise or anti-clockwise), and of course thinking about a contingency plan if it all went to shit or the world went back into yet another lockdown.

With my manager and assistant Yas, plus some volunteers on the end of the phone or on blurry Zoom calls, I spent the last couple of weeks of our time in the Alps with constant meetings and time behind the laptop. Yas and I met over five years ago when she was working for Pro Direct, supporting various brand photo shoots I happened to be involved with. We had minimal contact at the time, but when I was in the final stages of a previous adventure I was keen to find someone who could support me with brand partnerships, and to help organize a speaking tour following the journey. I happened to know that Yas had left Pro Direct to start her own business, and I reached out to see if she was willing to work with me. I was delighted to hear she was. The rest is history, as they say. Our temporary arrangement morphed into something more permanent, and Yas subsequently became my manager.

And so with the best of the snow melting, we eventually navigated the numerous and ever-changing laws and regulations and returned to the UK. Once back, I had just a fortnight to finalize plans, maybe go for a run (a little thing called training), and then gather the troops and head to the start line – a start line whose location at this point hadn't even been decided.

Start Line: T Minus 72 Hours

Just three days from the off, and the day after Andy's arrival, he and I spent the entire day loading the van that would be our home for the expedition, talking a lot about how things might unfold, and generally fizzing with excitable nervous energy. There was lots of packing and repacking, cramming large bags into small spaces, lugging stuff to and from the house, and trying, but mainly failing, to do everything logically and efficiently. Andy and I thought similarly in terms of space and access, but with the amount of stuff we were attempting to cram into a small area, we were fighting a losing battle.

The sleeping arrangements for the hundred days were simple. Accommodation would be the van. Not the van that took Nikki and me around Italy, but instead my parents' smaller, purpose-built campervan, my dad's pride and joy. (Yes – what could go wrong?) Nikki would live in our van (which quickly became renamed 'Nikki's van', or later 'the Palace Van', for clarity), along with Poppy. Andy and I would stay in my dad's van. This was in accordance with the 'No Responsibilities' clause stipulated by Nikki and me during the post-Italy turmoil. It was also her home, after all. This meant Andy was looking after me – totally looking after me – and Nikki was free to come and go as she pleased. All great in principle, right?

My dad's van was very quickly nicknamed 'the Council Van' (I'm sorry, Dad), purely due to it being more basic than the relatively palatial quarters of Nikki's van. To put it into context, Nikki's van had dimming lights, solar power, three-pin charging points, a freezer that could be adjusted from a phone, a luxury fixed double bed with memory foam mattress, and, well, just about everything you need. Dad's van . . . had wheels. The Council Van was 6 metres long, with a normal high driving position, small cab and snub-nosed bonnet, and looked like a bread bin on wheels. It was boxy, but at least it was constructed to make good use of the available space. There was a narrow single bed behind the driver, and an identical one behind the passenger. These of course could all be folded away to form a seated area around a small slot-in table. This we didn't need, and so under Dad's close supervision we constructed a permanent bed set-up; Dad even found two mattresses from an old sofa bed to replace the precious cushions in the van. This was a stroke of genius, as it gave us much more comfortable sleeping arrangements, and without the need to waste time and, importantly, energy making and unmaking the bed set-up. A small gap amounting to a couple of feet was our galley space between the beds – the only standing space in the van that wasn't next to the toilet or kitchen area, both of which were at the back. When in a sleeping position, my head was against the reversed and swivelled passenger seat with my feet against the wall of the toilet cubicle; Andy slept with his head the other end, next to the small panel separating the cooking area from the bed set-up. This came in handy because he could turn the hob on in the morning by reaching behind his head and finding the dial by feel, to begin our cup of tea ritual without getting up – a feat he became rather proud of. Needless to say, 'cosy' was an understatement. The small stowaway cabinets above us held everything we needed: food, medical supplies, clothes, cables and chargers, and miscellaneous sponsor-provided items. Bar a small upright cabinet towards the rear, the remaining storage was under the beds – good to have, but a pain to get to.

At last neatly packed and parked on the driveway of my parents' house, the van was tidy, things stowed where we thought best. We had jigged and rejigged more or less everything at least twice to cram in as many of our supplies as possible, but it felt organized, and all based around one priority: enabling me to run 52.4 miles every day. I wanted easy access to what I needed when I needed it, to avoid using more energy than necessary on anything other than running. This was crucial. Little did we know quite how much everything would change and evolve over our time on the road: the state of the van, how we'd live, how we'd sleep, how we'd eat. More or less all of our preconceived thoughts about our initial set-up changed at least once.

The following morning, turning the key in the van, Andy's eyes were focused and concentrated. He had the unenviable task of driving this precious box on wheels out of my parents' narrow wooden gates, down the 250-metre drive that led to the village, and onward around the entire country. His knuckles were white and his eyes wide as Dad ushered him out of the drive with the precision of airport ground staff, though he waved his hands in a way that made no sense to the rest of us. And just like that, the expedition was under way, and the van miles had begun.

From my parents' home in Dorset to the Eden Project is about three and a half hours by car, in a van about four and a half. With fuel, food and supply stops, it turned into six. Our convoy of family and friends meandered down the A roads until we eventually reached the Travelodge in St Austell at around 4 p.m., just a few miles from the Eden Project. The Eden start line had come about from a Sky News interview I'd done about a year earlier, after which I'd stayed in touch with the producer, James. On the same day I'd called Andy to ask for his support, I had a call with James and a chap called David, the media manager at the Eden Project. They were working together already and so James suggested I start and finish there – an iconic venue, with potential for Sky to get behind the media coverage. We settled on the start date of 17 April because we had a chance of making some big headlines. Two days post-lockdown we would pitch the run as a celebration of the return to freedom for much of the country. And it felt like just that, as if we were being released into the world again. We had discussed starting on 15 April, 'freedom day' – the actual day Britain came out of lockdown – but it was decided that all the headlines would be about lockdown rules being relaxed and we might get lost in the mix. So it seemed sensible to go for the slightly later date of 17 April to share our positive story about freedom, nature (with the biggest indoor rainforest anywhere in the world, the Eden Project certainly offered a fitting start) and Britain being united.

It was a good plan. However, as with all adventures, there's always so much out of sight, so much you can't plan for. On 9 April, Prince Philip died. His funeral took place on 17 April, and coverage of it dominated the news. We received virtually no media at all.

But back to the small car park, our now numerous vans and vehicles hogging the Travelodge's allocation, and in puffa jackets, bobble hats, and with bags of all shapes and sizes hanging off us, the team gathered. A pizza and some drinks down by a local harbour that evening was our brief but useful bonding time. A meeting in the hotel followed where expenses cash was dispensed, and roles and responsibilities were confirmed. I spoke a little about contingencies, and tried my best to show my gratitude once more.

The following day was full of photo shoots for supporting brands, last-minute prep, meeting David and James at Eden, buying forgotten items, and generally collectively panicking. On the eve of Go Day we had a final get-together in one of the hotel rooms. Yas hosted, kindly gave out little gifts to the team, and we dispersed from the room in high spirits, ahead of a 4 a.m. wake-up call to make the 6 a.m. start line at Eden. This being April, it was before sunrise, and none of us were really awake, but the excitable air of pre-adventure crackled in the chill. Sleepy smiles nestled under hats and layers of clothing. Go Day was upon us.

Day 1 – 17 April – 53.02 miles – 7,572ft elevation
The Eden Project, St Austell to Millbrook
5.50 a.m.

With ten minutes to go before the strict start time, the team scrambled to their positions. Cameras ready, a drone high in the air, people dotted around or dashing back to the vehicles.

The strict start time was self-imposed. I knew there would be days when getting out of bed and lacing up my trainers would be the last thing I felt like doing, so I needed to build a mental fortress, an impenetrable and unshakeable structure into which doubts and negativity could not creep. To keep myself going, having basic rules was a must – a framework for success, if you will. So, 6 a.m. every day, without fail, I would be running. No budging. Sure enough, at 5.59 and fifty seconds a few of the team began a countdown.

Ten, nine, eight . . .

My nerves buzzed and fizzed from my feet to my eyes, and my brain thought of all that had been before. Pain and suffering were coming of course, but so was the opportunity of a new challenge, and the chance to accomplish something that felt truly special.

With my friends around me, my family willing me from afar, and with nothing but blind faith in my heart and feet, I primed myself to begin this 5,240-mile run. My longest to date. But one thing stayed the same: I just had to keep putting one foot in front of the other. Over a hundred thousand times a day.

A smattering of applause echoed around the otherwise empty Eden as my left index finger reached to my watch on my right arm in what felt like slow motion, and the beep sounded. Eyes forward, a slight curl at the edge of my mouth, I took my first step. I was smiling, I was focused, and the team beamed back with early morning whoops and cheers. Here we go. I was layered up, buff up to my nose, covering my mouth, hat on, gloves on, leggings, a jacket, and phone tucked into my running belt. My breath in the cold, still air provided a hazy velvet cloud to run through. I turned, waved, blew a kiss to Nikki, and away up the hill I went.

As I found my stride, Andy was reflecting on the task ahead:

And that's it. With those first few steps past the frost-covered biomes, Run Britain is suddenly under way, and Nick's life for the next three months flashes before me. His Running the World expedition was an extraordinary and unprecedented feat, but this, in terms of physical and mental endurance, is on another level altogether. What Nick is now attempting is pushing the bounda- ries of what's humanly possible. He's just started his first mile of 5,240, slightly further than the total distance he covered running a marathon in every country in the world, which took him nearly two years. He's now attempting it in just over three months. With Running the World, the main questions I had over whether Nick could do it were around logistics, money, safety and remaining healthy in far-flung places. Now it's simply a question of whether a human can run two marathons a day for a hundred days – and I know Nick wouldn't have been at all offended if I'd voiced my doubts before the start. Obviously I didn't – that's not what mates do.

As we clap Nick up his first hill, heading out of the Eden Project, it's only then that it really sinks in that this is now also my life for the next three months. With all the preparation and focus on the start itself, I've almost forgotten that not only is Nick now running for a hundred days without a break, but I'm now in this too, for a hundred long, intense days, and although dwarfed by the scale of Nick's undertaking, the relentlessness of what I'm about to do sud- denly hits me. Goodbye life, goodbye normality. Hello inside of campervan, hello new job, and more importantly, hello adventure. While my preparation has focused on what will be required to sup- port Nick, what that actually entails as a day-to-day routine isn't something I've really set out in my mind yet, and as I climb into the van with all these thoughts flying around in my head, it occurs to me that I don't really know what I'm doing, and more immediately, where I'm going. We'll be using a combination of various different apps to track Nick and navigate the daily routes and using them effectively will need to become second nature to me very quickly. My first challenge is to find the correct exit to the maze that is the Eden Project, before making my way down to Par Sands where Nick will first join the coast.

Having passed the last of our team, set up to take photographs, it was within the first half a mile that I realized I didn't know where I was going. The Eden Project is around 3 miles inland from the coast. I knew I had to run south to reach the water and then turn left but that was it. The roads wouldn't be a problem because it was early, cold and a Saturday. The more pressing matter was getting out of the grounds of Eden. I reached a small mini roundabout within the complex, went left, realized it was a dead end, turned around, went straight over the roundabout this time, but wrong again. This wasn't the best of starts. I called Andy – no answer. The place was a network of little roads and tracks – I found myself cursing for starting in what is basically a maze. On my final attempt, on the only remaining option back from the roundabout, I made it out. I'd already run a mile more than the route planner we'd built to give us our daily distances and stopping points. Already the plan was out of sync. An ominous sign of things to come. Meanwhile Andy had mobilized, and a short while later he called me back, just as I made it to Par Sands.

'Hello, Andy.'

'Hello, mate, sorry I missed your call.'

'No worries. I got a little lost getting out of Eden, but I can see the vans parked along the beach. I'll be there in a few mins.'

I was now on the first bit of coast, and my first beach of thousands. Looking back, it never even dawned on me that I'd be running along or next to every beach in Britain. I knew I'd see the coast, but kind of forgot about all the beautiful beaches.

With the drone tracking my steady and comfortable stride along the shore, I approached the car park on the easterly end of the beach before heading towards the first bit of official coast path, where I passed Jack and Sarah, who were tucked away in the dunes snapping photos.

Jack and Sarah were our camera crew – and they come as a pair. Sarah is small, petite and smiley, half Scottish, half Singaporean and great with a camera. I'd reached out to her on Instagram about six months earlier, having seen some utterly stunning photos she'd taken in the Scottish Highlands. We'd exchanged a few messages – the usual initial chit-chat to see if we were both on the same page – and discussed working together when a trip became 'Covid-viable'.

A while later, with Sarah having committed to volunteering for Run Britain, she suggested Jack, a friend of hers who was also very good with a camera. Both of them were full-time photographers and had worked together on various shoots all over the world. This was a turn of good fortune and I was grateful for the intro. It was also a hefty bonus that not only was Jack keen to volunteer, he also had a van that could host the pair of them without any admin. No sourcing an extra vehicle, no insurance, no additional expense. Ideal. And so that's how Jack and Sarah came to be our camera duo.

We were also joined by Paul and Nicole. Paul and I had started chatting some two years earlier, after he got in touch to offer his help during my Running the World challenge. We'd spoken multiple times, and with Run Britain firmly on the cards he'd suggested coming along to act as cycle support, keeping an eye on me and offering encouragement, food and water, as well as help with navigation. He worked in a bike transformation workshop – a place where normal push bikes are adapted to be electric bikes – but would be sticking with pure pedal power on this occasion.

Nicole had responded to a short Instagram story I'd put out calling for volunteers to help with establishing a charity. Nicole is one of the loveliest people I've ever met and so generous with her time and energy. Later I asked her to get involved with certain projects in a paid capacity, and we haven't looked back since. Along with Yas, Nicole was crucial to ensuring that everything about Run Britain went to plan – or at least that when it didn't we were able to cope with it.

With sand crunching underfoot, the drone buzzing above, the ocean lapping and the sand dune reeds waving in the wind, I eventually reached the team waiting at the vehicles. This was stop one. Stop one of thousands. Only 6 miles into day 1, but the first opportunity to take some water on board, plus my specially mixed carbohydrate drink from Science in Sport that was designed to help me keep on top of my body's fuel needs.

Paul was waiting with his bike. I'd requested to have the first few miles on my own in order to get my head in the game. I was so grateful for his support, though still sceptical about whether a bike would be suited to the coast path. We'd soon find out.

We set out together, tracking along the coast anti-clockwise, east from St Austell, the Eden Project now behind me. Blue sky, a crisp morning, my body temperature slowly rising beneath the layers of clothes. The entire team, plus a handful of others, were gathered to cheer us off the initial short stretch of beach and up, up and away on to the coast path skirting the cliff top.

As I trudged the next few miles I weighed up the magnitude of what lay ahead. The next time I saw Eden I'd be a shell of the man that had started. A calorie deficit was inevitable. But just how much of a shell, only time would tell. What was this journey keeping secret? What would unfold? What would I learn? How much would I suffer? Running over 5,000 miles, even the strongest mind becomes frail. I knew I could push myself to keep moving, but I was praying the pain wouldn't appear until close to the end. Wishful thinking was an understatement. I knew only one thing: mind *had* to conquer body. There would be no other way to the finish line.

It turns out that much of the 'coast path' does in fact meander and weave all over the place, so sticking within touching distance of the water was hard, although the rule I'd set myself was only to remain as close to the coast as possible. Needless to say, the terrain, landslides, paths to nowhere, and some very overgrown shrubs made things a touch more challenging.

Paul's plan to stay with me was short-lived. Despite the energy he exuded, it quickly became clear that his bike, or any bike for that matter, would struggle on the path. Steps a couple of feet tall, long grass, rocks, outstretched branches reaching from one side of the path to the other, thorns, pebbles, more steps, more uneven rocky boulders – tough to run or walk on, close to impossible for a bike. We knew that later on there would be more accessible stretches, but for this section at least, no chance.

The day's route, like the other ninety-nine I'd be following, had been mapped on Plot a Route, a freebie web tool I'd discovered for planning hiking routes anywhere in the world. Simply drag your route, add way-points, and save. My mum and I spent a week drawing up and saving routes for the run, followed by checking and rechecking for paths, potential stopping points for a place to sleep, and of course roads, making sure they were safe to run on not just during the day but at night too.

It was this route that we uploaded to the website so the public could see where we planned to be, and could come and join in. It was also the route that Andy and the team followed. Andy had a complete digital and printed version; I, on the other hand, just had the coast path signs and the position of the sea. 'Keep the ocean on your right' was the motto which became my navigational mantra. That, of course, was a reasonable plan, but not the whole picture in practice. Estuaries, tributaries, rivers, river mouths, basically just any water, were getting in the way of that nice, simple 'Keep the ocean on your right' plan.

Having passed Fowey after 12 or so miles of heavily undulating coast path, with more or less no navigation needed, the little town of Bodinnick presented us with our first obstacle and promptly burst that bubble. To reach Bodinnick from Fowey you have to cross the river.

Let's put this estuary issue into context. Put simply, if I ran up, around and back down every river or estuary I came across, the coast of Britain would be a good couple of thousand miles longer than my 5,000-mile route. A handful of people have travelled around Britain on foot – nearly all of them walking – and they have covered varying distances, anything from 3,000 miles upwards. A few have spent four or five years completing the full circumnavigation in sections, covering well over 12,000 miles by hugging the coast almost to the pebble, and avoiding major bridges or ferries.

This option wasn't the plan for Run Britain. I wanted to run *around* Britain – along the coast, beside the ocean. For me, running tens of miles inland to cross a 20-metre stretch of water was unnecessary, and frankly detracted from the 'around' Britain concept. Besides, the magical two hundred marathons in a hundred days was the goal.

Our 5,240-mile route was perfect. It covered all the out and backs of headlands, but didn't go up and down every little inlet. I was happy with the plan. It was logical and that was that. I set myself one basic rule at the beginning of the challenge, though. That was to run around Britain as close to the coast as was sensible, while clocking no more and no less than two hundred marathons (5,240 miles). The caveat to this was that if I crossed stretches of water on ferries, when I wouldn't be running but my watch would still be clocking the miles, we agreed I'd need to run the equivalent distance covered by boat on foot, and add it to our total. In the end we rounded this up to 10 miles to be on the safe side. This made my overall mileage target a total of 5,250. I'm *very* particular about hitting the mileage I set out to hit, so every metre must be logged and accounted for. When I run, I *never* stop my watch until a day is complete. This then shows my true time. Besides, it's often a world record rule anyway.

For my own motivation I must know that we are obeying our own rules. Otherwise I'd feel like I was cheating myself. And what would be the point in that? Head to Strava and you'll see every step, along every beach, around the whole country. Andy spent many head-scratching hours trawling through the route to understand ferry points and operating times. He did this, by the way, without me asking, off his own back, in the weeks before I met him off the train. Andy is a saint. You will, however, learn that no matter how hard we planned, there were plenty of long miles up and down rivers that simply couldn't be avoided – but we did know they were coming.

If the route led us to a river that had a bridge that was close by, I'd take it. If there was a ferry from one side to another, I'd take it. If the river didn't have a bridge or a ferry, we'd have no choice but to go around.

It turned out there would be fourteen ferries to catch during Run Britain, and in fact nine of them all in the first few weeks, due to the topography of the south coast, where there are lots of rivers leading to the sea. As beautiful as they are, this did cause Andy much stress:

Ferry crossings are something I've been looking into in detail as part of planning for the trip, as they present potential stumbling blocks. One of the rules of the expedition is that Nick cannot be in a moving vehicle while his watch is recording; the only exception being that he is allowed to use ferries in order to avoid the unnecessary additional mileage involved in running inland around rivers and estuaries. A small adjustment will be added to Nick's target mileage to ensure the full two-hundred-marathon distance is covered on foot. Working out the logistics has been a headache. Is the ferry running on the right day (particularly with Covid restrictions still in place)? Do its operating hours coincide with Nick's ETA? Cash only? Tide or weather dependent? How long will Nick be without support after catching a pedestrian ferry while I drive around to meet him? It'll be a relief to get past Dorset, after which ferry crossings become few and far between.

Arriving at a ferry point to find out that it's not actually there, or that the boat is seasonal, or that we'd missed it by a minute or two, would either lead to wasted time or a potentially huge, unplanned, unmapped detour. Naturally this meant planning and replanning the route more or less constantly, with the 5,240-mile distance to cover in mind. No more, no less. As it happens, Andy's attention to detail is bloody marvellous so he knew exactly the miles and the route on a daily basis, even if I hadn't a clue, and even if he was guessing at times for some of it. This part of the job I hadn't thought about, but boy was I pleased Andy was there to resolve issue after issue. It wasn't long before I lost the mental capacity to problem-solve. Running will do that to you after a few double marathons.

The first ferry obstacle of the mission was just 12 miles in. It hadn't dawned on me that most ferries would be passenger-only, spiriting pedestrians across tiny rivers that vehicles can easily navigate with a small detour inland. I'd find that out over the coming weeks. This first boat, however, was a small car ferry – one of only four on the whole trip – which meant it was possible for the team to regroup and travel across together. As I ran towards the meeting point I could see the ferry was ready and waiting to leave, cars driving cautiously up the little on-ramp. As it was there, I ran to it and got on. I called Andy as I waited for the boat to leave, the chug of its engine idling with the propellers keeping it firmly against the side of the quay, the frothing white water turning over and over. I could barely hear Andy but he seemed to be saying we could all get the ferry together and it would leave in ten minutes. I hung up, having agreed, and propped myself up on a little seating area to wait for the others to appear. After a few minutes I realized Andy probably didn't hear me say I was already on the ferry. As that went through my head, the engine growled a little louder and the on-ramp rose into the air. I called him back.

'Andy, you know I'm on the ferry, right? And it's leaving now.'

He didn't hear me correctly, so I repeated the words. This stirred surprise in his voice.

'I'll be at the other side in about two minutes,' I told him. 'I'll just follow the path, and meet me when you can?'

Andy hesitantly agreed before hanging up to inform the others. It turned out the whole team had actually arrived at the harbour ahead of me and parked up just around the corner. The boat wasn't adhering to the scheduled times – why would it? It was a small ferry in the depths of Cornwall. This was our first lesson in advanced communication.

Up to this point Andy would appear every few miles, at a junction or where it was possible to squeeze the precious van down a narrow single-track lane. He'd feed me and offer a change of clothes, and I'd de-layer by one or two items as the day warmed up and my body put in more and more effort on the punishing paths. Fortunately, I'd learnt from Running the World always to carry a little cash. I broke my £20 note to pay the £1.80 crossing fee and cradled the change in my hand for the next 10 miles.

Running into Polperro, with the team having eventually caught up, I was approaching the first marathon mark. The miles had flown by. I was of course relatively fresh-legged, but I did wonder if I was pacing myself correctly. I was sticking to the plan, but were my legs ready for this pace for months on end? Day in, day out? I was unsure. Time and distance would tell. Having reached Looe with the first marathon distance behind me, my head was largely in a positive place, enjoying the views of baby-blue skies seeping into the deeper greenish blues of the ocean at the horizon. At my feet, the water was a clear turquoise, lapping calmingly against the bleached rocks as I passed, see-sawing up and down the coastline, sometimes just a few feet away from the shore before ascending the cliff tops again, where everything was a little more muted.

Meanwhile, on the road, Andy was mastering the art of interception:

It's already become clear to me that, although much smaller than Nikki's van, the Council Van has the turning circle of a medium-sized aircraft carrier, and is not well suited to narrow Cornish streets, as I discover when I get dangerously close to becoming wedged in Polperro. Even with this mini-disaster averted, it's already clear that on certain stretches of the coastline it's going to be impossible to get anywhere near Nick with the van. However, for these instances, we have a back-up in the form of Paul, who can provide cycle support for coast paths and places unsuitable for vehicles. There is also the option of Paul and I providing on-foot support, either running sections of the route with Nick or shuttling from the vans to the coast path to meet him. Having worked out roughly how far ahead I need to drive to have time to pack a bag with supplies and run down to intercept Nick, I trial a couple of support runs during the afternoon. It's hard work, as it involves running with a heavy bag, invariably down a steep hill, fast enough to make sure I get to a given point ahead of Nick, and then back up to the van, before darting ahead to the next stop. It's made more difficult by the patchy phone signal in these remote areas, meaning that a lot of the time we're having to try and work out where Nick is by the timing of his last-known location.

Dry, dusty, compacted single-track mud paths lined with bright yellow gorse and salt-washed grass were my meandering compass for most of the first marathon distance. I would cover over 7,000 feet of elevation on that first day, and although my legs didn't exactly feel tired, experience said the steep oversized steps and uneven terrain would soon become a pain point. I made a conscious effort to slow my steps, shorten my stride and put less energy into my forward

momentum. I was just allowing my feet to rise and fall rather than trying to propel myself forward.

Approaching Seaton Beach, the 500 feet of steep climbing instantly
confirmed my worries. My legs could manage a day or two of this sort
of ascent and descent, but not at pace, and I was all too aware that the
big elevation days wouldn't end until I was out of Cornwall and Devon.

The coast path here was gorgeous, largely empty and often right on
the cliff edge. Wooden stakes with horizontal riser boards formed most
of the larger steps where there weren't rocks to form them naturally.
My breath was laboured on the climbs, with my hands on my quads,
slowly and carefully crawling up each one. It was steep enough in places
to use my hands, as the stairs became more like a ladder.

Past Portwrinkle village, past the sprawling white sands of Tregantle
Beach, up and around past Rame and the fort of Polhawn, the military
base, and then to the first out-and-back section. 'Out and back?' I hear
you cry. 'Aren't you going *around* Britain?' Well yes, but there are many
places, hundreds in fact, where there's just one road, lane or path leading to a stretch of coast on a narrow headland. These peninsulas
usually consist of pretty steep cliffs with no coast path. You could
argue that it's possible just to skip the headland altogether, and that
did make sense for the tiny ones of less than half a mile, but just east
of Rame this headland made up several miles of coast, and if you
looked at a map, it would look like I was just cutting the corner, and I
would feel like that too. So it was decided that where it made sense, I'd
take in a headland, even if it meant doubling back on myself to rejoin
the main route.

Around 45 miles into day 1, I rounded the corner of the coast that
juts out before it dives inland around the Tamar Estuary. I was tantalizingly close to Plymouth and there were ferries across the half-a-mile
stretch of water, but the coast path went inland, and although a reasonably large detour, it was part of my mapped route. I would run back
past this point a day later on the opposite side of the water, which
might feel like painful progress if I weren't clocking up required miles.

At 48 miles down, Andy and I checked in for the last time before the
first day's finish line. My legs were OK, my head was in a good space.
The plan had been to finish each double marathon day within twelve

hours, allowing six hours for each marathon and plenty of stopping for food, water, changes of clothing, but clocking in at the finish of each day no later than 6 p.m., with twelve hours to eat, recover and sleep. However, as it turned out, this was a little overambitious.

With less than a mile to go, I'd run slightly inland to the town of Millbrook. Andy had informed me they had found a little patch of grass which used to be the car park of a local football club. I rounded the corner as the sun was setting, and stopped my watch after thirteen hours and forty-six minutes. At this time of year, I was starting in the dark, before sunrise, and finishing just as the sun was setting. It gave me a natural stopwatch, and a quick look at the sky gave me a good sense of whether I was ahead of or behind schedule. Although on this occasion I was nearly two hours behind, I was happy. I hadn't rushed, I hadn't let the vanishing light speed me up, I had minimized the fatigue in my legs for day 2. This was a hundred double marathons, not a sprint.

I found the team, joined by a new face – Amy, a friend of Yas's who turned out to be fantastic with a camera. They had also all been awake and alert for over fifteen hours, and were huddled around square camping tables with a few beers, cups of tea and the remains of some Chinese food Yas had cooked for my 6 p.m. target time. Mine was reheated upon my arrival. The few ripples of clapping and whooping from the team were enough to make me smile, and raise my arm slowly in the air in a fist, as we all congratulated ourselves on a good first day. Mileage-wise I was even a mile ahead of schedule.

As I stepped up into the back of the van, I remembered one of my dad's strict rules: 'Don't hold on to the sink and pull yourself into the van – it might damage the seal around the edges.' Of course he was right, but after running two marathons I needed something to grab on to. Andy, not wanting to flout the rules either, reached out and helped me up. The step at the back of the van had already got taller. It would be an Everest climb by the end.

Once in the van, I stripped off while chatting with Andy, who handed me various shakes, ice packs, a phone charger and clean socks. I was speaking with the help of the slight adrenalin rush my body had handed me as I came into the finish. This lasted about five minutes, enough time to change my clothes and prop myself up against my huge bag of running kit, occupying the swivelled passenger seat, which acted as my headboard each night. My legs outstretched and the massive Chinese meal consumed, my eyes started to close. Andy was pottering around, washing up, and had taken my empty food bowl away from me without me noticing. I was cold, my body having slowed the effort of pumping blood around my body. As I closed my eyes the three hobs of the little van stove were being lit – Andy's attempt to warm up our living quarters.

I knew I wasn't completely broken, far from it. I'd done 130-mile days before, and many more significantly harder single days than this one, but I was tired and my brain knew that we had completed just 1 per cent of the journey. This in itself was mentally tough. After all, I hadn't run more than 30 miles in a day for about eight months. My body was now in phase one of adventure running mode – the phase which is unavoidable: the adjustment window. I predicted it would take close to three weeks for my body and mind to adjust to the expedition and get used to the daily mileage, after which I hoped things would start to become easier. It's a bell curve, in maths speak. I was heading gently downhill from the top of the curve, deteriorating, and at the bottom of that curve my mind and training would need to kick in and I'd ideally rise out of the other side of the curve, with the plan then to maintain a balance and a nice flat trajectory with as few peaks and troughs as possible. This I'd done before, but there was no getting around the fact that Run Britain was a very different beast – my toughest physical challenge to date.

My eyes closed on day 1 and, in what felt like an instant, day 2 dawned.

2

The South Coast

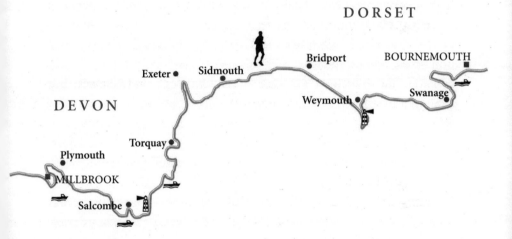

Day 2 – 53.24 miles – 4,844ft elevation
Millbrook to Modbury
Settling in

Despite my numerous alarms, I was woken by Andy preparing my breakfast. I later found out my bleeping gadgets, set to go off from 4.30 a.m., had woken him but not me. He is a lighter sleeper and obviously didn't have 50-odd miles in his legs.

It was our first night together in the van, and Andy clearly didn't think much of my wake-up system:

> *I'm woken up by the first of Nick's complex series of alarms, which start sounding at around 4.30 a.m. and continue marking various intervals until his actual 'getting up' alarm goes off at 5.30. Nick's explained to me that the earlier alarms allow him the small pleasure of knowing he can go back to sleep for a bit before he has to get out of bed. In reality, the effect is one of hyperinflation, with the multiple alarms devaluing the sound until his brain tells him that it's something he can ignore.*

Waking up in a confused haze, the first thing I wanted to know was, of course, what the time was. We had to stick to the 6 a.m. departure plan. It was crucial to keep a handle on the things we could control, which were massive mental boosters, and it gave us a clear start point from which to work out things like time on my feet, hours till sunset and calories per hour, and to easily compare these numbers from one day to the next. It was good to have that reference point – no messing around.

My first breakfast item on Andy's menu of elite sports nutrition was something I ended up having every morning, more or less without fail, throughout the entire trip: a sesame seed bagel, grilled (in the absence of a toaster in the van), with copious amounts of butter and topped with Marmite. Including mid-run snacking, I must have devoured at least two hundred bagels over the four months. Andy was a pro at breakfast prep from day one. It became a regular question, said without need: 'What would you like for breakfast?' Every day, the answer was, 'Bagel.' Bagels were to become the mascot of our British adventure.

Still in my cosy cocoon with duvet wrapped around me, I heaved myself up to a sitting position, letting out a few pensioner-style groans. My torso was instantly chilly, but Andy had all the hobs on again, the van slowly warming, the kettle just about to whistle to signal that my morning cuppa was on its way.

If this sounds like Andy was waiting on me hand and foot, you'd be right. We had agreed that my job was just to run. That's it. Barring basic bodily functions, the team would handle everything else. In the first few days I felt terrible that Andy was running around after me, but later I had no energy even to think about it, plus it soon became clear that I wouldn't have been physically capable of pitching in. I was just eternally grateful for food and drink coming in my direction.

With overhanging bedding and discarded socks and shoes on the floor, the walkway between Andy's bed and mine was virtually non-existent and left very little room for manoeuvre, and we hadn't yet quite nailed the choreography of our morning ablutions and the post-breakfast clear-up, which involved us trying to sidestep each other while Andy was closing the lid of the cooker ready for driving, and putting plates and cutlery in the small sink at the back ready to be washed in cold water poured from a 5-litre bottle. The sink, which of course was in the 'kitchen' (if you can call it that), was directly and immediately opposite the 'bathroom'. When I say opposite, it's no exaggeration to say that the bathroom and kitchen were basically the same thing. With the bathroom door open it was possible to wash up while on the toilet – albeit a bit of a stretch, and deeply unhygienic. It was a small space.

It soon became clear that while I was out of the way in the loo, this would be Andy's brief window of opportunity to move freely around the van and tidy the duvets, get my kit out from the box under the bed, and generally potter and clean. Once I re-emerged from the small wood-effect toilet cubicle, everything was more or less tidy. Another wave of feeling guilty and grateful in equal measure came over me. I thanked Andy a number of times, but it never felt like enough.

Two steps from the toilet and I was back next to my bed (and everything else). With my still-sweaty-from-yesterday clothes waiting for me, I pulled my socks and compression gear over my legs and gathered the accessories I'd need for the day – things like my phone, ear buds, some cash, and the all-important emergency energy gel. Fully clothed, I could resume my position in bed, legs horizontal for just a few more minutes. The small grey digital clock on the wall read 05:50, a time I would come to loathe and love at the same time. Ten minutes before twelve hours of running. But ten minutes of no running. Bliss. Of course the gods of time would hurry these minutes along as if to usher me out of the door early – they flew by every day.

A quick look at the route plan, and the last few sips of my now cold tea thanks to the bitterly cold van, to wash down my handful of supplement tablets, and that was that. I'd push my feet into my shoes, always the right before the left. My body was sore, surprisingly awake, but achy. Hunching at the back of the van and dipping my head so as not to hit it on the way out, I pushed the door open to see two cameras pointing at my face. Jack and Sarah were doing their job. I smiled and hopped out of the van with a loud and energetic 'Good morning!' The hop I regretted, and the words they knew were in jest. But it was a good morning. Dark still, but no wind and no rain. This I had to be grateful for.

As I ran round the corner and back to the coast path, Andy shouted after me: 'Day two, and already on your second county. You'll run into Devon after Saltash.'

I had no idea where this was in relation to where I was, but it would happen today, and that felt good.

Without really realizing it, Andy and I were already starting to fine-tune our expedition relationship. But it didn't take long before our neat plan of seeing each other every few miles, eating, drinking then moving on, started to unravel. The coast path, especially the southern part, is remote, to say the least, with hills, rivers and inlets continually getting in the way of a neat, easy-to-follow route. Today's obstacles included the small rivers Tiddy and Lynher that feed the Tamar, causing a diversion up and around eventually to cross over via the Tamar Bridge. Andy was already stopping much more often to ensure I went the right way.

Navigating myself was causing two key issues. Firstly, I was constantly having to get my phone out of its pouch, pop my security code in, open the map app, find where I was, and see which turning I needed. This was annoying, and could add up to at least an hour of extra faffing. There were, of course, thousands of turns and T-junctions, alternative paths, all of which were potential wrong turns. This led to the second issue: stopping to navigate interrupted my rhythm. Mentally, I was automatically clocking the distance I covered between every stop to look at the map. Sometimes it was further than I thought and that would give me a boost, but mostly I was all too aware that I was only 50 or 60 metres further along than when I'd last looked at the phone. This would make the day long, very long, and would also drain my battery, and that would eventually result in me having to carry a battery pack. Andy was of course in the van, on roads, and so it wasn't long before he stepped in to run some of the paths with me as navigator, abandoning the van in order to make sure the potential wrong turns were avoided. He did this well and with a smile, and while we had additional vehicles to shuttle him back to the van, this method worked well.

Once over the Tamar Bridge out of Saltash, and now into Devon, I started to make my way through Plymouth and around its complicated harbour complex, over the River Plym then through Oreston, Jennycliff, Staddon Heights, Heybrook Bay and towards Clitters Wood, where, once again, I'd need to take a ferry to avoid a massive inland venture upstream. As I followed the map, trudging slowly along a very overgrown and very narrow coast path, I saw Andy running towards me. With no phone signal, little did I know that he had raced ahead in the van to pay off a local ferryman to stay open a little later than usual, before running 5 or so miles back along the path to make sure I was going in the right direction. In these remoter parts of Devon, inter-laced with rivers, there are lots of water crossings operated by independent chaps with tiny boats, and you can only trust Google so much. Andy, being from Devon, knew that the best way to ensure a crossing was to get to the ferry point in person, make sure the ferry was running, and part with a bit of cash to make sure the ferryman didn't knock off early.

I call the ferryman to see if I can persuade him to stay open a little later to support Nick's noble quest. Sniffing an opportunity, he tells me he doesn't like to work beyond four o'clock as this is when he usually starts to get a bit thirsty, and although his hint tells me that a few extra quid has clearly piqued his interest, he sounds a bit non-committal. I decide it's safer to park as close as I can, run ahead and speak to him in person so he can see the colour of my money – in this instance, orangey-brown. It's a remote spot and it takes me a while to run down there, but the ferryman turns out to be a nice chap and eventually agrees to hang around to take Nick, Paul and Paul's bike across for some extra beer money.

This boat, by the way, could hold no more than four people including the captain. If Andy hadn't thought ahead, my double-marathon-a-day target would have ended there. The large inland diversion would have messed up the route.

You may notice a theme developing here. I am doing the simple run-ning bit, while Andy slogs out the all-important logistical stuff, including driving, parking and bribing. Having paid the ferryman to stay open twenty minutes longer, the River Yealm was crossed in sec-onds, and I was back running again. Although I'd made it over, Andy was then left to charge back to the van to begin the long drive around to catch up with me.

Darkness fell before Andy finally reached me a long while later. With simple navigation, my tired legs tackled over 4,500 feet of eleva-tion before I made it around Worswell headland, through Netton, and inland to cross at the nearest bridge over the River Erme. The little town of Modbury was day 2's finishing post. A welcome sight. Vans, food, team and bed, with the van prepped for a short night before dawn.

The day, despite the ferry hassle, tough terrain and navigational challenges, had been glorious. I'd literally prayed for good weather and I was gifted bright sunshine, a cool breeze and clear skies. My tan was increasing, it seemed, at a rate inversely linked to my bodyweight's decline. I was already in calorie deficit to the tune of around 2,000 each day. But two days down, and over four marathons completed, we were on target. Little did we know, Andy and I were both pondering the same equation:

It's been another bruising, hilly day, and with Nick having been out for over thirteen hours, we're already trying to cram his recovery into a very tight window. Within a couple of hours of running a double marathon, Nick needs to elevate and ice his legs, eat, drink and get his mind and body into a state where he's able to sleep. We're only two days in, and it's too early to make any educated predictions, but with miles and miles of rugged, punishing coast path to come in the following days, it already feels like the key to sustaining this unbelievable endurance challenge will be maintaining what can only become an increasingly fine balance between exercise and recovery.

Day 3 – 53.47 miles – 6,922ft elevation
Modbury to Brixham
Communication lost

This book is not intended to be a daily record, but the first six days of my brutal opening week were pivotal, to say the least. How a week of double marathons can change everything. The hills of Cornwall, Devon and the Jurassic Coast beat me up. Both mentally and physically. After today, day 3, my right knee was shouting at me. The steep uphills were bad enough, but the downs were slower, and more painful.

Despite having run the South West Coast Path before, and being all too aware of the devil that it is, the preceding months in Italy and the French Alps had not been ideal training. The path, in all its undulating beauty, racks up an impressive 115,000 feet of elevation. And remember, this is just the tiny bit in the bottom left-hand corner of the country. The overall up and down of the British coast was fast becoming the loudest among many screaming struggles. Four Everests in height, in the south-west alone, was starting to put things into perspective.

Jagged rocks, dense foliage tinted with thousands of pastel shades, bright yellow gorse, long lush grass and tangles of weeds and nettles, the path cutting from ocean to cliff top and back again. Within a mile my feet could be touching sand or jumping over streams of sea water and then be running along a cliff path while I looked down 100 feet to the ocean. The vastness of the elevation range was stark, and my legs noticed.

Close to half a million years ago a thick ice sheet covered northern Europe, encompassing much of Britain. Fifty thousand years later, a huge glacial lake had formed in the east of England, stretching all the way across to what we now know as Cornwall, and as the size of this lake increased over the next fifty thousand years, it eventually burst its ice bank, flooding and creating the English Channel, and shaping much of the south coast. The more resistant rock of the south-west, lying further away from this event, escaped much of its ravages, and its rugged cliffs have withstood erosion ever since, retaining the elevation which was now causing my suffering. Thanks, geology.

The scale and age of the cliffs I was running along, as well as hurting me, made me feel so insignificant, and yet it was an enormous privilege to be there, to bear witness to the beauty of this prehistoric landscape. As I ran alone along the empty coast path, it was easy to imagine what it was like for the first wanderers to cross the land bridge from Europe, hunter-gatherers looking out for the lions, hippos and mammoths that once roamed our land.

Looking out over the vast ocean, the wind in my face, with the occasional cry of an oystercatcher on the shores below, the place felt like a true wilderness. Nettles stung my lower legs, thorns from overgrown paths snagged my clothing and uneven ground caused me to correct my stride over and over again. After thirty-two years of living on this island, I was finally exploring it.

Day 3 was eventful. The first time I was left to my own devices without support for more than 10 miles. Just me, a backpack and the coast path. The terrain under my feet didn't let up for a moment. It was ankle-rolling territory for most of the way.

With me on the remote coast path out of reach by road, Andy took the opportunity for his first dip of the trip, an icy plunge at South Milton Sands, before dashing up to Kingsbridge for some food shopping and a trip to the bank to get some expenses cash for the team. He then headed back down to where he estimated I would be by this point, although as it turned out he was way off. I was a little lost, and as the miles clocked up and I plodded on in my own haze, I ran straight past the crew, who were parked a little inland in a small National Trust car park. The team were all using the Life360 app, which allows you to track the locations of members of your group – very useful, unless you have no phone signal. Andy had calculated that I would be further ahead than I actually was, and with numerous different paths I could take, even running back along the trail would mean no guarantee of bumping into me. The team and I had now been out of contact for several hours, and it was clear to them that either we'd missed each other or, worse, something bad had happened. They were worried.

Meanwhile, with no support and no shops, I actually resorted to filling my water bottle from a half-empty dog bowl that had been left outside an outbuilding. I initially ran past it, but doubled back moments later realizing that this water, albeit possibly dirty, might be crucial. After all, I was sweating a lot and rapidly dehydrating, and I had no idea when I'd link up with the others again.

Eventually, I saw a cyclist coming towards me, bumping his bike over the big boulders. Although his face, along with the rest of him, was shaking quite a lot thanks to the rocks, I could see that it was Paul. An almost childlike grin spread across his face; he was just happy to be around for the ride. It made me smile, seeing him come clattering towards me.

The others were now only a mile or so ahead and he'd come back to look for me, concerned that I'd either fallen or got lost, or both. I hadn't – it was of course just a breakdown in communication. Although I was in desperate need of water, I was generally fine, if a little concerned that these communication issues could happen again, and maybe in the middle of a crisis. I met up with the gang along the cliff path and shared some stories of the trail, which had been stunning. Turquoise water, fields of cows, horses and sheep, waterfalls trickling over rocks and across paths, all under big Devon skies. I was in a good mood, but physically it was obvious I was knackered. My eyes were a little sunken, my face more gaunt and sunburnt than ever, and my feet barely lifting from the floor as I shuffled along.

A late lunch on the grassy knolls near Start Point Lighthouse just south-east of Salcombe followed. I downed a can of Tango, inhaled an ice cream, and I was off again. After a rushed change of clothes a little later on in the ferry queue at Dartmouth, it was over the River Dart and on to one final, very hilly 10 miles to Brixham. It was a brutal 3,000 feet over the last few hours of the day. My knees were sore and becoming weaker, but importantly I was still moving forward at a pace I could sustain . . . for a while.

It had been dark for a couple of hours by the time I reached Brixham. Andy and I crossed the day's finish line together. He had parked up, greeted his parents, who had come out to cheer me on, and then run with me for four laps of Brixham town centre as I clocked a few more miles to reach the magic double marathon figure. Not only was I running around Britain, but the target was two marathons a day for a hundred days. And so although I had reached the planned finishing post, 49 miles wasn't enough, it had to be 52.4. Andy ran while carrying my kebab. Yes, you heard right. I'd seen a kebab shop and the temptation after 50-odd miles was too great – I'd earned the calories. Andy ordered while I ran, and caught me up as I plodded through the town.

During that last hour, through mouthfuls of kebab, we discussed my knee and agreed I needed to ice and sleep as soon as I got back. During this debrief, we decided that from now on we were going to need to aim for just twenty minutes between running and sleeping, despite the big question over whether the time that left for food and post-run routines was anywhere near sustainable.

As we approached the car park that was our campsite, I saw a small group of people outside the vans silhouetted by a street light, and a ripple of applause wafted quietly up the street as I ran towards them. I was hunched over by this point, wrapped in an oversized grey hoody. It was well past sunset and getting cold. It had been a fifteen-hour running day and the gang had been waiting a while, but the reception lifted my spirits. Yas's family own a local Chinese restaurant and had kindly cooked and ferried out food for all of us. I ate mine two hours after everyone else then fell asleep with my fork in my hand and the small plastic takeaway tray balancing on a pillow on my lap. With a kebab and a large (and incredibly delicious) Chinese in my stomach, no wonder I slept well. I had burnt nearly 9,000 calories though, and despite the mountain of food I was still in a calorific deficit. Probably around 2,000 short once again. My weight was of course going in one direction, and with it, my momentum.

I later found out that, while I slept, the team had a longer discussion about sustainability, following such a late finish. The question raised, very rightly, was: could I keep this up? At the time it would probably have upset or even broken me to hear everyone voicing such doubts, but looking back, it was a very fair question.

I was supposed to be completing each day within twelve hours. I was also supposed to be eating more and sleeping more, and be experiencing much less pain in my legs. But currently I was finishing in the dark, two hours at least behind schedule, and my right knee was becoming a problem. At this point, though, I simply didn't have the energy to think about all that. Run, eat, sleep, repeat. That was all I could do. And, of course, the next day came even quicker than yesterday.

In fact, time, despite seeming as if it was my nemesis, was also my guardian. You see, in my experience there's a threshold with endurance sports. It takes grit, desire and sacrifice to get deep into the hurt locker – deep into exhaustion, pain and suffering. It's the first few days and weeks that are the hardest. But once the metaphorical hole is dug, it's much easier to make it your home, to learn to embrace that dark, dirty ditch – easier than to climb out of it. People often ask me, 'How do you not give up? How do you get up every day and keep running?' Quite simply, I don't have the energy to give up. Quitting would hurt more and cost me more energy in the long run, because I'd have to start again, and I'd once more have to work hard to break that initial ground, and begin digging again. And so once started, I've learnt to lean into the suffer-fest, to learn to enjoy it. Coming to peace with pain is frankly the quickest path to success. In a way it is in fact the lazy way to do it. Once the hole is dug, I actually start to enjoy being there.

Day 4 – 53.54 miles – 3,174ft elevation
Brixham to Sidmouth
Marathon virginities and the Butter Effect

The average life expectancy for a human being is around seventy-three years. That's worldwide. For me, as a Brit, it's eighty-one and a half years. That means that, during my lifetime, if I'm lucky, the sun will rise and set nearly thirty thousand times. Waking up on day 4, I sat up slightly and pulled myself towards the small, slightly scratched Perspex window. The orange hues of the morning caused my pupils to shrink as warm light covered my face. I squinted and pinched the blinds' mechanism more firmly to open them fully. It was a glorious morning. Even once I'd wiped away the condensation there was still a thick mist that covered Brixham Harbour. With the van parked side on, I had a post-card view of the mismatched collection of multicoloured boats, sails, small terraced houses and large heaps of fishing nets, lobster pots and flotation buoys in various sizes and colours. The low-lying mist muted the landscape so that the orange glow of the sun was diffused and calm. There was virtually no motion to the water either. Just an occasional ripple from a bird taking off or landing.

My sleepy gaze across the harbour was interrupted by the sound of next door's van door sliding closed, followed by footsteps. The crew had ventured out to take photos of the morning view. Some days I didn't want to get out of bed, but today it was certain to be a belter. I also had a slight spring in my step, mentally at least, because I knew the morning's running would be along the flat seafront for a good few miles. Or at least I thought it would be.

The route from Brixham around to Paignton turned out to be not quite as flat as I was hoping. My tiredness and the increasing pain in my right knee were also making me grumpy. I was kind of limping, kind of running as I shuffled past a series of tatty multi-coloured beach huts on Paignton seafront. I had my earphones in, listening to a book, but was missing most of what was said because the pain had reached a threshold that my mind couldn't tune out. It also weighed heavily that it was still only day 4, and I knew a 500-foot climb out of Torquay was coming up, followed by the remaining 40 miles I'd need to cover before the day was over. My mind was weakening, and I knew it. This feeling, of your mental state beginning to deteriorate, is much like watching a car begin to roll down a hill. You might try to jump in front of it and break its momentum, but ultimately the laws of gravity prevail and you won't be able to stop it. It was a scary mindset to be in, especially with several months of back-to-back double marathons ahead of me.

Along Torquay's seafront, I weaved slowly around benches, bins, roadworks and the odd morning dog walker. In the distance I could see the WeSUP café and around forty people gathered on the bandstand-style terrace overlooking the harbour, a group of family, friends and fellow runners that I'd arranged to meet. I pocketed my earphones, gritted my teeth and got my head down. A short break and some smiling faces were just up ahead. Maybe this would reset my mood.

About 400 metres from reaching them, out of nowhere, the combination of the pain in my legs and the fatigue created a tension that suddenly had to be released. Without really realizing it, I let out a deep, gruff scream. It was loud, and I think I scared an elderly lady walking on the other side of the road. I immediately felt terrible, which of course worsened my mood. I was now experiencing a great deal of discomfort and was seemingly not in control of my actions. Not only had I startled the old lady, but I'd shocked myself. I hadn't been aware I was in such a mental cul-de-sac. Only once before had I let out such a scream of frustration, and that was with a broken ankle in the Sahara Desert many years earlier.

Desperately hoping that the happy gathering of people hadn't heard the scream, I got closer to them and eventually made it to the little café area. WeSUP had put on fresh pastries and drinks, and our group were grasping cups of tea and pieces of cake on small saucers. It was about 8 a.m. by this point and I'd covered 10 miles in two hours. Everyone was full of energy and keen to show their support. Upon reaching the elevated terrace, I made another of my sarcastically joyous good morning calls, and proceeded to dramatically crawl up the three or four steps to the small seating area and pretend to fall asleep. Ever keen to secure a little laugh at my own expense, this broke the ice while delivering my message of 'I'm knackered, leave me be for a moment'.

I rested there for about ten minutes, said a few hellos, and put on my best smile. They had no idea how much I was suffering. Note to self: you only have energy for running, and you don't even have that. This whole little situation had served as a reminder that I had to be ruthless with my energy, my legs, my time – the running was the only thing that mattered.

With that, I pushed down on a small wooden café seat and pulled myself upright again. I hobbled away from the cakes and people, and just started running with the water on my right as usual. I think everyone was expecting me to stick around a little longer, or at least say bye. I'd usually be a bit more communicative, but I just wanted to get my head back in the game. A bit rude? Possibly, but social etiquette wasn't very high on my list of concerns. I had a long road ahead of me, not to mention the hill out of Torquay, and my body was already close to breaking.

About a mile later I started to shrug off some of my antisocial over-tired mood, and Yas met me in her running gear, along with her old school friend Holly. Neither of them had ever run a marathon before, and were not intending to, but were suited and booted, complete with matching leggings and black Freetrain vests (designed to hold your phone against your chest). They were both in their early to mid-twenties, had energy to match – energy I could only wish for – and had come out to run about 10 kilometres.

Yas was good at being aware of my mood, and she could tell she hadn't chosen the best day to join me. In all honesty, my heart sank. I really just wanted to run on my own. But as the three of us trotted along, chatting to the girls, and having picked up a few more fellow runners on the climb out of Torquay, I found my spirits lifting. The sun was helping too. It was warm, with virtually no breeze, and their energy was infectious. They didn't know it, but they had turned my mood on its head. Even with the pain, the day was starting to become fun, and before long we were laughing about anything and everything, putting the world to rights, and even having a singalong as we ran. This, for those who aren't runners, is the runner's high, and is what running in groups is all about.

Meanwhile, Andy was trying to get the hang of life on the road:

From a viewpoint outside Teignmouth, I look out at Covid-emptied cruise ships moored in the bay. The morning haze has blended sea and sky, and with no horizon for reference, they look like ghost ships floating in nothing but mist. I wonder why there are stories of ships, trains and aircraft appearing as apparitions. Why have we deemed vehicles capable of becoming ghosts when they don't have souls? If this is the type of nonsensical metaphysical conundrum that will be occupying my mind in lay-bys and car parks over the next few months, it's going to be a long trip.

I was around 17 miles down when Yas and Holly reached their 10K mark for the day. They decided to stay on for a few more miles until we reached a scheduled pit stop at a local school up ahead. Both Yas and Holly were running strong, if a little slower now, and we chatted some more as the miles ticked by. We'd assumed the school was 'around the corner' when in fact it was around many corners, and over many hills.

Having picked up another ice cream, we made our way through Dawlish before rejoining Andy and the rest of the gang further up the coast. The girls had now, to their surprise, run over half a marathon, a huge milestone for them, and they were over the moon. I was too. My mood had lifted, and I was enjoying the running. All thanks to the collective efforts of Holly, Yas and the team.

There was no 'coast path' at this point, just a pavement running alongside the railway line that flanks this part of the coast. As the railway rounded the corner to follow the Exe Estuary, so did we, and just around the bend we could see and indeed hear a gathering of excitable school kids all waving and shouting outside their school. One of the teachers from Cockwood Primary School had got in touch with the team earlier and asked if I wouldn't mind doing a quick stop to see the pupils. It was lovely to have the support from the school. I signed some bits and pieces, posed for a photo, high-fived what must have been two hundred kids, and thanked the staff and head teacher. I love the thought that encounters like this might plant a small seed of inspiration, even if just for one child, encouraging them towards a life of adventure. It doesn't take much – maybe, just maybe, one or two of them will remember a chap running past their school. And maybe it will embolden them to try something different. This thought gave me a boost. Thanks to them, I felt stronger again.

The original route plan had me taking the small ferry from Starcross over the Exe to Exmouth. But because I finished yesterday slightly further into Brixham than planned, and with various bits of the coast path inaccessible today, my route was slightly more direct, so it actually made mathematical sense to run up the River Exe, cross the bridge further inland, run back down the other side and finish the day at Sidmouth as planned.

It's really not easy to plot a route along paths and over rivers, all while being entirely unaware of diversions, closed paths, new cut-throughs and various other changes of route along the way. Andy had done some careful calculations in a lay-by with his laptop balanced on the steering wheel and worked out that this reroute would put me on about the right mileage by Sidmouth. Back in line with the original plan, finishing day 4 more or less where we needed to be.

I ran on, expecting to leave Yas and Holly behind . . . but no. Yas had done her stint and was happy with it, so she hopped on Paul's bike to cycle along with us. Holly, meanwhile, was in beast mode, and despite never having run anywhere near the distance we'd already covered, wanted to get as close to a marathon as possible. Andy likes to call this 'the Butter Effect', defined as the phenomenon whereby runners coming to join me for a few miles invariably find themselves running considerably further than they (a) expected to, (b) have before and (c) have brought enough water for.

By mid-afternoon, as I approached the 40-mile mark, Holly clocked the magical 26.2 miles. She was in bits for the last 4 or 5 miles, but she made it. The path along the river served as a perfect place to finish the last 10 miles of her day on the flat, with no traffic and just the river for a view.

Holly and I hugged as she reached 26.2 miles. She cried, I cried for her, and we all felt a huge sense of accomplishment. In the closing miles of her marathon distance we had spoken of what running offers people. How running can transform a life. Holly won't mind me saying that it transformed hers. The fitness is the physical benefit, but the emotional and mental elements to running are numerous, and last long into the years ahead. We are all very good at living in our comfortable bubble, but marathon-running forces us to experience the overwhelming realization that being uncomfortable, suffering a bit, and pushing through pain is unfathomably and exponentially more enriching to life than taking the easy route. It teaches us, it evolves us, it opens doors to other aspects of life, it gives us strength. I saw all this in Holly as she finished her marathon. It hurt her, but it was worth it.

The day had started with a glorious view, then my legs had turned my mind to mush and frustrations followed, but once joined by Yas and Holly, and having met the kids at Cockwood Primary, and with Holly then reaching a full marathon distance, my mind was on a high again.

At Exmouth, Amy headed home and our team got a little smaller. She'd been fun to have around, not to mention very helpful, and we would miss her. What a rollercoaster of a day, and it still wasn't quite over. My legs still had another 10 miles to fumble through, and I was in for another pleasant surprise.

Looking back over photos of the day, we were blessed with blue sky from start to finish, the smiles were wide, and the sense of togetherness was high. We were all enjoying the journey as a unit, and to top it off I was joined for the last few miles by a fresh set of faces: Andy (known as 'the other Andy') and his partner Lucy. I'd first met this other Andy in the capital of Niger, Niamey, three years earlier, on my Running the World adventure. He worked for the UK government in the Stabilisation Unit, helping various communities in countries all over the world. We hit it off, and he'd since become a good friend and an occasional running buddy. I was honoured that he and Lucy had taken time out of their busy lives to come and visit me, and pleased that my mood wasn't still in the gutter as it had been in the morning. We covered the last 600 feet of elevation together, trudging up and over Pinn Hill, not far from the aptly named High Peak Park, dropping down into Sidmouth. It was great to have their company and they quite literally got me over the last hill of the day.

To my surprise, I finished day 4 in daylight, the first time that had happened on the trip, even if the sun was setting minutes after I'd taken my shoes off. I finished in about thirteen hours, not what had become the usual fifteen. I must give some credit for this to the lack of extreme elevation, and of course the kind weather, but the day was really such a success thanks to the people surrounding me.

I curled up in the van, having run eight marathons in four days. Holly had completed a marathon for the first time, I'd run with brilliant friends, Andy had managed to fit in a swim in the Exe, the team had gathered for a picnic at the finish line and I'd eaten fish and chips for dinner. We were all in high spirits. I went to bed with a smile, the van parked in a small council car park just off the esplanade next to a cricket pitch. It was one of those days that felt like a week. It was a slog, but we'd seen and done so much. Dare I say, I think I enjoyed it.

I had a word with myself that night, and a mental reset. My body was still battered, but I'd deal with that tomorrow.

Day 5 – 52.79 miles – 4,325ft elevation
Sidmouth to Portland
The unravelling

As I'm writing this, I realize that even now, day 5 doesn't feel like day 5 at all, it feels like day 50. The emotional peaks and troughs, the variety of the landscape, the countless little villages, the wonderful people, the pain, the logistical challenges, the near-constant intake of food . . . so much happened in the first few days that time felt warped. I assume this was partly because of the stark contrast with the days and weeks before the start line, when although I was busy prepping for the journey I wasn't doing any running. Running for between twelve and fifteen hours isn't just about the distance covered, it's actually shocking how much more of a day you feel like you've had. There's not a second that's wasted. But boy could I have done with some more hours.

Despite having gone to bed the night before on a huge pillow of positive energy, today would, sadly, bring about the true unravelling of my mind and body. I'm just pleased that when I set off from Sidmouth that morning I had no idea of the pain to come.

When you mention running to people, or more accurately running thousands of miles, the first thing people say is 'Oh that must ruin your knees – you're crazy' and 'You won't have any knees left soon', followed by familiar quips like 'I can't even run for a bus' or 'I only run to the fridge'. In reality, though, they're right. My knees and my legs *were* sore and aching, but there were also the more indirect effects of doing an adventure like this completing the picture, the masterpiece of pain. Day 5's first hurdle was mouth ulcers. I'd been drinking copious amounts of electrolyte sachets mixed with water, and taking salt tablets each morning in an attempt to avoid cramps and maintain my hydration levels. It's very easy to piss out all the good bits and bobs in your body through drinking lots of water, and without salt and electrolytes the hydration process doesn't work properly. It's truly not just about water.

I'm not entirely sure of the science behind all this, but having done a little research, my understanding is that salt, sugar and generally not paying attention to oral health (because you're knackered) can change things like saliva pH, the flow rate of saliva, and of course the bacteria count. Basically, one of the side effects of running super-long distances, which requires topping up my glucose levels and adding extra salt and electrolytes to my diet, is that my oral health is terrible. By day 5 I had around six large, painful ulcers on the inside of my lower lip, made worse by the fact that I've inherited the habit from my father of gently and slowly chewing the inside of my cheek when I'm nervous or thinking hard about things. I'd often find myself chewing on my cheek without realizing, only for the taste of iron from my blood to alert me and cause me to stop.

Before setting off, I hastily rooted around in my little box under the bed, full of supplies, medical bits, extra energy gels, tablets and spare water bottles. Alas, no luck. I'd packed everything under the sun, but had forgotten my ulcer cream. Five or so miles in, just as I reached the crest of the bastard climb out of Sidmouth, Andy appeared with a tube of Bonjela (other ulcer creams are available), along with water and a heavenly 'Maccy D's' – my usual order: double sausage and egg McMuffin meal with an extra hash brown and a hot chocolate. My hero.

With the ulcers settling down and 600 feet of elevation out of Sidmouth behind me, it was a hefty 5-mile descent towards Seaton. And yes, you guessed it, from there I'd be climbing back up again, totting up another 700 feet towards Lyme Regis. This second hill was eventually summited, and Andy handed me more ulcer cream on the brow of it before another steep descent. Parked in a shallow lay-by, he was leaning out of the van holding out his water bottle to say cheers with mine – I'd now run out of Devon and had made it to my third county in five days. Welcome to Dorset, home of the Jurassic Coast. These little wins worked wonders for me. Positivity is of course key at every moment of the day, and Andy knew it. Never miss a chance to celebrate a success, we said, no matter how small, and we didn't.

Andy pulled away, resting one increasingly tanned arm out of the window, a couple of beeps of the horn for good measure, and he was away down the hill. The next major town would be Bridport, or somewhere near it. But of course, not before another 500 feet down and then up again. It was at this moment, once Andy had disappeared around the corner, that my stomach started to churn and I began to feel decidedly unsettled. This was hurdle number two of the day. Oh dear.

As the weeks passed it became almost comical quite how many times I'd start to feel the need for a poo just as Andy and the van containing the toilet disappeared out of sight. I am ashamed and proud in equal measure to say that, throughout my time running around Britain, I'm sure that I deposited more brown parcels 'in the wild' than I did in toilets. Without getting too graphic, today I'd be notching up a fair few wild poos. Some, however, were not quite as wild as I would have liked. For this first one, I hastily found a spot just out of sight of passing cars, down a freshly trimmed embankment next to one of those metal dual carriageway barriers, which I nervously grasped as I squatted. Disgusted? Well, I'm just getting started. As were my bowels, unfortunately.

These occasions soon became routine. Naturally the usual wipe-and-flush was unavailable, so a good handful of leaves or grass would have to suffice until I could reach Andy and the van, and the sanctuary of toilet paper, baby wipes and hand sanitizer.

On day 5, this process was repeated every 2 to 4 miles. Fantastic. It was rather clear my stomach had had enough of the various quick and easy foods and nutritional substitutes I'd been shovelling down every day. My body had decided it was time for a purge. The miles ticked along, the wild toilet parcels were deposited like some kind of dirty Hansel and Gretel brown breadcrumb trail, and the elevation continued all the way to Bridport.

Happily, Andy was already thinking about how to replace those lost calories:

At Lyme Regis, I stop for fuel at an eccentric petrol station celebrating its location on Dorset's Jurassic Coast. Various dinosaurs, none of them Jurassic, are dotted around the forecourt next to the obligatory boat full of flowers and a big plastic Costa cup. It feels a bit like one of Alan Partridge's film ideas: Jurassic Service Station. *It's nearly lunchtime, so a little further on, somewhere near Bridport, I stop at another memorable roadside spot, this time a lorry stop, where I send Nick a picture of the greasy spoon menu so he can pre-order. He opts for the full English and a can of Tango, the trucker's special, and by the time he arrives his food is ready and I've bagged the most exclusive table in the picnic area, although there's plenty of evidence lying about to suggest that it's also used for certain other outdoor pursuits, the type you'd probably feel too full to partake in after a massive fry-up.*

With the temperature rising to deliver the hottest day of the journey so far, a roasting 19°C, and with the rest of the team at least 20 miles ahead, Andy and I voice-clipped each other via WhatsApp and he sent me a location pin to head for. The classically gritty lorry stop was just off route a few miles ahead. Despite my bowels protesting, my hunger won the battle for lunch. I arrived just as Andy was taking delivery of a large polystyrene box from a greasy spoon hatch. I was, oddly, craving a hot meal, despite the heat, so a quick break to scoff down some food, and another visit to the bathroom of course, would be the ideal lunchtime pit stop. Plus, it was just after the 28-mile mark, so the first marathon of the day was complete.

I sat down on one of the three or four rickety bird-poo-stained benches in the small set-back lay-by, large trees separating the busy road from the service area, muffling the noise of passing traffic. Various truckers and their trucks came and went as I spent about ten minutes downing the Tango and a full English with extra fried bread to the tune of air brakes and the chug of diesel engines.

Andy sat opposite me and we took stock. I was in pretty good spirits, but I think I had now entered the delirium stage of the journey. I'd completed nine marathons in four and a half days without a shower, having virtually pooed myself half a dozen times in a matter of hours. We laughed and chatted, realizing that we'd likely stopped for lunch in one of Britain's prime dogging spots. As I stood up to swing my leg back out from under the bench, I noticed a used condom stuck to my shoe. I opted not to revisit the grim, filthy double cubicle toilet block, and instead hobbled out of the lay-by and on towards the finishing post for day 5. Just 24 miles to go. I removed the condom before leaving, of course, by scraping my foot on the ground.

By 36 miles I'd completed the last of the five big hills of the day, at Abbotsbury, albeit very slowly. It was now downhill before a relatively flat evening run on to the Isle of Portland via Weymouth. These were places I knew well and had run, cycled and swum near as a kid, and in training in fact.

My body, however, had one final protest to make. The mouth ulcers hadn't stopped me, nor had the shits, but now my right knee was fast becoming a real show-stopper. This reached its peak agony as I began the long descent towards Portland, and it soon became unrunnable. My steps were now short and laboured.

I'd played it down for as long as I could, before eventually relenting to Yas's suggestion of putting a shout out on social media to any nearby physios who might be able to help. My knee was now unable even to bear weight without pain; bending it was eye-wateringly sore, making downhill running virtually impossible. It had swollen into a large puffy ball, like an oversized, overripe grapefruit. Step by step I gritted my teeth to the point my jaw and gums were starting to hurt. I was letting out audible moans as I plodded by. With the rest of the team having gone ahead to Portland Bill lighthouse to set up for the night and prepare for my arrival, Andy was staying close, edging ahead just a few hundred metres at a time, stopping anywhere he could to offer any support I might need.

To my surprise, only a few minutes after her social media request I had a call from Yas, who'd heard from a couple of local physios. Ideally, we were after someone who had the time to drop by in person to take a look at me at the side of the road. We couldn't afford the time to visit them, given that I was already behind schedule today. One of the physios was busy at that point, but kindly offered to keep an eye on my tracker and drop by once I got nearer Portland. The other, a chap named Tim, offered to do what he could over the phone, so, at our next stop, with my bed hastily converted into a treatment table, Tim talked Andy through the technique for examining my knee to try and determine where the problem lay. From what we could work out, it seemed likely to be a tendon issue, and Tim explained to Andy how best to tape up my knee and advised getting hold of some walking poles, as even taking a fraction of the weight off would help. It was helpful stuff and all Tim could offer without seeing me in person, but I still had a number of miles to cover.

Ignoring the stunning West Dorset Heritage Coast views and the setting sun twinkling on the Channel, I topped up on painkillers and anti-inflammatories and headed out with a heavily strapped leg. My mood was now the lowest of the low. I was quietly fearing the worst, but attempting to maintain a brave face. The worst, of course, was that my knee had been confirmed as needing attention, and might be too much of an issue for me to continue. I promptly tried to bury these thoughts, but they were never far from my mind.

It's probably time to take a reality check now. I was only five days into what was supposed to be a hundred-day, two-hundred-marathon mission, and I was in bits.

The record for a circumnavigation of Britain on foot was around 350 days. I was aiming to knock over 70 per cent off that, and in all honesty I was starting to have doubts. My thoughts began to follow a familiar sequence. Firstly, had I just been overambitious? Had I not trained enough? Had I been silly starting in the south-west, where all the bastard hills are, and above all – and worst of all – had I taken on something I couldn't possibly finish? This was a crippling thought, and every time it came into my head all the hairs on my arms would stand on end, and I'd shiver. The thought of not finishing was unbearable. Over the years, I'd learned to create a mental fortress to shut out any pain or doubt, or the temptation to quit when things get tough. The knowledge that all I had to do was keep plodding forward had allowed me to complete whatever challenge I had set myself. I'm an endurance athlete. And even though towards the end of day 5 I felt so far from that title, that's all I had to do – endure. Endure, and the finish line would come at some point.

The second thing that went through my mind, which usually happens immediately after I contemplate failure, was an internal pep talk that said, 'Man up, you're letting your body control your mind. Stop. Your mind controls your body.' I suppose only time would tell if that was true.

I'd come inland a little to avoid some closed paths and some areas where I'd have little or no support due to the terrain or lack of accessibility by vehicle. Sheep and cows roamed in the middle distance, while my legs painfully shuffled along into the night, my grubby, tired body complete with crusty knee from the lashings of anti-inflammatory gel and sticky KT tape, designed to hold the joint together, which bent painfully with every stride. My ankles and the backs of my knees were also frothing with sweat through my compression tights.

The finish line was still a long way off, although this wouldn't have been the case had I been running. It was only 8 miles away, but I was now only managing to maintain small, delicate, slow steps; and, as if the weather gods had felt left out, they too now turned on me, and as darkness fell the few fluffy white clouds of the day turned to a swirling mess of drizzle. This surely was the final hurdle. Surely.

On nearly every run I do, I carry my phone. It is a bit of a comfort blanket. I can use it to listen to podcasts, books and music, I can call people, I can navigate, I can speak to the team, I can take photos and videos. But rain stops me from doing this. I usually run with my phone in an Arch Max belt around my waist. It's just a small elasticated bit of fabric with some phone-size pockets. Simple but perfect, and I'd highly recommend it. However, when it's wet, very wet, the waistband rubs against my phone, and the water acts like a finger randomly selecting numbers to try to unlock it. Naturally this fails. This happens over and over again and eventually locks me out of my phone for a few minutes, or sometimes days. Nothing I've tried has ever stopped this from happening, so the solution was to drop my phone off with Andy in the van and continue without it. This, as you can imagine, made each mile extra long, and removed the last layer of defence against my dwindling mood.

But on I shuffled, and thirteen hours in, I made it to within touching distance of Portland. Following the call with Tim, I'd contacted my parents, who live fairly locally, to ask them to bring over some walking poles. My brilliant, endlessly selfless mum and dad had not only brought me the poles, they'd also dropped off a large homemade cottage pie with Nikki, enough to feed us all. Now that I had the poles, Andy drove ahead to park up and run back so he could provide constant support for the last few miles. Unfortunately, the adjustment clip instantly gave out on one of the poles, rendering it useless, and I ended up carrying them into Portland, where I was met by Andy running towards me to help me over the line.

My energy level at this point was much like my stomach, knee and pants – pretty shitty! I remember Andy commenting on the fact that at least my mouth ulcers were gone and that it was something to celebrate. I sluggishly held my poles in the air to acknowledge this smallest of wins, we giggled deliriously and plodded on, stopping often to re-strap my knee and generally search in the dark for the enthusiasm to continue.

To reach Portland, there's a fast causewayed road with a double-depth pavement running alongside Chesil Beach, possibly the most bleak stretch of tarmac in the country. In daylight I'm sure it's rather lovely – after all, there's just ocean and rocks either side, and it connects the Isle of Portland to the rest of the country. Lined with dim, flickering street lights, this road is at least a mile long. In the driving rain and wind and in my current condition, it felt like an endless treadmill, with the cruel reality that Portland is basically a large hill, meaning one final grim climb to the finish.

At 50 miles, with just two and a bit more to cover before I could sleep, a chap drove past slowly, braked and reversed back to us with his window down – our second friendly neighbourhood physio of the day, a tall, strong-looking chap in his thirties called Matt (at least I think he was called Matt. Sorry, Matt, if you're reading this, and you know your name is not Matt. I do apologize. I and the entire team were rather exhausted by this point.) After saying hello, he pulled ahead, parked up outside the front of a small kebab place and, without beating around the bush, said, 'That bad, eh?' He could see I was quite literally on my last legs – well, actually my last leg. My left knee was fine, it was just my right. I wasn't sure what I was expecting, but after a five-minute inspection on the kerbside he confirmed what the other physio, Tim, had explained to Andy over the phone: that rather than being a joint problem, it was more likely to be damage to the tendons around my knee, and possibly the meniscus. The meniscus is a C-shaped piece of tough cartilage that acts as a shock absorber between the bones and there was a possibility that it was either heavily damaged or had maybe even inverted. Could be worse, but not what I wanted to hear. I don't remember thanking Matt for his help. I was in a haze of exhaustion. What I can remember is nearly falling asleep during his inspection of my knee, as I lay on the pavement, in the dark, with the rain falling on my face.

I still had a couple of miles to cover to finish the minimum of 52.4, but I couldn't face the climb up on to Portland, so Andy called the crew to ask them to relocate down to a small, grotty car park we'd passed on the causeway, while we covered the final distance up and down the flat road. Over the last mile, before hobbling into the van and falling straight to sleep, Andy and I very briefly touched on the plan for tomorrow. We couldn't avoid it any longer. The truth was that if tomorrow was even vaguely similar to today, I wouldn't be running very far, if at all. Despite my mood, I decided just to continue and hope for the best, relying on the mysterious medicine of sleep, even if only a few hours. It was now close to 11 p.m. Andy was a little more hesitant about my blasé plan, but we did agree that no matter how I felt, I would try, and if I had to stop, then that was that. Not something I was ready for, even if my body was trying to persuade me otherwise.

There are, from day 5, some horrendous photos of me looking very glum and drenched by rain and misery. Jack and Sarah, in their infinite youthful energy, were like photo ninjas, darting about in the shadows. Already dressed for bed but with cameras in hand, they scrambled around the manmade embankment stealthily snapping my mood for posterity as I shuffled to the finishing post. This, as the pictures captured, was a dark, dark mile. None of us, crew included, were enjoying day 5, but the prize at the end of it was my mum's lovely cottage pie, which added some well-needed cheer before bed.

I recall very little after stopping my watch and being hoisted from behind into the back of the van. My only memory is hearing the wind and rain on the roof. The drumming, along with the slight sway as gusts of stronger winds blew over the embankment, rocked me to sleep.

Day 6 – 53.23 miles – 3,038ft elevation
Portland to Bournemouth
The day of the dead

Ignorance is bliss. Had I had any idea of what day 6 would be like, I would have cried like a baby before even sliding on a shoe.

A bird's-eye view of our little gaggle of vans looked exactly how an adventure crew set-up should look. Three vans side by side, parked closely together to shield us from the wind that was hurling itself over the sea wall behind us. A free overnight car park, no barrier and no other cars occupying the area. Puddles of wind-rippled rainwater lying in clusters around us.

I woke up sure that only minutes had passed since I'd drifted off to sleep, and that the darkness outside was night-time not early morning. Opening my eyes, I could see that Andy had my compression socks and shorts draped over the small piece of upright glass that acted as a separator between kitchen and bedroom. The smell was strong. Wet, dirty clothes drying next to the four hobs, foul steam infusing the van. The click, click, click of Andy pressing the cooker's ignition switch would stir and often wake me each morning, just as it did today. My heart sank when he offered me a bagel. That meant it definitely was morning. I thought it was some sick joke. No way could it be morning already. The rain still pelted off the roof and the gaps in the window blinds still revealed dark, bleak skies. Had it really rained all night, and was it already time to venture out again? Yes it had, and yes it was.

The problem with sleeping, especially only a bit when you need a lot, is that the journey from vertical to horizontal takes no time whatsoever, but returning from horizontal to vertical seems to take more energy and time than is available. Andy and I didn't need to say it, but we knew it. It was going to be a brutal day.

I set the expectations immediately: 'I'm going to be sensible today, but I *will* get to Bournemouth.' Obviously this was a stupid contradiction, and I could see in Andy's eyes that it made no sense. He kept quiet as I let it sink in. We both did.

This was the first full day of the route that I'd run before in one go, and I'd ridden it on a bike many times too. The significance of Bournemouth is that both my brother and I have homes minutes from the pier, just one road apart actually. The Butter family also have a beach hut built by my granddad just a short way up the coast. In fact, his memorial bench overlooks the bay from Bournemouth to Old Harry Rocks, just north of Swanage. When I was growing up, Bournemouth was the nearest town to our small tweed-and-wellies kinda village just 30 miles north. The last 20 miles of the day I knew blindfolded. So I knew what was coming, and that it wasn't horrendous given a fully functioning body, but with one leg out of the equation, I was heading into the rain at 6 a.m. on day 6 with nothing but good old-fashioned hope.

I am very fond of this section of the coast of Britain – when I'm not trying to run it on an injured leg, of course. The cliffs, rocks and bays that run from Exmouth all the way to Old Harry Rocks span the 96 miles of the famous Jurassic Coast. This stretch makes it on to the World Heritage site list, and rightly so. With around 185 million years of geological history visible from the sea, the coast from Portland to Bournemouth contains some of the best cliffs and rock formations anywhere in the world. As well as its incredible geology, this section of coast was pivotal in the Second World War, with Portland having one of the largest Royal Navy bases in the country. From Lyme Bay, where geologists have identified over seventy unique layers of rock, to the limestone archway of Durdle Door, the landscape is beyond special. It was a shame, then, that it was pissing with rain and my eyes were firmly glued to the few metres of road in front of me, my mind off in some hazy land far from here.

Day 6 has since been spoken about by the team and with close friends over and over again. It was physically one of the toughest days of my life. The usual daily limit of twelve hours was of course already out of the window, and we estimated a running/walking day of at least sixteen hours. You may recall that a day is twenty-four hours long, so this wouldn't leave much room for sleep.

From Portland to Bournemouth, the coastline is littered with National Trust protected areas and numerous evil-sounding hills, such as Stair Hole and Great Hill. My route plan had me climbing up and out of Portland, through Weymouth and over Osmington Mills, and following an undulating path along the cliffs at around 300 feet for 20 or so miles, looking down to the blue greens of the ocean below. Then down into Lulworth, past the Fossil Forest, past Kimmeridge Bay, up and over again to the famous Dancing Ledge, around Durlston Country Park and National Nature Reserve, complete with the Anvil Point Lighthouse, and into Swanage, before rounding Old Harry Rocks and then eventually across Studland Beach, take the Sandbanks ferry towards Poole, and finally reaching Bournemouth. My target for the day was Bournemouth Pier. A mere double marathon, again.

Andy's diary summed the situation up:

The only sensible option today is to continue avoiding coast paths, unless they're along flat seafronts, and we've taken to using the Footpath app to map routes at the start of each day. It's a good way of comparing the total ascent and steepness of different options, and although we try to minimize the ups and downs, there's no easy way of getting through this last hilly section of coast before the flatter terrain after Bournemouth.

With jacket on, hood up, hat and gloves on, and buff pulled up high, I checked the dash temperature: 1°C. It was still early of course, dark and raining, and although my teeth were freshly brushed, the rest of me was tired, sluggish and grim. It took all the morning energy I had to pull on my damp shorts, calf compression, quad compression and socks over my feeble and frail limbs and squeeze my aching toes and feet into my shoes. My knee was already throbbing and swollen. The bagel, a cup of tea, my usual cocktail of tablets (extra painkillers), water, a quick loo visit and a good old-fashioned pat on the back from Andy sent me on my way. I pushed the back door open, placed my tea on the side and stepped out straight into a puddle. My right foot was instantly soaked. I shut the door but it didn't quite close, so I slammed it harder the second time. Poppy was at the window in the neighbouring van while Nikki made her own morning tea. Poppy growled, not recognizing me with my all-black robber-like running gear on. The van's fifteen-year-old engine chugged into life. Andy looked at me from the driver's window for an eye-to-eye acknowledgement that I was grateful for the support he was about to give. His eyes were tired, with hefty bags, but his expression was one of reassurance and readiness for the day ahead. I set off under the street lamps, hobbling around the puddles, knee already screaming and knuckles white, gripping the now fixed walking poles.

Andy had spent most free moments over the past twenty-four hours learning how to correctly strap this sort of injury and, in addition to the advice from the two physios, had also turned to the ultimate teacher: YouTube. While Andy supported me through the first miles, Nikki dashed into Weymouth and later dropped off around £100 worth of assorted physio and support tapes and strapping, everything Andy needed to patch me up. Once again the silent supporter was working diligently to push me closer to the finishing post.

Using the poles to bear some of my weight as I progressed back along the lonely spit towards Weymouth and beyond, I made a list of the benefits of having an injury, any positive thing I could think of. Most notable was the fact that I would be able to eat more, shortly followed by new parameters being set for pace. The team knew I would be slower, and therefore there were no time pressures to meet people at particular places. Not that this was a big pressure anyway, but it might help preserve the rest of my body, if not my dodgy right knee.

After only an hour, and after much debate as to whether or not I should even continue, I'd sucked up the pain and made it the few miles to Weymouth for a stop for breakfast. Pathetic really. I'd only covered a short distance, but at least I was making headway and so that ticked the principal criterion: forward progress. The extra calories helped too, and many hours later, after several knee treatment stops, I rather shocked myself by reaching Lulworth, some 20 miles into the day. My knee was very angry with me. I had been using every trick in the book to keep the pain away from it and disperse the injury load into other parts of my body. You're always told to 'try not to overcompensate' with an injury, but let's be real, you'll do anything to relieve the pain, even if more pain elsewhere is the likely result. And yes, you guessed it, that's exactly what happened.

Having limped, walked and basically crawled to complete my first marathon of the day, it had taken me over eight hours to reach the midway point, not far south of Wareham. These eight hours were made up of painkillers, frequent stops to strap my leg and slow climbs up and over several 300-foot hills, Andy all the while staying close enough to provide a hobbling buffet, never more than a mile ahead. I powered myself on chocolate. Plus pastries, crisps, and basically any junk food that would make the day less painful. At this point I could see the light at the end of the tunnel. I knew I could run a marathon, I'd run hundreds, I'd just done one that morning – what's one more?

Those first 26.2 miles were completed thanks to Andy's support, Nikki's text message encouragements, and a healthy helping of stubbornness. Which, in the endurance world, is packaged up as the impressive but largely bullshit concepts of determination and resilience. I was continuing because I couldn't face stopping.

At one point a lovely mother–daughter combo had stopped by to hand me some products from their local chocolate business. I was lifted by both their special tasty treats and their kind words. They'd followed my journeys and challenges over the years and had seen that I'd be passing. Most days I'd have local folk who'd stumbled across my little jog around the country via social media, or maybe the radio or the telly, come out to wave and say hello, or even join me for a few miles. Some days we'd have hundreds of interactions with people, and on others just the occasional hello from a family or couple wanting to wish me well. We never had a day without one of these encounters, which is pretty amazing really. Everyone was well-meaning and lovely. It was heartening to meet so many brilliant people who had selflessly gone out of their way to offer support and urge me on.

The company-to-energy ratio was not a constant. Some days, the more company I had, the less energy I'd have. I loved company, but too much would finish me off and I'd mentally sink into my own head. Other days, it would spur me on. Largely, the emotional intelligence of whoever joined me was of key importance – meaning an awareness of my pain and exhaustion and understanding when I was too tired for chatting.

As I finished the chocolate, something clicked in my mind. I was becoming ashamed of my slow progress. Talking to the two ladies had jolted me. I was going too slowly for this to be sustained. It hit me hard, and I tried to dig myself out of a mental trap. In hindsight this was largely down to fatigue and the lack of time my brain had to clean and tidy itself from the previous day's futile battle to finish before sunset. This mental housekeeping is utterly vital to remaining positive. The extra glucose that I'd been shovelling down me, and which had pushed me on past marathon one of the day, was now delivering a sugar low, and I fell into a gloomy quicksand of negative emotions.

The brief chat with the chocolate ladies was a trigger point of some kind, and the remainder of the day was a struggle at best. This was made worse by the fact that I knew the big hilly miles were still to come. I had only just about finished the easy bit.

Flagging Andy down, I explained that I was in a bad headspace, and to make matters worse, my left shin and Achilles were now, like my knee, becoming unusable. Perhaps not quite yet, but I recognized the signs.

On day 30 of the Italian Grand Tour challenge (a hundred marathons in a hundred days), my right shin had given out. A stress fracture, and I was literally crying in pain. Later it got worse and the fracture larger. It caused me to have six days off, requiring a week of double marathons to catch up. And yes, six days may not sound like much rest, but it did prove that it was possible to recover and run again quickly, and indeed catch up.

This pain in my left shin felt familiar. About an inch up from my ankle joint. The front middle of my tibia. The first thing that went through my mind was of course the realization that catching up after missing a few days of single marathons was very different from catching up with doubles. There was no way I could string together weeks of quadruple marathons. I really had to keep this leg safe. The problem was, I didn't have any legs left to lean on.

The message to Andy, however, remained the same: we make it to Bournemouth Pier and finish my twelfth marathon in six days, no matter how long it takes. The rain had, thankfully, cleared and I'd at least have some sunshine before it started to get dark. It was a long afternoon and early evening, and by 8 p.m., as I limped slowly into Swanage, I had just over 10 miles still to run. Andy had made it to a seaside chippy just before closing and handed me what had been the last sausage in the shop, along with some dryish chips. It was my last taste of enjoyment until the following day.

I say I had 10 miles left to run, but running was not really what I'd call it. I was using my arms in cooperation with my poles just as much as my legs. My morning's positive thinking about regaining some weight and topping up my body's fuel had gone out of the window, because I was actually now burning through far more energy than usual. I was propelling myself along using my upper body as a stabilizer to reduce the load. My wrists, forearms and shoulders were totally shot. I must have changed clothes, bandaged my hands and stretched my shoulders at least ten times by the 40-mile mark. Even my fingers were cramping. I was sweating through every item of clothing.

With one final hill before Studland and the ferry to Sandbanks, Poole and Bournemouth, the shit really hit the fan. And not in the day 5 way. The climb at around 44 miles that took me up to the midpoint between Swanage and Studland had drained the reserves of whatever was left in my legs. I had 8 miles to go, but I just couldn't move forward without pain searing up both legs. The knee was my right leg issue, and the Achilles and tibia my left.

These last 8 miles became even worse than the previous day's hobble into Portland. And to add insult to injury, literally, the roads into Studland had no street lights or pavements. It was now dark. Dark in a famously wonderful dark sky zone. Absolutely no light pollution – great for star gazing, not great for being visible on narrow roads to passing cars, with me moving slower than walking pace, dressed in black and feeling even darker. All Andy could do was chuck a fluorescent jacket on me, plus a head torch so I could see and be seen, and simply watch me struggle in his rear-view mirror. He knew instinctively to stay close, but to leave me alone and let me slog it out.

A lovely friend of mine, Vee, had hopped on her bike to offer support for a while, having cycled at least 40 miles to be with me. I wasn't expecting her to turn up, but I'd had my live tracker on my website so anyone could see where I was. By this point Paul had ditched the bike idea and resorted to helping out with shuttling crew to and from shops and supporting with general team needs. The bike just wasn't a goer on the coast path. And honestly, I think Paul was realizing that supporting a mission like this is far from the fun and games it appears, actually quite the opposite. I hardly saw him for much of days 4 and 5. He, like the rest of the crew, was burning out.

Vendagi (aka Vee), however, was a cyclist who knew her stuff and wanted to drop by for twenty minutes for a chat by way of support. Vee has cycled around the world solo, been chased by bears, and has many, many stories to tell. She's a kind-hearted, strong-willed, lovely soul and a great athlete. But – and it's a big but – I just wasn't ready for company, even the understanding type. She was waiting for me around the corner just before the last few miles of the hill towards Studland. She smiled and shouted 'Hey Nick, wooo!' before asking if she could cycle along for a bit, naturally expecting a yes. Instead I had to say, 'I'm so sorry, I'm just hurting too much.' I said this without looking at her, without smiling, and in a pretty grumpy, shitty tone. I couldn't bring myself to say 'No, go away', but she knew what I meant. She stuck around for five minutes and then politely wished me well and cycled on. I really hope she wasn't offended, I hope she understood, but the guilt made me feel like screaming. Great people were giving up their evenings to come and support me and I was being rude and blunt. It broke the principal rule of adventure, the rule that states that the adventure is the journey, not the destination. And yet alone in my own miserable, angry, deeply negative head, it felt like the right option. It just goes to show what lack of sleep and severe exhaustion can do to your decision making.

I continued into the darkness, head torch swaying as if on a deep-sea fishing vessel in a pitching sea. Despite doubling up on painkillers, I was moving at half the speed I had been going at an hour earlier. It wasn't just my legs that were getting to me now. It was also extreme physical and mental fatigue and the fact that I'd been running for over sixteen hours, on the back of eleven marathons in the last week over some of the hilliest paths in Britain. Had I been at 20-odd miles, I'm pretty sure I would have pulled the plug. But I now had just 5 miles till my sixth day of doubles was complete.

I'd climbed and descended more than the height of Everest in six days, and I was beat up. Unable to do anything for me, and still understanding that it was best to keep out of the way, the rest of the team were already at the finish line. In fact they had been there for four hours and had had their dinner. It was nearly 10 p.m. Oddly, at the time, I don't recall thinking about what this would mean for the next day. How would I do this again tomorrow? It would have been a sensible thought. But my mind just blocked that out. It was literally one step at a time.

More stops for new KT tape on my knee, blister plasters, salt tabs

and an apothecary bag of medical assistance. It was at these van stops
with Andy, in the dark, adding new layers as it got colder, that I started
to verbalize how shit I was feeling, and how useless I felt. How my legs
were in agony, and how miserable it was. This is not my style, and I'm
all too aware how this kind of talk can sabotage even the strongest
mind, as well as drain the life from a team. It helps nobody. Andy was
also still awake, driving through the night, and not having any fun
doing it.

As I mentioned earlier, I knew this route, but, with my mind a mess,
I can honestly say it was like I'd never been there in my life. I was sure
the next corner would bring the all-important glimpse of the ferry to
Sandbanks and then the stretch of beach to the day's destination,
Bournemouth Pier, but no. Every corner, every junction, every time, I
was wrong. I was close to tears. The kind of tears babies shed when
they are overtired and don't really know why they are crying. My pain
was bad, but I'd had it for hours, if not days. It wasn't the pain. It was
mostly the overall misery of the miles seeming to stretch when I needed
them to contract.

At some point before reaching the ferry – I can't remember when
because time was so warped – a chap with an Eastern European accent
in a Ford Mondeo flashed his lights and beeped his horn as he slowed
and drove past me. He was yelling something that sounded vaguely like
support, but I had my earphones in and couldn't hear him. It was now
close to 11.30 p.m. To my disbelief and instant rage, he stopped and
wanted to run with me. He was in jeans, so wouldn't be sticking around
long, but I was ready to shout at my own reflection let alone anyone
else. Enthusiastically he asked how I was. His accent was strong and I
struggled to understand. I replied in an unsmiling, miserable tone,
'Terrible.' I stole a look at him while my answer sank in – he was disappointed in me. He was trying to be nice and all I could do was be short
and blunt, closing him off and hobbling away in silence. I think I apologized before I sent him packing, but his tone was less upbeat as he
waved me off, beeping his horn again as he drove off.

When I finally, *finally*, made it to the ferry, which by some miracle
ran a very late service, to my astonishment the same guy was waiting
there for me with a huge smile on his face. The entire ferry was

otherwise empty. Just Andy and me, and a dim light glowing in the control booth, and this enthusiastic chap in silhouette against the street lights of Sandbanks on the other side of the small stretch of water.

I said I'd be honest, and it's with a heavy heart that I'm ashamed to say I totally ignored him. I have no acceptable excuse, but I wasn't thinking straight. I was now in the depths of my own mind, suffering in the hurt locker with little to no physical, cognitive or verbal energy, barely able to hold myself up. I could hear the slow underwater groans of the engine holding the car ferry against the boarding ramp mixing with the deafening concoction of negative thoughts in my head. The two-minute crossing went by in a flash, and my thoughts then had to turn to the final stretch of flat seafront. Not a single incline now, just a promenade. A promenade I have run countless times before.

It was now past midnight as I downed more painkillers and briefly tried to explain to Andy where he should wait for me. I needed support, at the very least someone to keep an eye on me, my own eyes barely open at this point. My sole visual memory of getting off the ferry was my brother in his work clothes with his bike suddenly appearing from around the corner of the tatty old ferry ticket office. Initially I thought it was someone else wanting to ride with me to the end, and I closed my eyes and mentally bit my tongue. It's hard to explain this type of frustration, because having support is a good thing. When broken, however, in pain, on the verge of collapsing and depleted of all energy reserves, it's just too much. I no longer had the capacity to talk, to be polite, or to engage in, well, anything. The act of placing one foot, balancing, and then placing the other was all I could manage. And I was only doing that thanks to walking poles holding me up. So not only was I hugely relieved that it was Chris rather than some eager runner, but he couldn't have timed his arrival better, at the point when I desperately needed on-foot support.

Chris hopped off his bike and asked, 'You all right, bro?' in a tone that didn't require a response. He hugged me gently and I mumbled something like 'You won't be needing that', referring to the fact that he was cycling. I was now covering about 2 miles an hour, and not just due to injuries. I'd stopped eating, I'd stopped talking; my brain was desperately needing sleep and I was depriving it. If you have a dog or a baby, you'll know what I mean. If a dog or baby is crying at you for something – food, for example – their tone gets sharper and the volume louder the more you deny them. My brain was doing something similar. Running on about four or five hours of sleep per day, and draining my carb reserves, living off fat, and nursing two or three lower leg injuries, plus, now, issues with my wrists and arms from holding the poles . . . I was only just hanging on. My mind was crumbling and, as for my body, collapse was starting to feel like the unavoidable next step.

Chris works as a nurse practitioner and is highly experienced at critical care. Having spent a decent chunk of time in A&E, he's very good at remaining calm when the situation screams the opposite. He simply and directly said, 'Andy, you go to the end and I'll walk with Nick. We'll call you if we need anything.' Without noticing it, my mood lifted tenfold.

Chris and I walked along Banks Road, famously one of the most expensive places to buy a house in the country, adorned with large, fancy glass-fronted mansions. Banks Road leads to Canford Cliffs Beach, Branksome Chine Beach, then Alum Chine Beach, and stretch upon stretch of white sand. One uninterrupted, flat seafront all the way to Hengistbury Head, some 20 miles further east. I only needed to make it to Bournemouth Pier, which I could already see in the distance. At night, slightly stumpy seaside-style street lights look like a curved landing strip stretching for miles. Close together and more orange than white, their light illuminated the beach and, very faintly, the gentle ripples of water at the shore. The light falling the other way also lit our path and the hundreds of small wooden single-door beach huts. The place was deserted.

We exchanged a few surprisingly cheery words, with Chris joking and making remarks about how running isn't good for you, and saying things like, 'See, that's why I don't run marathons.' I laughed as much of a laugh as my energy would allow and remember feeling proud to have him as a brother and reassured to have him with me. I also felt rather pathetic, frail and weak. I was now stooped over my walking poles. Chris would occasionally ask things to check I wasn't about to have a heart attack (again), and he certainly didn't want me to collapse because there would only be so much he could do without a hospital full of supplies at his fingertips.

Inching closer to the pier, I stumbled a few times, my knee flooding with pain as I gripped my poles tight to stay on my feet, my hands cramping some more. It was at this point I started to have vivid hallucinations. I saw that lion on the beach, I started to speak total gibberish to Chris, and naturally he was worried that I'd have a stroke, pass out, or just fall and hit my head. I was worried too. Everything was blurry, in slow motion, and I remember having to sit down a few times to let my heart slow. Having a couple of drunks slowly overtake me, despite their uneven stagger, was one last bit of humour for the day. Chris and I looked at each other, him smiling at the absurdity of it all. I smiled too and got my head down. A few more metres of little to no talking and eventually we made it to the pier. The icing on the cake was that I had passed the magical 52.4 marker, but at that point I didn't really care. The Pavilion Theatre car park was where Andy, Nikki and the others were parked up.

Eventually, incredibly, Nick staggers into the car park at gone 1 a.m., and collapses on the tarmac, where unless moved he will happily sleep, having completed what have been the 53 most gruelling miles of his life.

I thanked Chris and told him I loved him. He said the same. Had I had any fluid left in my body I think I would have cried. I lay fully clothed on the ground outside Nikki's van. She hugged me, comforted me, and got some dry clothes ready. During the few miles with Chris along the seafront I'd asked if we could crash at his house and if I could have a bath. I'd told him, but nobody else just yet, that tomorrow wasn't happening: I would not be running. And as those syllables had left my lips, I felt that all my efforts for that day were for nothing if I was just going to stop. But I meant it. I said it, and I meant it, and it felt like a relief more than anything.

Having been hauled into the van, I fell asleep within a minute. The journey to my brother's house is about eight minutes by car, no more. So I managed to bank seven minutes immediately. Once parked up with the engines off, Nikki woke me up, and I told her what I'd told Chris.

Sitting slumped in my brother's living room, I explained to Andy, Chris and Nikki what was going to happen. They had all rightly avoided trying to make a plan, as they knew it had to come from me, especially as they knew I would decide regardless. I said, 'It's game over. Tomorrow we sleep in, we see a physio in the afternoon, see what he says, and we take it from there.' It was a rubbish plan, because it didn't really fix anything, but mentally I had to believe we were going to continue. The gang were dubious, but they humoured me, assuming the physio would become the one who had to deliver the bad news.

Nikki ran me a huge bubble bath while Chris and Andy scoured the internet for the last remaining Indian takeaway that was open. They found a place which delivered. Andy isn't fussy when it comes to food, and Chris, having just finished a twelve-hour shift in A&E, was happy to eat anything, but they both agreed it was the worst curry they'd ever had – one of the perils of ordering takeaway in the early hours of the morning.

When meeting people for the first time, it doesn't usually take long before I'm asked, 'What do you do?' and I say I do a lot of running. I then expand a little, and the conversation generally prompts phrases like 'you're a machine', 'how do you keep going?' and 'why?'. There's a photo I often show to people during these conversations, one which really does paint a thousand words. I don't recall the photo being taken as my eyes were glazed over at the time. Nikki took it, once she had lowered me into the bath at my brother's house. I'm up to my chest in bubbles. My arms are limp and draped over the sides. My chest is red from the heat of the bath, my hair wet. My face, however, says it all. I look like I've just come off a three-week drinking bender. My eyelids strain to stay open, the skin on my forehead is wrinkled into a frown of immense effort. My eyes have rolled back and my jaw is floppy. I'd run 53 miles that day, in about nineteen hours, but it looked like I'd just finished off fifty-three pints and was being bathed before being ferried off to rehab. The picture shows that I'm not a machine, and in fact it's the rising out of pain and suffering that is the hard part, but also the most rewarding.

The last thing I remember is Nikki's face as she knelt by the bath holding my hand, making sure that I didn't slip under and drown. Her outstretched hand was a symbol of love, energy, effort and unfaltering selflessness. It was her hand I was holding, but it symbolized the whole team and everyone's efforts over those six long days. It was a week none of us will ever forget.

As I slipped into oblivion, Andy wondered if it was all over:

One thing is already clear – there will be no running tomorrow. The last thing I remember hearing Nick say before turning in is: 'It's game over.' It's even more disappointing than the curry, and I go to bed with a strong sense of loss for what has already become a great adventure, realizing just how much I don't want it to end.

3

Changes Afoot

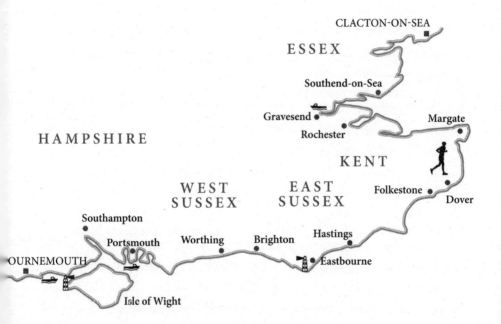

The remaining pages of this book are a sign that the journey didn't end with me in my brother's bath looking like a drunk. It didn't, but there was a lot that changed.

Days 7 to 9
Bournemouth
Pain is merely a perception

I woke before Andy, Chris and Nikki – which I wasn't expecting – a little disoriented from being in a house, not a van, and being clean, not filthy. It was also 10 a.m., not 5 a.m. I'd had nearly seven hours' sleep, more than I'd had any night since we left the Eden Project. I'm pleased to say my first and lasting thought of the day was a positive one. I referred to this blip in the plan when speaking to the others as hitting the pause button, not the stop button. It gave me and everyone else a good solid understanding of what this weird, unexpected time was all about.

Over a very late and very big fry-up breakfast, Nikki, Andy, Chris and I chatted about the previous day's madness. Chris wasn't working for a few days and said we could stay as long as we wanted. It was a glorious warm morning and with the doors open to the garden we lounged around waiting for Tim the physio to call us back. The last message to him had been sent by Andy around midnight, not expecting a response but instead asking him to call us in the morning and explaining that I was in a bad way.

Jack, Sarah and Paul, the other half of our on-the-road crew, were in their vans parked up on the seafront just around the corner. Chris simply didn't have the space to host everyone. Yas, Nicole and Danny were all, as planned, working remotely (Danny had reached out to offer help with anything and everything – another much-needed kind supporter. Later, as you'll read, he stepped up even more so.) This trio made up the off-the-road crew, supporting with the charity, social media, brand commitments, PR and the general nitty-gritty of the public-facing side of the challenge. After all, what's the point of attempting something like this if it's not to raise some money and awareness for a good cause?

It's here I'd like to drop in a little plug for my charity, the 196 Foundation, of which I'm enormously proud. Run Britain was designed to raise awareness of it and to raise money for the causes we support. Each year's beneficiary is chosen by our monthly donors, who kindly pledge £1.96 per month – no more, no less, although you can pay for three years up front if you wish. Throughout the year we accept applications for support. It could be something small like helping a neighbour to buy a wheelchair, or something bigger like building a school in Uganda. We collate these requests and whittle them down to a shortlist of three, based on what funds we have available. Each April, these causes are then presented to the donors, to vote on which one we should support. We call it the democratic donor model. A simple, cheap way to make a big difference while the donors have the deciding voice on exactly what they are funding. The foundation is doing great work and growing at an impressive rate.

In the first week the team fitted into their roles rather well. Pretty much exactly as planned. I suppose we were a big crew, but me, Andy, Nikki and Poppy were the core unit, with Jack and Sarah in their own van, providing photography and videography. Paul had borrowed a small orange van and had chucked his bike in the back; he was now helping any of us as and when needed. Danny and Nicole would link up with Yas to make sure they had social media content, while Yas liaised with sponsors and shielded me from the toing and froing of requests to meet schools and give interviews, and helped answer questions from the public who wanted to run with me. Our website carried a basic form for runners to complete if they wanted to come and join me on a certain date. And so, despite the others doing brilliant things in the background, my day-to-day contact was 95 per cent Andy and

5 per cent Nikki and Poppy. Other than that, I'd have phone calls with Yas and see Jack and Sarah taking snaps of me five or six times a day. Well, sometimes I'd see them, and sometimes they'd just be hiding in bushes or flying the drone overhead.

By 1 p.m., Tim the physio had called. We were all delighted to find that his practice was only a couple of miles from my brother's house, so I shuffled into the van, and we drove to his clinic. Tim was a highly experienced physio, having supported many well-known endurance athletes, including one or two celebrities over the years. Not only was he willing to see me for free, he was incredibly helpful, both on the phone and now in person. This was a chap who'd reached out to us following our social media plea, and I'd ended up down the road from him at my brother's house. For a change, it felt like fortune was on our side.

I had no expectations of our appointment. If truth be told, I'm a bit of a sceptic when it comes to 'rehab/recovery/repair' specialists. Over the years I've seen physios, osteopaths, surgeons, doctors, multiple alignment and balance specialists, plus chiropractors, and spine and hip experts; I've had acupuncture, hydrotherapy, sports massages . . . you name it. And you know what? They generally advise different things for the same problems. Now, every one of these areas is founded on a sound scientific understanding of the human body, and they do work. However, the bit I find that's missing in the road to recovery and, importantly, in the advice that's provided, is that every human is different, that one method for someone may not be right for another. The problem lies in the fact that human beings are built differently – aligned, unaligned, mobile, tight – and everyone has a different pain threshold, a different attitude to pain, different diets, different ways of interpreting the advice, and so on. I guess historically I've not had much success or felt like I've not seen benefits greater than my own interventions. Maybe that's just me.

What I'm trying to say is that I was desperately hoping Tim would fix me, but I knew the fixing really lay with me and my body. His words and one appointment weren't going to do much good. Or were they?

Tim's firm handshake and his 6ft 5in. stature wobbled me as I took one hand off my walking poles to say hello. Andy followed me in like an anxious parent. It was a small, smart, highly functional practice. I commented to Andy about how I'd passed the building so many times when running around this area over the years and never taken much notice of the place. It's weird how the world does that.

I hobbled into Tim's room, adorned with framed photos of him with Paula Radcliffe, Eddie Izzard and various skiers, runners and tri-athletes, plus medical certificates and anatomy posters. After a brief examination of my knee and various surrounding ligaments and alignment pinch points, he confirmed what we suspected: it was a tendon problem, not joint or bone. This was a good start. There was a slight worry that I'd need injections or similar, and that I'd have to wait days. While being examined, I explained the ins and outs of our current situation, our objectives, and how I was keen to get on my feet asap. He was impressed with what we were doing, glad to help, but most importantly he knew that telling me to stop running was a waste of his breath. He recounted stories of getting Eddie through various injuries during her forty-three marathons in fifty-two days.

Both Andy and I were impressed with Tim. I would go as far as saying the short time we spent with him was unquestionably the best forty minutes of advice and treatment I've had from any medical person in my life. It was to the point, based on science, and positive. Tim understands athletes. He's not just a brain that has studied and then administers. He could see the bigger picture, and ultimately gave Andy and me the tools to get us back on the road.

Andy was relieved too:

After just a few minutes with Tim, it becomes apparent how lucky Nick is to have had this forced pit stop in the town where he has his practice. Tim's is exactly the voice that Nick needs to hear today, and having previously worked with many athletes on similar (if lesser) endurance challenges, his focus is on active recovery. The phrase 'active recovery' is music to Nick's ears. I know that he has no interest whatsoever in being told how long he'll be out of action or how long he should rest for, and all he'll want to know is how he can keep going while his knee recovers.

It was fascinating to hear Tim talk, to hear him discuss options and methods, but more interesting was his deep understanding of how the brain interprets and in fact creates the concept of pain. He explained how pain is merely a perception, a thing conjured in the brain, and talked about ways to trick the mind into bypassing this chain of command. I've listened to podcasts, read medical journals and accounts by adventurers, and watched programmes dealing with the subjects of pain, the science of outlying athletes, how to control fear, the secrets of a strong mind, but although I already had a basic awareness of what Tim was saying, *how* he was saying it made me believe that I was back in control. It was like a switch had been flicked in my head.

One of the options he suggested, which we later used heavily, was capsicum jelly, which when mixed with Deep Heat and applied to the skin around the injured areas overloads the skin's pain receptors and overrides the pain signals being sent to the brain from the underlying injury. Simple but clever. The capsicum jelly came in a small translucent plastic tub, an angry-looking bright orange. You do not want to get this stuff in your eyes or, worse, anywhere near your privates. It's like smearing fire on your skin. My knee hurt, so the solution was to set my leg ablaze, to make my pain receptors forget about the tendon. Capsicum is an active agent – the more the surface of the skin moves the more you feel it.

Our time with Tim also allowed Andy to get trained up on how to correctly and securely tape my knee, Achilles and shin. In short, the assumptions we'd made about my injuries were more or less correct. My shin was fragile, my Achilles was taking too much load from over-compensating, and the meniscus in my knee was either flipped or torn. Obviously rest was the easy way to repair these issues, but that wasn't even discussed. Tim pulled out a razor and proceeded to shave my leg. His matter-of-fact approach we both found funny but totally on the right level. He shaved my leg so the tape would stick well, and of course not cause any more pain when it was pulled off. It was the first time I'd had my leg shaved, and it made it look even more frail. Andy had a go at taping my knee a few times under Tim's supervision. It reminded us of the uncomfortable occasions when he'd had to massage my calf and, in Tunisia, disinfect a dog bite to my lower bum area with iodine and antiseptic. This was another occasion to consign to the repressed memories locker.

I moved with much more positivity when exiting the practice. We thanked Tim over and over. He bundled handfuls of physio tape along with a large tub of capsicum jelly and a tube of Deep Heat into Andy's hands as we left. He was happy to provide this help, but we were even happier to receive it. Andy made a comment as we left about how he had now taken on yet another responsibility as my 'dangerously under-qualified physio'. We laughed. I was buoyant, smiling and ready to get running again.

All the talk about how capsicum overrides pain, and how everything can be controlled through the understanding that what we experience is a perception, an interpretation of the mind, got me thinking. From that moment on my perspective on mind and body changed a little. I had always been keen to keep my mind and body separate when think-ing about endurance. The mind controls the body. But this meeting with Tim altered that way of thinking for me. I'd forgotten that my mind isn't just in control of my body, it's *part* of my body. In the days that followed I would place more focus on 'brain foods' and anything I could eat that would support my brain's strength. Obviously sleep was also key. Just that slight shift in my thinking has stuck with me ever since.

I also, coincidentally, had just finished listening to a book about the 'Happiness Concept', i.e. to be happy is to think happy – the idea that it's a decision rather than a long, winding road. Truly believe, and it will be. Fake it until you make it. Whatever you want to call it, just will it into being. This was a way of thinking I'd always been a big believer in. My mother instilled it in me from my school days. Whenever I had a hard time as a kid or struggled with something, through various bouts of sadness, depression or unsettled feelings as a teenager, I'd return to the thought that happiness is a decision, and I can make that decision. It's not linked to success, attainment, money or accolade. It's a simple decision. Not always an easy one to make of course, but a simple concept nonetheless.

Thinking about this, along with the chats and laughs with Andy, the support from Tim and the tools and tricks he had given us, lifted my spirits to an even higher point than before day 1. Although my body was far from ready, my mind would carry it. My mind was back in the emotional Goldilocks zone – strong, positive, aware of recent struggles, and while not forgetting the pain, very ready to take back control.

Despite the metaphorical spring in my step, I was, however, still using poles to walk, and so we regrouped, made a plan, voice-clipped the entire team, and that was that. We decided I'd have three full days off, and return on day 10. Days 7, 8 and 9 would be spent eating, resting, eating some more, and keeping my leg elevated and covered in ice, trying to restore fat, carb and glucose levels, catching up on sleep, and improving whatever else would be useful. I also put out a short video on social media explaining the 'pause-not-stop' message, and thanked Tim once again for his help. I would start at 6 a.m. sharp on day 10 from Bournemouth Pier, where I'd stopped my watch after the brutal slog on day 6.

How far I was going to run on a daily basis was briefly discussed. One marathon at least, two ideally, and then try to catch up the miles I'd missed as soon as possible. First things first, though. Let's see if I could run at all.

My brother's living area and kitchen are open plan. He's brilliant at making things, so a large eight-seater bench-style wooden table, complete with fancy joinery, stands proud, separating the living room sofas from the U-shaped kitchen. Beyond are bifold doors and decking on to freshly laid grass. This was now our 'crew quarters', rapidly resembling a messy bachelor pad, complete with empty crisp packets, takeaway boxes and BBQ leftovers. It was a few days to regroup and bond that we all needed. I was able to shower, go to the toilet on a toilet, and even wear clean clothes most days. It was starting to feel like this, as always, was happening for a reason.

Having had lunch with the entire crew to discuss next steps, and how to learn from what had happened, we were keen to crack on. We also started to calculate what mileage I would need to run in order to catch up. I looked ahead months to work out the best points at which to add miles and slowly claw my way back to the original plan. It looked like a very long road back to plan A.

I'm all for head down, crack on, but I also love to reflect and assess, and so I started to make lists that evening before bed, jotting down pages of notes on my phone. What could I do differently? What was my focus now? How could I support the team more? What else might happen? I tried to think of everything to avoid another slip-up. The hazy message that seeped into the forefront of my mind was always, however, that whatever the prep, the journey would always be bumpy, horrible even, but at the finish line the sense of accomplishment would outweigh those bumps in an instant. A positive mind can always achieve more than a negative one.

With my thoughts in a great place, and about to head to bed before one more full day of rest ahead of the restart, my phone chimed. A WhatsApp message from Paul. I still have this message, and frankly it angers me every time I think about it. The headline takeaway was that Paul, along with Sarah and Jack, would not be continuing to support the challenge. They were heading home that night, having collectively decided it wasn't for them. It had not been what they were expecting, and I think they were disappointed I'd already picked up an injury. They didn't see how I would finish the journey, they weren't being paid enough, and they were being overworked. Paul was also offering advice about how I should run more efficiently, suggesting a different diet and requesting a better van for him to stay in. Needless to say, this riled me. Maybe it shouldn't have. I'm aware I can be very standoffish with differing opinions, but I do feel my frustrations here were, at least in part, justified.

I can appreciate that the reality of our expedition may not have been the romantic cruise around the coast that it first appeared, but from my perspective, our terms, in advance of the challenge, were simple and explicit: on-the-road support crew would be present for eighty days over the course of the hundred-day trip, and everyone would receive monthly expenses to cover basic fuel and food costs paid every thirty days in advance. Given that the run was raising money for charity, I couldn't afford to pay proper wages and provide better kit than we had access to, and I knew from the start that I owed a debt of gratitude to everyone who had given up their time and put their own lives on hold to be involved. I also knew that I wanted to have a single crew present for most of the journey to lessen the possibility of any breakdowns in communication and to support continuity. Naturally, having 50 per cent of that crew disappear after the first week was rather stressful, especially given the emotional and physical energy that had gone into completing those first six days' running.

For the record, I am grateful for Jack, Sarah and Paul's efforts. They were lovely, brilliant people to have on such a challenge. They did their job well, and perhaps their expectations of what was to come swayed their decision. With only 6 per cent of the run complete I was barely mobile. I wasn't exactly inspiring confidence, so maybe I should have seen this coming. Losing hope on an expedition makes a hard task almost impossible. As I've said, the lack of sleep, the effort, the collective team exhaustion, the extra patience you must have for others . . . the whole concoction of a journey like this is daunting. It requires everyone to dig deep. I can only assume this wasn't for them and, although frustrating, that's fair. But to disappear just hours after having lunch together and planning the coming days was, I felt, out of order.

I never heard from Jack or Sarah again. They did send hard drives with the photos from the initial days to Yas a week later, but they left with their month's supply of expense money and ignored any requests to return it. As for Paul, I politely asked Yas to shield me from various follow-up messages. I needed to focus on the task at hand.

Our on-the-road crew had halved, placing additional burdens on Nikki and Andy that they weren't expecting. I felt my shoulders sag with the extra responsibility, as I'm sure theirs did too.

Yas and I had gathered a handful of sponsors to support fuel costs, modest salaries and expenses for the team, food supplies, and the occasional luxury of a shower at a Premier Inn. You'd be surprised quite how much a journey like this costs. An original team of close to ten, all requiring some form of subsidized sustenance, was one half of the expenditure, while the other lay with expenses and fuel for the vans. The journey was over 5,000 miles on foot, but close to double that in the vans due to drives to and from start/finish spots, wrong turns, food shopping trips, detours around passenger ferries and similar. We budgeted around £30,000 and spent over £55,000. Extra campsite costs, parking costs, much more food than expected, and expenses for the team being slightly higher than planned all meant the money became tight very quickly. It's worth noting too that we only had around £20,000 in sponsorship. The remaining money came out of my (now empty) pocket.

And so with the budget on my mind it was paramount we delivered for our sponsors. Without their funding the trip was unsustainable. We now didn't have anyone to take photos and thus promote the brands supporting us, so responsibility for this fell on the remaining team, none of whom really had capacity. Filming content for a long-form documentary was immediately struck from the list. I also very much needed to focus on running and getting my legs back to full health. I was conscious that if there were any more delays I would be close to pulling the plug, due to finances. The last thing you want when you're battling for the energy to continue is a neon sign stating 'quit now and you'll save thousands of pounds'.

Having by all accounts thrown, kicked and spat my toys out of the pram that evening, I went to bed knowing there was one more day of full rest and recovery before rejoining the challenge. I was deflated, money was now a growing thorn in my side, and I found it hard to shake the feeling of disappointment – the mess the journey had become in just a week. I was ultimately responsible, and that saddened me.

Having used my last non-running day for sleep, tidying the vans, resupplying and generally checking the rest of the crew were happy, I thanked my brother for the use of his home. We were all refreshed, showered, clean-clothed and well fed, but the trip, and my appetite for getting back on the road, had taken a knock.

I went to bed ahead of day 10 trying to remain positive, mentally preparing myself for running again. I am proud that by some miracle I can't quite put my finger on I woke up the next morning, put on my kit and set off.

Day 10 – 27.69 miles – 553ft elevation
Bournemouth Pier to St Leonards
Back on my feet

Today is the day when Nick, still limping fairly heavily, has decided he will get back on the road, for better or worse. The decision to run

*again today is driven more by his fidgetiness than by careful assess-
ment of his fitness to run, but as anyone who knows Nick would tell
you, there's no point trying to stop him. It's been incredibly kind of
Chris to allow us to descend on his house like a swarm of locusts
with a dog, and this break from the initial relentlessness of the first
week has given us time to reflect on the sustainability of what Nick
is attempting. The recovery period he's now entering will be a bit of
an unknown, and even when he's back up to full strength (assuming
he gets to that point) the level of endurance running he's aiming to
sustain may still prove impossible. However, for today, the target is
simple: a single marathon. Nick sets off strapped up, painkillered up
and with his lower right leg smeared in hot sauce.*

Hobbling down to Bournemouth Pier from the car park where just a
few days earlier I had been hauled into the van looking like a zombie, I
was greeted by about twenty fellow runners in various garish running
outfits. Headbands, water bladder backpacks, compression sleeves, and
even sweatbands. They had cottoned on to the fact that the best way to
follow me was to use my location tracker rather than the pre-planned day
routes. Whoops and cheers made me smile as I approached to say my
hellos. While they looked ready to film an eighties fitness video, I was
dressed for winter, knowing it was to be a slow day. I had a big grey oversized hoody on – a treasured Afghanistan Gym top given to me by a lovely
ex-military chap called Glen, with whom I'd run in Kabul a few years
back. My buff was pulled high, almost meeting my orange woolly hat.
    The elevation for the day was flat, very flat – an absolute blessing.
And to make everything a little easier I also knew the entire route. I
wanted to start at 6 a.m. even though I was only intending to run 26.2
miles. It was good to get back into the habit, in anticipation of the
longer running days ahead. Besides, I was secretly hoping my knee
might be up for a few more miles.
    Having made it to the Mudeford ferry, about 6 miles up the coast, I
was relieved to find that the ferryman had, as promised, opened early.
I'd called him the night before and offered to pay him £40 to open two
hours ahead of schedule. He'd seemed reluctant, but I played the charity card and he kindly obliged.

Above: Two days before Go Day my dad put up a map at the back of the van. Pointing to our start in St Austell.

Above: Day 1. The team gather minutes before the off. Spirits were high.

Left: Running out of the Eden Project – the first of more than eleven million steps.

Above: 07:00 on the morning of day 1, running through the dunes of Par Sands.

Below: Cycle and run support for the first leg of day 1. As always, the ocean on my right, Britain on my left.

Above: Climbing up the bloody Cornish coast.

Right: End of day 3, hobbling into Brixham. Andy comforts me with some encouraging words, and a kebab. Nikki's waiting for a hug at the end of a long day for everyone.

Below: My brother Chris and Andy helping me up from the ground after a brief collapse of my knee.

Left: My right knee, not looking like the other knee. Pain followed.

Below left: The beginnings of strapping my initial knee injury.

Below right: Needing to lie down, or else I would fall down.

Bottom: Resting and taking directions. A snapshot of life in the Council Van.

Left: The knee. The pain spot.

Below: Day 6, nineteen hours into what should have been a twelve-hour day. Navigating by head torch through utter agony and hallucinations on the Jurassic Coast.

Above: My frail, withered body. It's as though I've just come off a drinking bender. I have no memory of this photo being taken. I was hallucinating and very dehydrated.

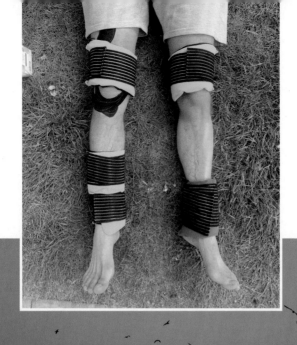

Left: Ice packs and compression velcroed to my legs. I rested like this at every opportunity.

Below: The peace and solitude of early mornings in Britain.

Above: Stopping my watch after one of the slowest days of the challenge.

Left: Nikki helping to top up the sun-cream. No matter how overcast, twelve hours outside and my face weathers.

Left: Twenty days in: Andy using his Stanley knife to pop a blister and remove some grit from my foot.

Below: A van with a view. Seascapes like this were the reward for sleeping next to the ocean every day.

Bottom: The dolphin show off the coast of Aberdeen.

TO THE SEA

Above: Even when out of sight, I was never far away.

Right: Asleep with my MyoMaster leg sleeves on after another long day.

Below: Greeting Poppy on a stop for refreshments, wearing my Supersapiens glucose monitor. The hottest day of the year on record – over 37 degrees.

To my surprise, I reached halfway through the first marathon pretty promptly. The group of about eight that ran on with me were a mix of all ages, genders and energy levels. They stayed to act as my invisible crutch. They knew I would be suffering and so did everything they could to keep my spirits high. It worked, despite the frosty early morning start, and even with the strong headwind we were leaning into, we made good time. I suppose, unlike on day 1, I had just had a week of intense training.

The last of the merry running crew tailed off around 20 miles in. I did the last 6 miles without my headphones in, just taking in the surroundings. I ran through the forest and farmland near St Leonards, east of Lymington, and stopped my watch at just over 27 miles. It was quiet. Weird actually. Paul wasn't around, Jack and Sarah weren't jumping out of bushes accompanied by the sound of camera shutters. It was just Andy and Nikki marking the finishing post, two vans parked on a grass verge near a farm entrance. A few New Forest ponies greeted me as I slumped down next to a barbed-wire fence on the gravel at the edge of the road to wrestle my compression sleeves from my legs. A tractor rumbled past over a cattle grid, but apart from that and a passing stoat, we were alone. It was only 11.30 a.m. I'd finished before lunch, and my knee, although sore and stiff, was functioning, some of the soreness masked by painkillers and ibuprofen gel. I'd also stopped to top up with the special capsicum mix every 5 kilometres or so. Re-tape, take things slow, repeat. I was still using poles too, but it all seemed to be working. It was all rather spooky.

Andy had heated a large fish pie ready meal, complete with some vegetables. More brain food, plus two big protein shakes. Running one marathon a day on a gentle flat coastline in the sun felt like child's play after unrelenting double marathons complete with hills. The average daily elevation of the previous week had been ten times greater than day 10. Even with my bad knee, and running with a slight limp, using my poles as best I could, this was the confidence boost I needed. I felt fine. In fact I felt great. I suggested I try a few more miles after food, a suggestion which Andy and Nikki shot down in an instant. 'Rest and repair!' they shouted. They were right, of course.

The afternoon light seemed to last for ever. The vans were parked

tightly together with both sliding doors facing away from the road, providing a sheltered little grassy space for camping chairs. I sat with both
legs elevated and multiple ice packs velcroed to my quads, hamstrings,
calves and knees, alternating anti-inflammatories and painkillers every
two hours. We vowed to keep this up for as long as it took.

Long after food, and long after the ice packs had warmed in the sun,
it was still only 5 p.m. It felt like a summer's evening. Andy had a cider,
and Nikki joined him. Poppy even had a little run with Nikki while I
napped. It felt like I'd discovered the best, if the most extreme, way to
train for a marathon. Run twelve marathons in six days, add some
crazy elevation and some tough terrain, and you'll be able to run an
easy marathon on day 10. Even with an injury. Who needs a twelve-
week plan, eh? In a mad moment of sense, I suggested an early night,
and shut my eyes around 7 p.m. as Andy and Nikki finished off their
drinks in the dwindling light, with the doors and windows still open. I
didn't stir till 4.30 the following morning, as I heard the sound of Andy
reaching to fire up the kettle. It was good to be back in our little
routine.

Days 11 to 14
St Leonards to Brighton
The return to double marathons

From our little farm parking spot just shy of St Leonards, the immediate route ahead had the potential for a perfect recovery run: a mix of
quiet roads and flat, easy-to-follow footpaths around the River Beau-
lieu and on to the Solent. I didn't stop for lunch until 30 miles had
ticked by. I took an hour out for some food and to repeat the same
drug-and-tape ritual, while we spoke fondly of Tim, and how his magic
capsicum–Deep Heat concoction seemed to be keeping me on the road.
Spirits were high. So high in fact that I managed to persuade Nikki
and Andy to let me run another 8 miles in the afternoon. There were
just 1,093 feet of elevation over the day as I clocked up a total of 38.26
miles.

During our lunch stop near Southampton, my thoughts had turned to making up some of the lost mileage. Our mission was to circumnavigate Britain and to do so by totalling at least 5,240 miles – aka two hundred marathons. That was the goal. Ideally, within a hundred days. I hadn't been able to keep my continuous streak of double marathons up because of the injuries. That was unavoidable, and to say it was a huge disappointment for me would be an understatement. It continued to eat me up for weeks, before that passage of time allowed me to sweep it under the rug, gone but not forgotten. It was, however, still possible, though improbable, to run the distance of two hundred marathons in a hundred days. Once repaired, maybe in a few weeks, I could start running 57-mile days instead of 52-mile days. For the remainder of the day, and feeling like my knee was hampering me less and less, this was all I could think about.

Post-run, I got the laptop out before I'd even changed my clothes. Andy could see I'd been attempting the maths in my head and I explained we should compare spreadsheets and see when might be a good time to start clawing back the miles. Andy was . . . well, he was Andy. He knew it was madness to start talking about running more than double marathons, and in the back of my head so did I . . . but just thinking about it couldn't hurt.

The following day, three days before the start of May, I set off from Weston, south-east of Southampton, with a fresh bunch of runners. About fifteen, as I recall. I went through the motions of answering the usual questions about how I was feeling, how the knee was, and what the plan was. Most days, the runners who joined me assumed I knew where I was going. It became quite funny. They'd say, 'Are you running up past the big Tesco and turning right at the such-and-such pub?' Or, 'Are you going over the bridge?' Every time, my answer would be the same: 'I'm not entirely sure which county I'm in, so I'm afraid I don't have a clue.' This then prompted local runners to advise me, offering suggestions and giving their time to navigate me through specific routes they knew. This was kind, selfless and, occasionally, unhelpful, as it interfered with my mapped-out route for the day. I may not have known where I was going but we did at least have a plan.

As we progressed, Andy had pointed out that our start and finish points would have to be carefully thought out. If they weren't, then we could end up running around the country and back to Eden in 180 marathons rather than 200, or worse still, 230 marathons. Just keeping the coast on my right sounded like the sensible plan, and that's pretty much the only navigation I did, but for Andy the job was far more complicated. He was tasked with staying on track with the mileage plan while keeping as close to the coast as possible, and making decisions about which bridge, ferry or tunnel to take. And so, each post-restart morning, Andy and I would draw up various options for the day's route on the Footpath app, trying to find the most efficient, enjoyable, sensible, safe and flat route we could, although generally we'd settle for ticking off two or three of these specifications. Safety was most often dropped, followed by enjoyability. We opted mostly for closeness to the sea, efficiency in terms of low navigation, and wherever had the most flat paths.

It's fair to say I went the wrong way at least two or three times a day. Fortunately, Andy was on hand to pull on my reins and steer me back to the path, either through phone calls or messages, guiding me through various junctions. Every so often those kind locals had route suggestions which did make more sense than our plan and we'd take their advice. Mostly, though, we stuck to our plan. Andy drove ahead to every junction in busy areas, and ahead 3 or 4 miles in simpler sections. For now, day 12, Andy stuck close, as did Nikki, more or less for the entire journey. I didn't ask for it, but they knew it would help.

Despite the good company, the ice cream stops, the odd banging tune played from a runner's backpack and friendly chats with fellow nutty runners, my leg, specifically my other Achilles tendon, the right one, was now becoming sore. Another classic case of compensating for an injury in the other leg. The team were now taking bets on which part of my legs would get injured next. Both quads and my left tibia remained intact. That was about it.

With injuries on my mind, it was an easy decision for me to stick to a single marathon on day 12, and after a steady seven hours I totted up another 27.64 miles. A slow one, even with an injury. But I'd taken my time, and hopefully it helped in some way to aid the recovery of my growing collection of injuries. Short strides and a slow pace felt like the simple recipe for getting back on track. I'd even ditched my poles.

After 700 feet of elevation and some tricky navigating around Lee-on-Solent, Anglesey (the other one) and Gosport, I called it a day at Southsea Common, just outside Portsmouth. We parked up with a view over the shipping lanes, with the Isle of Wight in the distance. A large, empty, sheltered car park made for a good night spot. I can fall asleep just by looking at a pillow, but Andy is affected by sounds and light more than me, so this was a good opportunity for him to get a good night's sleep too.

He was also making good use of the shorter running days:

For the last couple of days, I've been looking longingly over at the Isle of Wight (one of my favourite places), knowing that we won't be setting foot there, as islands are out of scope for Run Britain. The main mission parameter is to cover the equivalent distance of two hundred marathons around the coast of mainland Britain. It would have been logistically impossible to include islands, as there are thousands of them, and there would be no value in just selecting a subset. Nick will run on those that call themselves islands, but are actually joined by land, e.g. the Isle of Grain, but won't run on actual islands connected by bridges, e.g. Anglesey. The only exceptions will be Canvey Island and here, Portsea Island, as although technically islands, you wouldn't really notice, as they are only separated from the mainland by narrow creeks, and form a more natural part of the mainland route.

With Nick having only run 27 miles, we have most of an after-noon still to play with, and while he eats, ices and recovers, I track down a leisure centre that has relaxed Covid restrictions and re-opened its swimming pool. I go for a token swim to maintain the façade of somebody who is interested in exercise, before sloping off after three lengths to indulge in my real reason for going there: my second shower of the trip!

I feel a bit like one of those parents who start going to church just to get their kids into a good school.

One last little motivational boost for the day was a fire crew from the local station. They sounded their sirens as they pulled up next to us in their fire engine. Andy wondered if they'd heard about his cooking and sent a crew over as a precaution, but no, it was just some local firefighters, one or two of whom were also runners, come to wish me well. After a few quick photos with me in my scruffy, dirty post-marathon clothes, complete with ice packs strapped to my knees, the nee-naws were sounded once again and they drove off. We were all asleep by 9 p.m., making the most of any opportunity to catch up with sleep.

Day 13 was a tactical day. Less mileage today would mean I could attempt a double marathon the following day. With just 227 feet of elevation it was the flattest day so far by some margin. I decided to start on time and finish just one marathon, ideally in less than six hours. I did: 27.14 miles in a moving time of four hours and fifty-three minutes, plus an hour of breaks for strapping, taping, painkillers, and an interview with the BBC, plus lots of new running faces to chat with, including a friendly chap called Gary, who would go on to be affectionately nicknamed Pop-up Gary. More on him later.

It was a day to recharge my batteries, to rest the aches and pains and to get the day done in good time. This would allow us more rest before a double day tomorrow – 30 April, the end of the month. Once again, Andy was enjoying a little extra free time:

With a few hours to spare, I go for what turns into a long walk down to Medmerry Nature Reserve. This takes me through one of those peculiar little communities you only really find on the British coast, a long row of mismatched houses, ranging from grand designs to glorified beach shacks. Many of the larger houses have that vaguely nautical architecture, with features loosely resembling the prow of a ship or a sail, while the humbler abodes are bedecked with the standard driftwood and flotsam. They all have that most British of qualities: quirkiness, and you can tell we're getting into the more affluent parts of Sussex now, with lots of 'Private Road' signs and other abrupt messages reminding passers-by of the area's exclusivity. These places are paradoxical – extroverted, yet insular.

Day 14's runners made the miles enjoyable. I later realized, only as I finished, that it was nice to have company again. I was able to chat for hours, without my mind thinking about my legs too much. This was starting to look like progress. From West Wittering, around Medmerry Nature Reserve, through Selsey, Bognor Regis, Littlehampton, Worthing and Shoreham-by-Sea, my legs, working rather well now, hauled my body towards the double marathon finish line into Brighton. Just a week after my show-stopping injury, I'd totted up 52 miles with an easy 337 feet of elevation in under twelve hours, including two hours for stops, food and, you guessed it, taping and icing my legs. It was working.

Andy's diary was all about the wildlife today:

Along the pleasant seafront paths, Nick and his group can enjoy the sights, including a pod of dolphins at Bognor Regis, glinting in the sun as they surface. The wildlife sightings continue in Worthing, where a peregrine falcon is being relentlessly mobbed by gulls until they eventually force it to drop the pigeon it's just caught, leaving it free to flash its talons at the nearest gull to scare it off. Whatever the result of this falcon v. gull contest, you have to feel that the pigeon is probably the loser overall.

It's turning into an enjoyable day's running for Nick, which he really needs, and we're all looking forward to a visit from Nicole later. After a few days with just the three of us on the road, it'll be good to see another member of the team. Nicole is fun. She has a wonderful way of looking at the world and can always make you laugh.

The final miles of the day followed Brighton's famous seafront, a colourful blend of Shoreditch and Miami. Running past clusters of bars, ice cream stalls, arcades and small independent eateries, I passed roller bladers, long-boarders in baggy clothes, and hula-hooping, Lycra-clad acrobats. The place was full of the juxtapositions and contrasts of the English seaside, with quirky, overpriced gin pop-ups alongside chain pubs selling alarmingly cheap food and drink.

Nikki had gone ahead to meet a friend for a well-earned drink, and had hit the Pimm's long before I finished. I ran past and high-fived her, before running back to steal a quick kiss. To hit 52.4 miles involved running a little further up the seafront and back. Having driven ahead to park up, Andy had come to join me for some fresh air. After changing and shovelling down some food, we joined Nikki, her friend Lara, and later Nicole, who lives in London but has family in Brighton. Having been diligently beavering away in her support role in the background, it was great to see her in person again. Most of what she did for Run Britain wasn't that much fun, but it was crucial.

Sticking slightly to the tacky paint of a blue seafront bench, our group sat and enjoyed a gentle drink in the evening sun. I, as usual, was in my slippers, to let my feet breathe and hopefully avoid potential developing blisters. I was a right state, but it was good to be out.

Covering a double marathon for the first time since that soul-crushing day that ended with my collapse at Bournemouth Pier was, if I'm honest, a surprise, even to me. The mind was still in control. My body was to do as it was told.

The others were on the beers and Pimm's while I sipped a protein shake with ice packs strapped to my legs. It dawned on me that if this trip was to be a success, we needed more little moments like this. Frankly I couldn't care less about 'fun' – I get my kicks out of the challenge – but I appreciated that we as a collective needed brief interludes to keep spirits high.

I stayed for a short while but took myself off to bed after about half an hour of chatting. In fact, for the first time on the trip I slept in Nikki's van. Our home. I craved my own double bed and some space, plus I knew she'd be out for a while. I could cuddle the dog and then cuddle Nikki when she got back. I was beginning to compromise on little things to keep the overall mission alive.

Andy, Nicole and Nikki were all out until at least 3 a.m. Despite appearing like a slightly irresponsible thing to do when supporting a big challenge, the evening had been fun, it was needed, and it bonded the team. It acted as a stress ball, relieving some tension from the previous weeks. I took note.

Days 15 to 20
Brighton to Burnham-on-Crouch
Finding rhythm, new injuries and a new photographer

Day 15 had snuck up on us, me waking up at 4 a.m. in the furnace, and the others with sore heads. I left Nikki and Poppy in a deep sleep as I pushed the latch of the sliding door and stepped out into the new day. We had parked right on the main beach strip. Leaving the Palace, I shuffled back to the Council Van in my PJs, which I'd been wearing since finishing running yesterday. I always slip into the most comfortable garments possible as soon as the run day is complete. There's something very satisfying about taking tight-fitting compressions off and slipping into soft baggy pyjamas. Freedom.

I'd gone to sleep to the sound of music, evening banter and laughter, and the general hum of a Friday night in Brighton. Stepping out to shuttle myself back to my own van to have breakfast and run through the usual morning rituals, I was struck by the calmness of the place. Seagulls, ocean lapping on sand, and the distant beeping of a road sweeper. A few foil kebab wrappers blew past my feet. I allowed myself just a few minutes to stroll to the railing and look out to sea and breathe in the smell of the ocean. I was smiling. It was exactly two weeks since we'd set off from the Eden Project.

Day 15 was a day of two halves, totalling 48.09 miles, with some of the biggest elevation since Dorset and my initial knee injury. We'd made it to our sixth county yesterday, and we weren't far from our seventh. Cornwall, Devon, Dorset, Hampshire, West Sussex and now East Sussex. Rounding the corner of Kent and heading towards the Thames was just a few days away – if I could stick to decent mileage, of course.

The morning was quiet, with blue sky and the occasional dot of fluffy white cloud. The seafront out of Brighton was flat too. I had with me another group of fifteen or so runners that made for great company. The 2,218 feet of elevation on today's route came in two big horrible peaks, the first of them at 20 miles, which left my legs feeling sore. To make matters worse, from around midday the rain came, and my head, just like my mood, dropped. For the final big hill out of Hastings, around the 43-mile mark, the now torrential rain and the swelling in both my Achilles and one knee were making the remaining miles rather bleak.

I did, however, have one extra mental boost button in my back pocket. That was the experience of having met Karen earlier in the day. Karen Penny, aka 'The Penny Rolls On', is a hiker in her mid-fifties who was also circumnavigating Britain on foot. She was hiking solo with a big pack on her back and walking poles in each hand, but even without the kit, my eyes picked up the familiar shuffle of someone who had been on their feet for quite a while. Besides, a flag and a laminated sign on her back with an Alzheimer's charity logo was a giveaway. I had been told about Karen just the day before and I had been hoping to bump into her. She was travelling clockwise, while I was heading anti-clockwise, so while there was a good chance we'd meet each other, it would have been just as easy to miss each other. The coast route may sound simple, but there's a vast range of alternative pathways and roads all the way along it.

I was over the moon to see her. She'd been on the road on and off for years, I believe. Covid interrupted her efforts of course, but she was a great example of someone who put determination to complete the mission just ahead of her enjoyment of it. She stayed with kind people who'd hosted her, walking about 15 miles a day, taking shelter if she needed to and raising valuable funds for Alzheimer's Research UK. I was impressed and inspired by our encounter. And it was her kind words of encouragement I called upon at 48 miles, with my injuries flaring up to the point where I was hobbling again, and the rain beginning to cause a cluster of blisters and the usual chafing under my arms and between my inner thighs. 'What would Karen do?' I thought. Sod it. The extra 4 miles today don't matter. I don't need to ruin my legs any further. Think of the long game. And so, very close to the end of the double, I stopped. I had learnt a new way of looking at the day. A way of turning weakness to strength. Strength to look at the bigger picture, and importantly to enjoy the miles. Because if I didn't, it was going to be a very long way around.

Ice, elevate, compress and rest. And do it again tomorrow.

And sure enough the sun did its thing, and tomorrow happened. As usual, Andy was up first:

At first light on day 16, Nick warms his hands over the gas hobs as the now familiar routine of bagel, Deep Heat and physio tape gets under way, ahead of another chilly start. I always have a slight feeling of daunting disbelief when Nick steps out of the van each day to cover his mileage quota, almost a feeling of 'sympathy dread'. It's bad enough when he's feeling relatively fresh and confident, but on days like today, where the state of his legs and feet add such a big element of uncertainty, it's almost unsettling having no idea how the day's going to pan out.

With mainstream supermarkets a bit scarce around here, my first stop of the day is at a convenience store attached to Pontins at Camber Sands, deserted due to Covid – a faded wonderland. On a sign next to the chained-up gate, a crocodile tells me 'The fun starts here!', but he's not fooling anyone. Crocodiles are notoriously insincere – hence crocodile tears.

It all feels a bit post-apocalyptic – the shop still has plenty of Easter eggs available though.

Day 16 was one of bleak beauty. That's the politest way I can find to talk of the barren wasteland of Dungeness and its surrounding coastline. I headed off from just south of Winchelsea, through Rye and Lydd, before passing the only noteworthy landmark of the day: the Dungeness Power Station. Need I say more? But 30.87 miles with a mere 87 feet of elevation was, despite my moaning about the scenery, rather useful. It was outstandingly flat, and it settled my injuries again. I made good time too: seven hours, with plenty of stops to retape my legs included.

Once again I'd decided on the Karen approach. I put enjoyment at the forefront of my mind. Not something I was familiar with to be honest, but it seemed to work. I rewarded my near 31 miles with two of my favourite things: I had a kale salad and did some yoga. I joke, of course. I scoffed down two McDonald's meals – large, of course – and watched the Portuguese Grand Prix. Ahh. Now this was better.

I did, however, have a few more miles to cover today. The rest and
enjoyment was all very well, but I now had many, many miles to catch
up on. For once in my life I didn't let this bother me, though. I just
ate, watched Lewis Hamilton win the race, then kitted up again and
out I went. I was consciously trying different approaches to the day, in
an attempt eventually to land on a method that worked and was
sustainable.

In stark contrast to the flattest 30 miles of my life, the additional few
miles I ran had over 500 feet of elevation. My knee and my mind
weren't up for that, so after an extra ninety minutes of slogging it out,
I stopped at 7.11 miles. A total of 37.98 miles for the day. We parked
up near a small town called Capel-le-Ferne, between Folkestone and
Dover. Better than Dungeness, the sign could have read.

At the top of the bloody great hill out of Folkestone, Nikki had
found a pub and negotiated with the owners to let us park there if we
had a meal. The place was more or less abandoned, partly because of
Covid, but the people were nice and served drinks to us outside. A little
tipple for Andy and Nikki, and a couple of pints of blackcurrant
squash for me with my legs elevated over the back of a well-used yellow plastic chair.

We discussed the concept of this careful balance between enjoyment and progress for an hour or so before bed. I actually slept with
Nikki and Poppy that night, which gave Andy a Nick-free van for the
night. This was luxurious because the van was small when empty, and
we were now sleeping among very dirty clothes and half-finished
packets of biscuits. Andy could just chuck everything on my bed and
spread out.

In bed, I half dreamed a half-baked equation to try and understand
the intersection between progress and enjoyment and my personal
threshold specific to this challenge. The weather, elevation and distance
governed the likelihood of injury, the main limiting factor to progress.
That's pretty much as far as I got. Not much of a formula for success,
but it did put more emphasis on the balance of weather, hills and distance. The enjoyment part would come when I understood the rest of
the formula properly. My brain was too knackered to think much
more. I was kicked out of bed in the early hours by Poppy, who had got

used to having her own side of the bed and demoted me to the seating area. And just like that, another day was upon us.

Day 17 confirmed my suspicions that I had started this challenge in the wrong part of the country. Through lack of good research on my part, I'd foolishly agreed to start in St Austell. Had I started in, say, Bournemouth, I would have had a week of running to get used to the mileage on routes with 1,000 feet of elevation, not 5,000. This could, and probably would, have allowed me enough time to get into stride and likely avoid injury. Hindsight is a wonderful thing, but wow this annoyed me. My own stupidity and lack of decent planning had resulted in Andy and me strapping my knee and shins hour after hour, day after day. We were also spending about £30 a week on KT tape. On the bright side, lower mileage the previous day meant I could target a double marathon today, even with 2,710 feet of hills. I did have plenty of blisters now but I was getting there. The balance felt closer.

By now we had our morning routine nailed. Wake up, eat bagel, drink tea, visit toilet, tape knee, tape Achilles, tape shin, clothes on, map check, shoes on, swallow tablets, open door, run. On this occasion, with some interesting legwear:

Nick's running clothes live in a huge bag that occupies the passenger seat of the Council Van. Lately, I've been trying to organize it into sections with similar types of garments grouped together and then subdivided using various things as partitions in an increasingly futile attempt to separate relatively clean from really quite foul. However, despite now knowing roughly where everything is, I can't lay my hands on a pair of comfortable running leggings. It's another cold morning, so Nick sets off running in his pyjama bottoms.

While he settles in to his first few miles, I head for a nearby Waitrose. I find they tend to have the best-kept facilities of the large supermarkets, and their toilets have become my throne of choice. My food shopping includes a local delicacy: Kentish Gypsy Tarts. They taste of sugar and disappointment.

Just like waves, clouds and all of Mother Nature's wonders, no two days were ever even vaguely the same. Yes I was running, and the mornings followed the same routine, but the people, the route, the elevation profile, the roads, the paths, the frequency of stops, all created so many differences. Today the hills were unique. A big down which buggered my knee a bit, a big up which buggered my Achilles, and another big down taking me to 11 miles . . . and the rest of the day was pretty much a gradual 2 per cent gradient uphill. Which buggered my shin.

From Capel-le-Ferne I plodded around the Kent coast, ticking off Dover, Walmer, Sandwich (where I had the titular snack), Ramsgate, Margate and Herne Bay, and finished in Whitstable (where I had a Chinese). Without noticing, I was no longer on the south coast. Andy mentioned this to me just past Margate, where for the first time I was running west. This was the mental lift required to get me through the remaining miles. I looked at Google Maps on my phone, and zoomed out two or three times. I'd run the whole of the south coast, more or less (apart from the bit at the far west, which I'd do at the end). Not only had I got here, but it wasn't even the end of week three, and I was carrying multiple injuries – a little reminder that my mind was holding me together. This was its own little reward. Never had I imagined I'd be so pleased to be in Margate.

I mentioned earlier that I often like to run with audio books. Sometimes music, but mostly audio books and podcasts or nothing at all. Now well into Kent, our seventh county, I had already listened to eight books. To our surprise, Andy and I found we were now on the same book, Andy reading an actual paperback in his few minutes of downtime per day, and me listening to it as I ran. The book was Simon Jenkins's *A Short History of England*. This was my attempt, and it turns out Andy's too, to broaden my knowledge of English history as we travelled through its historic places. I'd picked the book randomly months ago, as part of a spending spree on about fifty books to listen to throughout the challenge. An audio book is usually about ten hours long and so in theory I could listen to one every day. Obviously, interruptions in the form of company and food stops meant I was averaging about half a book a day. Still, not bad for a non-multitasking man.

This book in particular was perfectly timed for this corner of the country. There were sections on Vikings and various other invaders, and once finished, I downloaded a few more books about Vikings ahead of hitting the east coast. I was alarmed by how little I knew, and how much there was still to learn. Similar books on broader topics, such as Andrew Marr's *A History of the World*, were equally informative, along with Bill Bryson's *A Short History of Nearly Everything*, which I've now listened to three times.

Andy was clearly getting into the spirit too:

We stop for lunch at Pegwell Bay, where there's a full-scale replica of a Viking ship. It was also apparently the place chosen by Caesar for his arrival in 55 BC. It's obviously a popular spot for an invasion, so we descend upon the grassy car park in our battle vans. Bet the Romans and the Vikings didn't have to pay and display.

On day 18, marathon one from Whitstable to Rochester covered 1,834 feet of elevation and 27.16 miles. Marathon two from Rochester to Cliffe covered 1,459 feet of elevation and 27.15 miles. Both not dissimilar in elevation and distance, but the second marathon was a killer.

The day taught me that the ground surface I was running on should probably also make it into my equation for success. From Faversham to Rochester, a 20-mile stretch, I was running solely along the pavement of London Road – a sign that the capital was now not far away. From Rochester onwards, however, having stopped for lunch for an hour or so, it got rather difficult. Boggy and uneven marshland with flooded sections and hard-to-follow signage made for what would be a slow slog of an afternoon. But above all, day 18 would become remembered as the day of the Poo Incident.

One of the problems with running west was that I was now facing into the prevailing weather, which that morning had taken the form of a fierce headwind. For the first few miles I leaned into the battering gusts, having to expend far more energy than usual to make headway. I flagged Andy down to try and use the van for shelter, but it was too unsafe running in the middle of the road. After a few miles, the route mercifully cut inland around the impassable creeks and boggy ground of Graveney Marshes, taking me on to slightly less exposed ground where the wind wasn't as bad. I made a quick stop to tape up my big toe, knowing that preventing blisters is far better than reacting to them. It was annoying to stop and de-sock, but I've learnt my lesson over and over again. It's far better to get on top of foot maintenance before problems develop. Then it was on to Watling Street, the old Roman road running between Canterbury and London, making navigation for the remainder of marathon one of the day easy.

Rochester was the halfway point, and frustratingly I was still experiencing Achilles problems and quite a lot of shin pain. Andy suggested I should probably start doing some mid-run stretching. Andy knows I am notoriously bad at this thing he calls 'stretching'. He says I view the scientifically well-proven, beneficial practice of warming up and stretching as some sort of alternative New Age nonsense, a bit like homeopathy. This is of course an exaggeration. I know full well that stretching works, I'm just rather lazy. I'd rather just run. However, desperate times call for desperate measures, and I decided to give this wacky concept a go.

The start of marathon two of the day saw me turn east again to round the final headland before following the Thames Estuary back towards London. It was still very windy, and about to get worse. This section took me around the Isle of Grain, which is no longer an island. It was more or less a full loop, so Andy parked the van up at the end and ran across to meet me.

The coast path here is flat and fairly even, but running along the top of flood banks it is also very exposed. Once Andy met me – a welcome sight, as I was now in a bit of a mental slump – we were instantly battling against stronger and stronger headwinds and now rain. We found ourselves out on a bit of a limb, in one of those places where, if we did have to turn back, it would involve a lot of extra miles, rather than just heading back to the nearest road. At the edge of a military area, we double-checked with an unofficial-looking official on the gate to make sure we could get through. He assured us we could, so we put our heads down and ploughed on, both of us wearing waterproofs that were already soaked through, buffs up to the bags under our eyes, hats and gloves. It was miserable. These marshes were becoming a memorable beast.

Andy had run with me when he could over the past few weeks, for sections of anywhere from 3 to 10 miles. This would be his longest to date, totting up nearly 20 miles, while carrying supplies of water and snacks on his back. To get back on to the road, we had to cut through a grim static caravan park, where we stopped for a quick break from the wind behind two large Biffa bins. This was the first available bit of shelter we'd encountered in miles and it was a relief. We could hear each other again, our clothes weren't buffeting in the wind and causing that annoying flapping sound, and of course we could sit for a few minutes and have some water and food. Andy had bought some custard creams, part of his elite sports nutrition menu.

As he was rummaging in the bag for biscuits, a scruffy dog appeared, having already sniffed them out, and came over in the hope of a snack. It was a little odd, because we hadn't seen a soul for miles. As Andy pulled the packet of custard creams out of the bag, there was a soft thud, and something landed on the back of his hands.

'Is that . . .? No . . . surely not,' Andy said.

'Yes, yes it is,' I said, struggling to contain myself.

It was a bag of shit.

Andy froze and stared down at the brown missile in horror and disbelief. Where had it come from? A critic? Had we made an enemy? Then we heard eager apologetic words. It was the dog's owner, who, on his way over to retrieve his dog, had launched a poo bag towards the open bin, but failed to account for the strong sidewind. By the time Andy had worked out what was going on, I was already in tears of laughter, my belly hurting. It was the funniest thing I'd seen in years. There was something so perfect about it. After the serious effort we'd put in to navigate the brutal wind and terrain, to then have the simple pleasure of custard creams interrupted by the sudden appearance of an extraterrestrial bag of shit . . . just like newsreaders getting the giggles, I couldn't stop. Neither could Andy, once he'd seen the funny side. The dog's owner was of course mortified, and having retrieved both dog and dirty bomb he continued to apologize profusely, while we attempted to dry our eyes and slog our way to the finishing post. We literally laughed until I stopped my watch to close the final marathon of the day.

I'm sure Andy generally doesn't like having faeces thrown at him, but I'm so glad it happened. The Poo Incident became a story frequently recounted, a light-hearted, joyous bit of misadventure amid the misery of the rain, and a gentle nudge to keep things fun.

Andy did manage to see the funny side:

In the course of one's life, there are low points. Having dogshit thrown at me is up there as one of mine. But from this mire of wretchedness, a ray of sunshine: I've genuinely never seen Nick this happy. Tears of joy stream down his little face. To have a still-warm dog egg mould itself over my knuckles, with just the thinnest layer of plastic in between, is worth it, just to see the unbridled pleasure it has brought him.

It was dusk by the time I made it to Cliffe marshes, where Yas and Amy had come to join us. Yas and Amy, both in their mid-twenties, know each other from school and are good friends. Yas was still working hard to keep the back end of this mission going, and Amy, a keen photographer who had been with us briefly a couple of weeks back, had agreed to support with photos on and off if we could cover her expenses and she could sleep in the van with Nikki. We sat around eating pizza in the Palace Van that night before I left the gang and took myself off to bed about forty minutes after I'd stopped running. Yas and Amy would be around for a few days, so our little crew was nearer to full capacity for a while. It was a change, and it would lighten the load for Andy and Nikki for a while at least. And today had been a success. This was my first back-to-back double marathon day since Bournemouth. A sign of recovery perhaps. Or perhaps not.

Day 19 was full of more boggy terrain and bad weather along a badly signposted and partly cut-off coast path. A grim lorry stop for a chip butty with a side of effluent stench was the highlight of my morning.

Prior to breaching the Essex county line in the second half of the day, Gravesend was as close as I had to get to London thanks to the Thames crossing, a small passenger ferry that took me to Tilbury. Andy drove ahead to buy a ticket in advance and I hopped on after killing a few miles running around Gravesend, having just missed the previous crossing. With Andy waiting to make sure I was able to get the ferry, Nikki had driven ahead to meet a friend of ours, Dani, on the other side, while she waited for me to arrive. Meanwhile, Andy would get across via the Dartford Tunnel, which would take him a while.

Dani is one half of a couple Nikki and I met in Brighton just before the first lockdown, while I was in town to give a talk. Dani and James, who are from Essex, were on a mini holiday in Brighton with their two-year-old vizsla, Woody. Being new vizsla parents, we made a beeline for Woody and introduced ourselves. We've been friends ever since, and they've even looked after Poppy for us a few times. Vizsla parenthood is a strong bond. Dani was waiting eagerly to run a few miles with me and I'm sorry to say I was a little grumpy, having been battered by rain and caught out by uneven terrain hidden under grass for mile after mile. Dani cheered me up though, over the 10 miles he spent with me. I was grateful that he was there to drag me along.

By the end of the day I'd clocked a total of 42 miles, inching closer to finding that happy medium of avoiding and even repairing injuries, while making progress and finding that elusive sense of enjoyment.

Each evening we would mark our progress on a big paper map of Britain at the back of the van, a little ritual that was supposed to add to our positive energy. But on this section of the coast with all its twists, turns, loops and switchbacks, these few days didn't feel much like progress. Andy's diary records the mood:

With Nick having clocked 42 miles, a dreary train station car park serves as an apt night spot for what has been a fairly dreary day, and we opt for another Chinese takeaway to cheer us all up. After dark, we're joined by a fox who's sniffed out our food – she's particularly fond of chicken satay.

Similar to the previous day, day 20 was uneventful, just more miles around the bleaker parts of Essex, where the 'pleasure pier' was a highlight. A relative highlight. Fortunately, there were a couple of light-hearted moments to brighten up our day.

Andy had stopped, quite deliberately, next to a couple of signs, one pointing to the town of Foulness, the other saying St Nicholas. Andy was looking very chuffed with himself at having found this photo opportunity. Foulness and me, by now, were synonymous. Having run for three weeks with just one bath, wearing the same wet, sweaty, crusty clothes every day, with wild poos aplenty, running around Britain was far from glamorous. Foulness summed it up perfectly, and also describes the day's only other noteworthy incident.

I'd been struggling for a while with what I thought was some grit lodged in between my big toe and the one next to it. I couldn't quite see it, but could feel it, and so without messing around Andy reached for his surgical instruments, rummaging around in his toolkit before triumphantly pulling out his grubby old Stanley knife. He prised my manky, unwashed toes apart and rooted around with the unsterilized blade, hacking away dead skin, while Amy took photos of the disgusting procedure and Nikki looked relieved that this responsibility had fallen to Andy and not her. It was indeed a cluster of grit and some thorns that were buried into my thick crusty layers of foot skin.

Andy and Nikki got along well. Barring my parents, they were, and are, the only two people in the entire world who know me inside and out, and they were starting to delight in the fact they could predict my mood, my food orders and finish my sentences, pretty much reading me like a book. They bonded over it and are still good friends now. You couldn't ask much more from two people I deeply care for, and who have cared for me more than many friends or partners would.

A quiet yacht club car park served as our resting place for the evening, Nikki having scouted out a perfect spot. We were in Burnham-on-Crouch, and I'm afraid I don't remember a thing about the place. My photo library, along with my diary and Andy's, is rather short on memories from here. I just have photos of feet and food. For his part, Andy's diary reads:

It can often be a challenge to park the van close to Nick's finishing spot. I usually ask him his exact mileage at the last stop before finishing, subtract this from his intended total and then drive ahead for the remainder, to find the closest possible place I can stop. Today, a quaint petrol station is the nearest place I can stop to the end of his second 26.2 miles of the day. Nick trots up and down the road to make sure his watch has ticked past the magic number while I park on the forecourt and wander around the shop with my best browsing face on, pretending I have the intention of buying something. Nearby, Nikki has found a nice little car park attached to Burnham-on-Crouch yacht club. We're not members, but if questioned, we're ready to drape jumpers over our shoulders and wear shoes with no socks, so we at least look the part.

Despite the generally bland day, it was another double down. The crew (Andy, Nikki and now Yas and Amy) had a few beers to celebrate, while I enjoyed my treat of choice: sleep.

Days 21 to 22
Burnham-on-Crouch to Clacton-on-Sea
Week three complete

Nikki and Poppy joined me for 10 kilometres of the final day of week three. Officially three weeks completed, although it already felt like months. None of us could believe we'd only chalked up twenty-one days on the road.

A journey by car, plane, train or even push bike is very different to a journey made on foot. You see, smell, hear and feel everything. I will accept I am a little biased. I love running, in case you hadn't noticed. But the way the journey unfolds is so much more intimate. Tarmac under your feet, your legs brushing through grass, smoke from nearby wood burners and diesel engines being dragged into your lungs, hearing the foaming crest of white-capped waves breaking on rocks. It's a sensory overload. It doesn't have to be pretty to be experienced. There's something so deeply enriching to the soul to be outside, with whatever weather, geology or other obstacles in your path. Most notably, these factors combine to impact your perception of time. Time elongates and contracts. And we all have one short life, so who wouldn't want to eke it out. It almost feels like I've found the elixir of life, a way to live longer, by packing as much stimulation as possible into a twenty-four-hour day. This I am grateful for, and must remind myself of when I start to wish away the miles. Having Nikki join me, with Poppy pulling on the lead out front, was a joyful start to the day. And in turn I was pleased that I was acknowledging my fortunes.

A stop to address some pain in my feet brought me back down to earth a little. Having covered the initial 26.2 miles of the day my feet were sore. Very sore. I'd already changed trainers twice during the trip as they'd passed their optimum duration, and even though my current pair still had around 100 miles left in them, I tried a new pair in a bid to ease the pain in my feet with a little more padding.

The pain, we deduced, was probably from the hundred thousand-plus steps a day bruising the bottoms of my feet, from heel to toe – my latest nemesis. I set off again with new shoes after the midday interval, but I was back to a hobble within a few steps and, keen not to over-compensate once again and develop even more injuries, I reluctantly closed the day on my worst mileage of the week. But I accepted it, and reminded myself: it is what it is. Keep moving forward, and the finish line will come to you.

Pulling my compressions off over my ankles was a struggle, my back also sore from clenching my posture as I ran. Changing into fresh boxers and slipping some new socks on, I at least felt comfortable again, because I was horizontal, but the pain level was, worryingly, not dissimilar to that of day 5 or 6, when I could hardly stand. It was a different pain, and only for the last few miles of the day, but it was notching up to a solid eight out of ten.

Food, followed by immediate sleep, is what I needed, and the only options I had anyway.

At least Andy still had his sense of humour:

With a few hours to kill, I take Poppy for a walk along the edge of a golf course by the river, where she shouts at some golfers. Although she appreciates the progress that golf has made at becoming a more inclusive sport, as a strong independent female dog she can't forget

the sexism that has blighted golf throughout much of its history,
and barks her views across the fairway. Or it might just be that one
of them is wearing a yellow jumper.

Having spent a good few days with us, Yas headed off before I was awake, wanting to beat the traffic. When I did finally wake up, a little later than usual at 5.30, day 22 began to the all-too-clear sounds of heavy rain pelting the roof of the van and wind gusting hard. It felt like we were on water, not land. Getting up so late was, oddly, a blessing. I didn't have time to wallow in the sound, and instead rushed to get dressed. Taping my legs took up most of the time, and was largely in vain because the strapping wouldn't last long in the rain, even under my compressions and leggings. The wet morning was also chilly, but I still started the day with a group of hardcore early bird runners.

The weather got worse and rapidly developed into the wettest day of the trip so far. By mid-morning, items of clothing were being wrung out and I resorted to putting my phone in a plastic bag. The moisture had been causing it to repeatedly call my emergency contact, which had resulted in an earlier than expected start and numerous nuisance calls for my dad. He called me back a few times, but of course I couldn't answer because the phone was too wet. I may as well have taken it diving. It was useless.

In rain this heavy, there's no point stopping for clothing changes as dry clothes will be soaked in a matter of minutes, and besides, I was keen to keep going to avoid getting cold. If you look at Strava, all of my quickest runs will be because of either rain, the cold, or both.

With the phone out of action and therefore impossible to use for navigation, Andy was now stopping wherever possible to point out turnings, which was particularly difficult around the busy town of Hythe – the third Hythe we'd been through in as many weeks. Andy had taken to parking anywhere and everywhere, more or less burning the Highway Code. Today, this included the crosshatching between the lanes on a roundabout approach and the grass island between carriageways, sticking his hand out of the window to point directions at me. Luckily there were no police about. None that we saw anyway.

The rain is a good speed motivator, and having bashed through the morning marathon in under four hours, it was a good opportunity for some decent recovery time before setting off again. The quicker miles felt like I was racing. I was giving it my all, which frankly was stupid. But joined by four guys in their early twenties eager to get out of the rain too, it was fun. Yes, really.

My foot, however, wasn't a fan. Although painful, it was no worse, but the danger was that I was getting fed up with it holding me back and more inclined to risk injuring it further.

With Andy's help, I used the last bits of my morning energy to dry off and have some food, followed by a nap. The intention was to run as many miles as comfortably as possible in the afternoon. No pressure, just getting out and maybe even enjoying the rain would be enough of a win.

Meanwhile, poor Andy wasn't having much luck with water either:

While Nick has a nap, I take advantage of the fact that we're parked up next to another leisure centre, an opportunity for my first shower since Portsmouth. This one is a bit of a pain though, and I have to sign up as a member to use the pool. The title options available when I'm entering my name details include various levels of nobility – I opt for 'Lord' and go for another pretend swim, only to find, to my dismay, that, although the pool is open, the showers are still closed due to Covid restrictions. I'm so disappointed, I feel like renouncing my peerage.

In fact the rain had stopped by the time I woke from an hour's nap. I was groggy though, and the rain soon returned as I made my way down Essex's final headland towards Jaywick. According to the internet, Jaywick is the most deprived area in Britain. It's a bleak and bewildering place, with a strip of flat-roofed buildings with single header boards in simple uniform block capitals, bearing not the names of the establishments, just a literal description of what they are: Café, Grocers, Bakery, Tattooist, Sweet Shop, Public Toilets. Everyone here seemed angry and suspicious and a few locals gave us the 'shiteye' as we, clearly outsiders, moved through the town. We passed through quickly, and I mean no disrespect to the place, but I felt anxious, and threatened.

After I'd had my bout of judging and turning my nose up, I soon felt ashamed, and a wave of guilt came over me. I was born into a lovely home, with wonderful parents, and given every opportunity I could dream of. High crime and low school attendance were a world away from my childhood. The people here didn't deserve my derision. I thought about my place in the world for several hours, and vowed to be less judgemental.

With my head off on a tangent, my legs and specifically my feet were nearing the limit of what they had left. I ground out a few more miles, eventually arriving in Clacton-on-Sea, an afternoon stint of 14 miles, bringing the day's total to 40, which, considering the end of yesterday, wasn't bad at all. Andy was impressed. I was too. Having changed into the same old scruffy PJs, I limped along the seafront with Andy to find a takeaway.

As we walked, we couldn't help but marvel at the locals making the most of the newly reopened bars following the lifting of Covid restrictions. On a Saturday night in Essex, you know you're in Essex on a Saturday night. It's Benidorm Britain at a beauty pageant, and we enjoyed the contrast of spider-leg eyelashes, fake tan and revealing outfits against the sight of our straggly and unwashed frames sauntering down the strip.

Opposite the sprawling restaurant frontages, complete with outdoor upright heaters and gaudy signage, there was a classic seaside amusement park with stalls where you chuck darts at balloons to win prizes, speakers inviting punters to get their tokens at the cash desk, bumper cars and cheesy chips served out of greasy hatches. We wandered for some time, lost among all this Essex finery. Eventually we stumbled on a Prezzo and ordered more stodgy food than we could eat.

We headed back to the van, acknowledging that the joke was very much on us. We both looked like hobos. I'd accidentally tucked my grubby, off-white T-shirt into my pants, I was sockless in boat shoes, and wearing pyjamas and a baseball cap that had been chewed by the dog. To complete the look, I'd somehow, during the day, managed to smear a dollop of green snot up my right cheek. Andy looked slightly less down on his luck, but still fell into the general category of 'crumpled'. And neither of us had been clean for weeks.

4

Heading North

SKEGNESS ■

Boston ●

Stiffkey ●

Cromer ●

King's Lynn ●

NORFOLK

Great Yarmouth ●

Lowestoft ● ✳ *E*

SUFFOLK

● Felixstowe

Harwich ●

CLACTON-ON-SEA

Days 23 to 26
Clacton-on-Sea to Stiffkey
My fragile limbs

By the end of day 23 we had come to rest in Suffolk. I couldn't believe I was now further north than London. Not long now and I'd be in Scotland. Well, that's a slight exaggeration. It was just another 800 miles till then.

Rather than break the day into two halves like I had been recently, I opted for bigger mileage in the morning. This acted as a psychological booster and was actual physical prep for regaining longer stints, back to doubles without breaks and ideally beyond. I managed 37 miles in the morning, and just 5 in the afternoon.

Today, and over the next three days, my body suffered. In anatomy speak, the lower body is divided into three regions: the thighs – anything between the hip and knee joints; the legs – anything between the knee and ankle joints; and the general term 'distal', denoting the ankle and below, aka stuff far from the centre of our bodies. From top to bottom, it's pelvis, femur, patella, tibia and fibula, the smaller lower leg bone that kind of hides behind the tibia.

Feeling like a fraud a few years ago, and in some faint effort to keep up with or at least stay within sight of my brother in terms of medical knowledge, I started to download book after book on anatomy. As a runner with a heart problem who has suffered with multiple injuries, a minor heart attack, and also has hypermobility and Osgood-Schlatter disease, I thought I should begin to have a vague idea about what's going on in my body. My memory from childhood education is absolutely zero. Something about blood cells and photosynthesis . . . or maybe that's plants.

Osgood-Schlatter disease is not a condition that'll lead to me growing a third head, or a second for that matter, it's caused by playing
sports that put repeated stress on the patellar tendon – sports such as
running, which I did a lot of as a child, and of course still do. It's a
fancy word for the pain when the tendon in the knee pulls against the
top of the shin bone, particularly when bone is forming and growing
during childhood. This is called the growth plate (apparently). The
rubbing and pulling along this growth plate causes inflammation and
thus pain. If you look at my knees, you'll notice my left has a large
hard bump just under the knee joint. It flares up sometimes, usually if
I rest for too long and then run too far too soon. Now, having clocked
over 70,000 miles in my life, it's a pain my mind tunes out. I don't even
notice. So that's a bit of science on my knees out of the way.

So you can see how, on day 23, and in the three days that followed,
my leg health took a nose dive. I kept up with the miles more or less,
but I had the fear the pendulum had swung back away from recovery
and towards an unavoidable cliff of more injury. With 41 miles covered
on day 23, 37 on day 24 and 41 on day 25, I was making steady progress, but limping heavily.

Fortunately, Andy was staying positive:

*Nick is still moving, and despite not running as far as he'd like, is
still, on a daily basis, putting in mileage that most people would
consider absurd. Stamina and sheer grit are never in short supply
with Nick, and the only thing missing from the perfect formula at
the moment is consistency. Although the original end date is now
more or less confirmed as unachievable, if Nick can start stringing
together a good run of form, he'd be able to run more comfortably
and work towards a new end date, making the mapping and schedule for the remainder of the trip more predictable. However, Nick's
assortment of injuries, minor niggles and pains are making that
very difficult for him. But now, with the flattest stretch of the
whole trip ahead of him, the largely elevation-free expanse of East
Anglia and Lincolnshire, Nick is hoping to capitalize on some easy
terrain to 'run off' some of these problems and improve his form
and fitness.*

This morning, he makes his way around the marshes of Orford Ness before rejoining the coast path, where I meet him by the nuclear power station at Sizewell. Here, a colony of kittiwakes have found an unlikely nesting site, using one of the old offshore cooling platforms as an artificial cliff. It's a good example of the way in which areas where industry prevents human habitation can become great places for wildlife. It reminds me of the deserted city of Pripyat, a place Nick and I were fortunate enough to visit on his Ukraine leg of Running the World, which the Chernobyl exclusion zone has inadvertently made a wildlife haven. This sort of unintended, passive rewilding is surely the best advert for the concept, demonstrating how little human effort can be required to produce incredible results.

Over those few days we crossed rivers, navigated past more marshes, Nicole visited again, along with her mum Marion, and I even indulged in the ultimate luxury: a shower. Yes, you read that right. A shower! My first since Bournemouth. A Travelodge special. This was, of course, the highlight of the month for my nether regions.

On day 25 we reached a real milestone, our first of four compass points. Suffolk is home to the most easterly point in mainland Britain. Having set off from the previous day's Travelodge shower celebrations a little late – my first post-6 a.m. start, in fact – we reached a boring huge tarmac compass set into the ground on the edge of an industrial estate in Lowestoft. Nikki and Poppy arrived to celebrate the moment with a photo and a kiss. And as Andy pointed out, Poppy was unfazed about being Britain's most easterly dog. She just wanted to run. After a quick blurry selfie with a sweaty phone lens, off I trotted.

Andy later joined me with Poppy at Waxham in Norfolk, answering her call to stretch her legs. She'd been getting fidgety to be out of the van, having smelt a huge group of seals basking on the other side of the sand dunes (I believe the term is raft of seals, although I find this confusing because the seals did not form a raft, nor were the seals on a raft, but anyway . . .). I have never seen so many seals in one place. Seals of all ages and all sizes were neatly lined up on the tucked-away beach.

Andy, Poppy and I ran under the afternoon sun. We humans were in good spirits, despite my slight limp, while Poppy was well behaved despite the nearby seals, but was kept on the lead in line with the guidance and out of respect.

The day ended in a small car park in Happisburgh. A delicate, freshly painted lighthouse was our backdrop. The sunset with the lighthouse in the foreground was a mood booster. Despite my legs now very much worrying me, especially my shin bone, I hobbled out of the van before sunset and snapped a few photos on my camera. Amy, Nikki and Poppy were all larking about in a small play area, their bodies silhouetted. I later learnt that the Happisburgh lighthouse is the only independently operated lighthouse in Great Britain, and is by far the oldest in East Anglia.

Andy was impressed too:

Amy has managed to find what will no doubt remain one of the most perfect overnight spots of the entire trip: a small cliff-top car park at Happisburgh, next to the most photogenic lighthouse I've ever seen, and a small children's playground. After a while watching Amy and Nikki playing on the swings, Nick and I wonder if we should call them in for tea, but they seem happy, so we leave them to it. They'll come in when they're hungry.

As you look at a map of Britain, we spent the night right on the upper butt cheek of the country. Due east of here is Amsterdam; due west, inland to somewhere between Leicester and Derby. With few inlets to navigate, we seemed to zip along that smooth, sweeping butt cheek rather quickly. It had been only days since we were level with London.

My legs that evening felt more frail and fragile than ever, and for the first time in a while I told Andy the real pain rating and just how bad they were getting. Andy used this as a motivational prompt. We opened the back doors of the Council Van to reveal the large map where we draw our progress line each day. We'd not done so the last few days and it was a nice little nudge of encouragement to see how far we'd come.

I iced some more, we both spent a few moments having a rather far-cical tidy and sort-out, then went to bed after a big bowl of ravioli covered in thick cream cheese. A high-fat, high-carbs meal to send me off to sleep. We spoke only briefly about my legs, and how much I was worried about them. There wasn't much to do really. As usual we just had to see how the next morning went. The good old phrase 'one step at a time' sounded about right.

I was on to a new pair of trainers before stepping out on day 26, plus new insoles, the laces tied loosely to allow for swelling in my feet. I esti-mated that the extra blood and some inflammation of the ankle and foot would account for an increase of at least half a size over a mara-thon distance. It's one of the things I've always seemed to get right. I was wearing Brooks Adrenaline, the 2021 model. They offered the per-fect cushioning, but with enough width inside to allow for extra insoles, and they grip around the heel enough but not too much. Plus the heel-to-toe drop suits my natural short-stride running style. I've tried so many brands but I like Brooks because they aren't a fashion shoe. Nor are they popular because of their looks or fancy branding, but simply because they are great trainers. They were doing a sterling job of defend-ing against any worsening injuries. Or was I speaking too soon?

At 31 miles, after much discussion, a few route changes and some joyous runners for company, I had to call it a day, unable to run many more miles due to severe shin pain.

The situation had all the hallmarks of my fractured shin in Italy. I ran through the early warning signs then, and I was pretty sure I was doing the same now. Much like Run Britain, with big hills in the early days, I'd made it over the Dolomites when my shin became swollen. Within a few days a red patch had formed just above where my ankle meets my shin. The patch had localized and was tender. The more I ran, the more it hurt. The muscles attached to my tibia were basically start-ing to pull away from my shin. This obviously gives less support and thus eventually leads to a stress fracture, and then a fracture. At the time this was made worse by wearing very unsupportive shoes, but by the time I switched them and bought extra insoles for cushioning, the damage was already done. Now I was worried about a repeat.

Having stopped and changed, I hid my leg under ice to prevent the others from inspecting it. Once the painkillers wore off, my shin was throbbing and the pain ratcheted up the notches, from painful to agonizing to immovable. I drifted off to sleep after my evening supplements and more painkillers with my fingers crossed for the morning. I felt so rubbish that I hadn't been able to up the mileage. I was beginning to get dejected again. Andy noticed too. He didn't acknowledge it directly, but he was putting more energy into words and movement in a hope I'd mirror his upbeat mood. I was grateful, but it didn't work.

I remember saying a few quiet words accidentally out loud. I was willing myself to get well. I'm a believer in visualization and compartmentalizing big problems. It's something that's now second nature to me. My brain just let slip a few audible words: 'Come on legs' and 'Nicholas, it's OK, you've got this'. I was reassuring myself that my legs were just an extension of my mind; rest and repair would follow – keep the faith. I must have seemed mad muttering such things gently under my breath like Voldemort casting a spell. But it was needed.

Day 27 – 7.62 miles – 252ft elevation
Stiffkey to Holkham
Crutches on the salt marshes

On the north Norfolk coast, I left the Stiffkey salt marshes on time. I made an early decision to take my poles, following an inspection of my shin at breakfast, and managed 7 measly miles before crumbling. The day was not what I had hoped for as I'd drifted off to sleep the previous evening.

Andy noticed my shin as he set about taping in the usual places – the shin I'd subconsciously tried hard not to look at because the feeling was all too familiar. We looked at the raised red swollen lump on the middle of my tibia a couple of inches up from my ankle. The skin was tight and hot. Identical to the Italy injury. We then looked at each other. Andy mentioned that it was something we needed to think about, and that it could be the start of a fracture. All in a gentle tone. For Andy that's as direct as he gets. I owned up and explained that I'd been thinking the same thing.

Having finished breakfast, which of course was a Marmite bagel and a cup of tea, we continued to tape my leg as usual and spoke no more of the big lump protruding from my shin. We were in tune with each other, and knew it was simpler just to brush this potentially serious problem aside for now. Until I had at least attempted to run, there was no point us discussing stopping. That would always come from me. Andy knew it, and he allowed me to make those all-important decisions myself. This is something I never gave Andy enough credit for at the time.

I've been on challenges in the past with a crew that were not quite synced up with my way of thinking. They didn't understand the highly sensitive words and phrases that could either lead to a huge positive uplift or cause deep degrading damage. This naturally changes morale, mental strength and ultimately belief, in seconds. If Andy had said 'I think you should stop' or 'Nah, that's fine, carry on', neither option would have helped. He knew I knew my limits. He also knew I would push them to the very edge, but trusted me to be sensible enough, just enough, to make a hard decision if I needed to.

I hobbled into action, while Andy, unbeknown to me, got on the phone to look at options for getting my leg looked at. I found this out 5 miles down the road as I hobbled with poles again, along a straight road in a posh part of north Norfolk, just past a village called Holkham, where Andy, Nikki and Amy had parked up. They watched me stumbling towards them, all looking concerned. I gritted my teeth and clung to my poles like a frail pensioner as I approached them, in a dejected, frustrated mood. They were all grimacing.

My head was low, and with one eye on being sensible, I considered stopping. But I just wanted to continue. We couldn't afford to waste more time on injuries. If we did, the hundred-day finish line would definitely be out of reach. Andy walked with me for a few steps and began to explain that, although he'd been speaking to a few clinics and physio practices, it seemed that the best option for a quick and definitive assessment was good old A&E. Choosing his words carefully, Andy used a clever ploy to get me to agree to go to the hospital. His train of thought was, the earlier we got there, the less chance there would be of having a long wait. If we carried on now, we might waste more time in the long run. Smart move, Andy. He was of course right, too. It wasn't even 9 a.m.

A drinks company called Berczy were sponsoring me at the time, and had sent their owners out to come and run with me for a day. The obvious idea was to get some PR, enjoy a day's running, and bond a little. They were nice blokes. Oddly, both named Nick too. The only problem was, I was at a crunch point, a big fork in the road of a mission into which I'd poured every bit of energy and money I had. They were lively, awake and geared up with running bags for a big day out. They turned up just as Andy and I were discussing going to hospital. Sponsors make trips like this possible, and although I knew they'd understand, I felt shit. An endurance athlete that can't endure. A broken one at that.

I managed basic politeness, even a smile, but within a few minutes of hobbling along with them, it was game over. I'd told Andy that I'd try a few more miles because the Nicks were here, but it felt silly. They were struggling to walk as slowly as I was moving.

About a mile down the road, Andy drove past us and I flagged him down by raising my arm in the air, pole included. I called it. I must get my leg seen to. The Berczy boys understood and I miserably waved them off as Andy gave me a hand hauling myself up the step at the back of the van. The roads were quiet, not a cloud in the sky, and it was looking like a gorgeous day to be out running on the Norfolk coast. Instead I spent the morning in the waiting room of King's Lynn A&E.

As suspected, it was a fracture. I informed Andy, and waited for the results of a second X-ray to confirm the details. Although expected, it was still a crushing blow. Sitting in the cream-coloured corridors amid antiseptic-smelling misery, tired faces lining the walls on old tatty chairs, my waiting-room companions and I repeated the same ritual over and over: we shifted in our seats, we sighed, we looked at the clock, checked our phones, glanced at the clock again, and looked around at each other pondering our individual stories. All, of course, with masks on, causing our faces to sweat. And we couldn't even have a skim through three-year-old copies of *National Geographic* because Covid had removed them all.

I was waiting for the second X-ray because they were unsure what they were looking at. When I was told the news about the break they'd explained 'the good news and the bad news'. The bad news was that my tibia was broken; the good news, as peculiar as it was, was that I seemed to have an extra bone in my leg, about three inches long and attached to the side of my fibula.

The haggard-looking doctor was generally rushing through the details and didn't allow me to look at the X-ray as he explained it was rare, but usually seen in dancers like ballerinas. I got the impression he didn't really know what he was looking at. My suspicions were confirmed when he beckoned over another chap in a tunic, and then another, a woman this time, in a different-coloured outfit. They were like a family of stethoscope-wearing Teletubbies, all peering around the monitor at me looking rather bemused. They said they wanted to X-ray it again because I might have moved, and that it seemed a 'little strange'. Always a reassuring phrase to hear from a doctor.

It turned out that I definitely did have another little bone, and that too was fractured. It seemed to have split longitudinally. I never did get a proper explanation. My assumption was that my lifetime mileage, plus early years doing lots of skiing, combined with Osgood-Schlatter disease, may have had something to do with it.

That was that. I was simply told to rest for six to eight weeks, and that I could either have a big boot, some kind of external splint and cast, or just crutches. They advised I come back in a few weeks so they could check progress, and if it wasn't improving, they'd intervene. The doctor fetched some crutches, I hobbled around the maze of identical walkways, and eventually made it to the car park. Andy was napping in the front seat, having tidied the van and parked right outside the main entrance. Top bloke, as always.

After rather proudly showing off my 'special' leg, we talked about when I'd be able to run again. I liked the fact that although I'd been told six to eight weeks of rest, neither of us even mentioned the word 'weeks' during this discussion. We were both on the same page. Rest today and tomorrow and see how it feels.

I think Andy was shocked at my mood. I wasn't angry, crying or even despondent. This was because I'd been here before. Not King's Lynn hospital, but the same situation. I knew I didn't need six weeks.

Last time, a grumpy Italian woman had told me I should stop running altogether and that I was stupid to damage myself like this. Within five days I was back running marathons every day, including doubles, for another two months. This was different because I'd be going back to bigger mileage, but I was accepting the situation and was now back in active recovery mode, with physio Tim's voice ringing in my ears.

It was Thursday, 13 May and my leg was broken – and, I now knew, in two places rather than just one. But after having had a few hours to think about it, I set a target to be back on my feet by Monday.

Andy's take on the day reveals his reservations – though he knew better than to share them with me:

By the end of yesterday, Nick could barely walk. His shin was causing him discomfort to the point where he was only able to run 31 miles, and in Nick's eyes, that's shameful. His solution is just to pretend everything's fine and start running as normal today, with the intention of covering 40-plus miles.

As I tape his leg, post-bagel, I get a close look at his shin, and even to my untrained eye it looks like he already has a stress fracture. There is very light swelling and inflammation around the shin itself, rather than a joint or tendon, and it worries me to the point where I mention it, but in a very British, matter-of-fact way, so as not to cause alarm. Nick reveals that he had been thinking the same thing, but hadn't said anything to avoid putting a downer on breakfast with something as trivial as a broken leg. With this minor inconvenience swept under the carpet for now, Nick limps into action, while I get on the phone to see if there's anywhere we can get his leg looked at without going to a general hospital.

By 5 miles, Nick's walking with sticks, and at Holkham, in possibly Britain's poshest car park, a wide tree-lined avenue of gravel, Nikki, Amy and I pull in and give each other nervous sideways glances as he approaches, suggesting that none of us is comfortable watching this ordeal. Nick, of course, will happily carry on until (a) it becomes tomorrow, or (b) his leg comes off. After mile 6, just when I'm wondering if it's time for an intervention, Nick, to my relief, flags me down, realizing that he has no option but to sort out some healthcare. Having taken advice from a few clinics and physio practices, the consensus is that we cut out the middleman and proceed directly to A&E, and I figure the earlier we get there, the less chance there will be of Nick having a long wait. King's Lynn seems to be the best option in terms of distance and expected busyness, and I'm relieved to find that Nick seems receptive to the idea, although I suspect it's more out of curiosity about what's going on inside his leg than self-preservation. He bids goodbye to the two runners (technically walkers) who had the misfortune of joining him today, stops his watch, and I hoist him into the van. Nick sleeps for most of the 30-mile drive to King's Lynn hospital, and therefore doesn't see the look of horror on my face as we pull into the largest and busiest hospital car park I've ever seen. I'm suddenly glad it's still early.

Surprisingly, he's seen relatively quickly, and I only have time to give the van a quick clean and have a half-hour nap before he messages me. With bad news. As suspected, it's a fracture and he's waiting for the results of the X-ray to confirm the details. Although expected, it's still a shoulder-sagging moment, and I'm suddenly back in Bournemouth at the end of day 6, desperately hoping this isn't the end.

Nick's natural dislike of authority and unwavering self-belief mean that being told he can't do the thing he was born to do goes against every fibre of his being. Anticipating the fact that, whatever the prognosis, he'll be feeling pretty low when he emerges from the hospital, I call Nikki, as she'll know better than anyone how to help him, and we discuss what we can do to cheer him up.

Expecting the worst, I'm surprised and relieved when Nick reappears only an hour or so later, on crutches, but in remarkably good spirits, with a very unusual, although still bad, diagnosis. Two X-rays have confirmed that Nick has a stress fracture of his lower tibia, but also, no doubt due to his ridiculous lifetime mileage, that he has an additional piece of bone that has grown adjacent to his fibula, and this has also split – possibly an unrelated injury. The X-ray must have looked like the London Underground map, and Nick seems as delighted by his extra bone as he is disappointed by his latest injury. If you count the separate pieces, he has five bones in his lower leg instead of the standard two, 150 per cent more than a normal human, and this is definitely a badge of honour to him.

After marvelling at Nick's weird leg, we eventually get round to talking about when he can run again. On initial examination, Nick was brusquely told 'you won't be running on that for months', and then, post-X-ray, that anything other than hobbling on crutches should be avoided for at least fourteen days. The reason he doesn't seem too upset is that, naturally, Nick has taken the NHS prognosis and modified it using his own formula, which can be expressed as

$$r = \frac{(min\{a,b\})}{4}$$

where r is recovery time and a and b are the two NHS estimates of the number of days before 'you'll be able to run on that leg again'. So by taking the lower of the two rest periods suggested by trained medical staff, and dividing it by about four, he's magically turned two weeks into three days. It's Thursday, and with a leg essentially broken in two places, he's decided he'll be back on the road by Monday. Two words you won't find in Nick's vocabulary are 'namby' and 'pamby'.

Days 28 to 31
Stiffkey salt marshes
Injuries: two. Broken bones: two. Counties complete: ten.
Miles run: 1,010

It was safe to say that month one hadn't quite gone to plan. But what an adventure, albeit with some hiccups.

I have already expressed how the mental element of running plays such a crucial role. It's a widely known fact. Or at least it is for super-long distances. These few days of rest and recovery were a good example of how a positive mind not only forges a path to progression, but generates smiles and laughter that echo among those around you.

My body was breaking but my mind was now stronger than ever. A little bit of adversity goes a long way.

Driving out of the hospital, I had a few moments to myself on my single bed behind the passenger seat. I was positive, but I can't lie, I was searching my mind as to how I could possibly catch up the miles. It would take a minor miracle to get back on track now.

It was thirty minutes or so back to where we'd stopped the night before, and I must have fallen asleep, having been rocked by the twisty turns of the A roads. Although I couldn't remember what it looked like, where it was or what the place was called, Andy assured me that Stiffkey was the best place to be holed up for a few days. He was right.

Looking out over the salt marshes, on the remote north Norfolk coast, the odd container ship peeping over the horizon was the only indication that the sea was there, beyond the wide, sprawling marsh. We were in a small gravel car park at the end of a long track. It's a National Trust place, with room for about ten cars, no more, but we were the only ones there. Nikki was parked with the back doors of the Palace Van open, framing the view. It's a stunning place, and teeming with wildlife. We parked next to Nikki, side door to side door, the meandering, steep, banked creeks that criss-cross the sandy marsh resembling First World War trenches at low tide. The last visible point before the land and sky meet is Blakeney Point, where a colony of seals could just be made out on the beach. Wind turbines broke up the crisp horizon, faint in the distance.

Over the past few weeks, the rest spots had become key to the happiness of the crew. That was the only time they were in one place, and spent any time together . . . and here, there was something for everyone. I could lie down with a cracking view. Amy could take photos of the landscape and go on various walks. For Nikki and Poppy, it was like a playground, Poppy running wild in the marshes, chasing birds and rabbits. She'd begin her day fresh and smooth-coated, and she'd return covered in grey mud, smelling of dead things she'd rolled in. And once flooded with the tide, she'd have a swimming window too. She was now 'The Hound of the Stiffkey Marshes'. A sequel, perhaps.

And as for Andy, it was as if I'd taken him to Legoland. He is a big twitcher . . . aka bird watcher. We'd only have to be parked up a minute and he'd have his binoculars to his face, scanning the sky. Since day one of the journey, he'd been making a note of birds he'd never seen before. Andy does things off the back of an envelope, and this was literally the case with his bird list. I'd see him reach for a small folded envelope tucked under the sun visor flap, scribble on it with a stubby pencil and pop it back. The only things on the passenger seat were my big Ikea bags of clothing, and Andy's bird-watching book and binoculars. They were never beyond reach.

The little plaque next to the car park informed us that the salt marshes had been acquired by the National Trust in 1976 as part of the Blakeney National Nature Reserve. I was surprised to see only a four-star rating and twelve reviews on Google. There was nothing here, but that's the point. Nothing, unless you look closely, as Andy did.

Despite trying to use my leg, just for a few moments every day, it took a while for it to heal. Or at least begin to repair. We were hoping to spend no more than seventy-two hours at the marshes. It took a little longer, but we didn't care. In the end, this glorious place was our home for four days. A holiday, a retreat, an unexpected slice of peace and an invitation into nature. This was reminiscent of injury one, of course, when we basked in enforced rest at my brother's. Also, it took me back to a bump in the road from another previous adventure.

A long time ago, ten years or more I think, when I first attempted the Malin to Mizen world record, I got pneumonia, lost a decent chunk of my lung capacity and had to bail out. A brilliant woman called Mimi Anderson had the record at the time, and I was trying to break it. The mission was to run the length of Ireland in three days – 350 miles: 115 miles on day one, 115 miles on day two, and 120 miles on day three. Mimi's time was three days and two hours, I believe. Halfway through day 2, and running constantly in unrelenting heavy cold rain, my body, every part of me, dismantled. I had a great crew, and some utterly selfless people supporting me, but we had to bail, having not even reached halfway. It taught me a lot, possibly the basis of much of my success that followed. The similarity with our time on the marshes was the small window of togetherness that felt like warm hugs, a profound unity that derived from setbacks and kindness.

Although we relaxed, my routine was strict. The Palace, Nikki's van, the one we'd lived in until this adventure, had, and still has, a penthouse. A company called TentBox, as the name suggests, produces vehicle-mounted tents in the shape of a box, which basically contain a memory foam mattress with canvas walls and a hardtop brushed-cotton-lined ceiling. Imagine a four-poster bed stuck on the roof of an 8-metre-long van. Scale it down a bit and that's what we had. The difference, of course, is that the walls and ceiling are on gas struts so it collapses down and squishes the mattress to just a few inches for when we drive anywhere. To use it, undo the clips and up it pops.

It was at this point that the tent box became a bit of a lifeline for me. I bought it not for running challenges but instead to host friends when they came to visit. We could sleep four inside the van comfortably, plus a big hound. But it would be helpful to free up some space and give guests their own double bed. The tent box became our spare bedroom. Friends from all over the country could visit us anywhere and have a place to stay. No cost to them, and we enjoyed hosting.

Now, though, it was the biggest bed of either van, and with warmer weather now appearing I could fold away the window flaps of the tent box walls and spend the whole day lying down with my leg raised, ice packs on, and have fresh sea air waft over me as I slept.

It was during our short time in the marshes that I started to sleep in the tent box every night. This became a regular resort to help stretch my legs and get better-quality sleep. Andy had his bed, I had mine, and Nikki hers, plus Poppy. Despite our understanding that Nikki had the freedom to come and go as she pleased, and so therefore, on paper, the original plan was to stay with Andy and hardly rely on Nikki, she was becoming a key team member, willing or otherwise, and I was grateful for the extra space and the much-needed sleep.

This is probably as good a place as any briefly to touch on Nikki, me, and what was slowly becoming our unravelling relationship. By now, there were lots of daily stresses and Nikki had got increasingly sucked into the vortex of the mission, all the while trying to continue to run her business and requiring internet connections to speak with clients. Worse, we had little time to discuss or restore a sense of balance.

Nikki and I separated shortly after Run Britain. Not as a direct impact, more the result of a collection of things, but the pressure cooker environment and my attitude can't have helped. We parted very amicably and by mutual agreement, but it was tough. We cared for each other, but we were simply going in different directions, and I was too focussed to compromise on what had now become an obsession, moving from one expedition to another with little thought for the impact this was having on her and her own dreams.

We had great adventures together. We are still close, and suffice to say that without Nikki's support for me and the journey, her care for Poppy, and her endless moments supporting Andy and the team, the challenge would have come to an abrupt end within days. In fact, the Italian Grand Tour would have, too.

I spent every moment at Stiffkey doing everything I could to repair myself. Amy taught us a card game called kaboo, which we played for hours, drinks in hand, sat around the small wooden pull-out table with the lights dimmed and the mood merry. Poppy frolicked on the mud flats, and we ate and ate and ate, Nikki, Amy and Andy all chipping in with the cooking, as I lay there feeling fat and lazy.

By this point, although we hadn't verbalized it, we knew our magical hundred-day target had now moved from unlikely to the realms of needing a miracle. We would focus on shifting the plan around further down the line. Let's walk before we can run.

On the morning of day 32, it was a tough goodbye to this little bubble of togetherness. I think we all had a little tear in our eye as we drove to where I'd flagged Andy down, what felt like weeks ago. I'd stopped my watch before being pulled into the van and heading off to the hospital, which meant I could pick up from where I'd left off. Amy was heading home for a break and would be back in a week or so, Nikki had driven ahead, and that was that. Out of the van with no idea if my legs would now work, I took my crutches as a support and began, the misty morning and dark skies providing a mirror to my uncertainty.

Days 32 to 35
Holkham to Skegness
On the road again

Having had four days to recover, we were all a little anxious to see what would happen. The pressure was on. It's possible that you may think four days isn't enough to mend a broken bone, and obviously you're right. But I didn't need it to be fixed, I just needed to be able to make forward progress. As long as I wasn't making it worse, and as long as it could mend even just a fraction a day while I moved forward, that's all I needed. The mending could happen, albeit slower than might be ideal.

Putting weight on my leg for the first time in days was a gradual process, initially just softly and delicately with my crutches to support me. Knuckles white gripping the crutch supports, I did this for about 3 miles. I forgot about speed and instead just tested the waters. I was able to put weight on it, but with a decent chunk of pain. After these first 3 miles, my morning meds began to kick in and things started to loosen up. The anti-inflammatory gel concoction, co-codamol, strapping and compression were holding me together, but I was fortunate with the terrain. Norfolk, and the following county Lincolnshire, are two of the flattest in Britain.

This first day back was an unknown. We had the route on our side, the weather too. Gentle hills, nothing major, and Andy staying close, strapping and re-strapping, while simultaneously chucking tablets down my throat. I was in a haze most of the day, using my crutches for more or less every other step. It took me ten hours, but I covered the 26.4 miles, our basic target. I was knackered. Full body knackered. I'd burnt through about 4,000 calories just hobbling along. It didn't matter. I was elated. The marathon distance ticked over just outside a campsite and so we called the number on the gate and they had spaces. Of the three years I'd lived in a van, I'd stayed in a campsite about three times. I hate them. They just defeat the object of camping for me, which is to be free and to be in nature. Now, though, who cared? A shower, somewhere to top up the water tanks and, handily, no time wasted looking for somewhere to stay. Just sleep.

The following day, Nikki had to leave for a few days, for a friend's birthday and a few family bits and pieces. We said goodbye early, before the day began. I was emotional and knew I'd miss her energy. Having her around pushed me on. It was like I'd had my blanket taken away. I kept most of this to myself of course, but I was acutely aware of how the people around me really were my cradle of hope and positivity.

Starting day 33 a little mournful with Nikki not being around, and feeling a bit down within myself, I re-engaged my brain. It took a while, but it dawned on me that today was a crucial moment. Had I done too much or had I protected my leg with yesterday's slow and steady approach? Maybe other injuries would come to the fore with my other muscles having unknowingly overcompensated. The second day back felt more important than the first.

King's Lynn, where the hospital was, was cruelly still ahead of us. I'd not even made it that far yet. It was so demoralizing, because driving there to have the X-rays done had taken about thirty minutes in the van. I was slogging my guts out yesterday, and I hadn't even got to the hospital.

Despite lots of stops, I made it, and felt like I could put King's Lynn behind me, literally. Having crossed the Great Ouse and then the River Nene, Andy parked up along the riverbank near a spot called Guy's Head. I'd been focused. I'd taken my poles for a while again to try and protect my leg as much as possible, but ditched them and tried to do something that resembled running for the last few miles of the day. I did, but I was sore and my upper body was now even more tired from holding myself up for the past two days.

I hadn't really been looking at my watch because all the numbers were either too high, depicting my pace and thus slowness, or they were too low, confirming how far I hadn't progressed. When I got to Andy, I asked for a change of clothes because I was getting too sweaty again. I generally changed clothes at least five times a day. It was about being as comfortable as I possibly could be. Andy suggested I should stop, and I must have looked surprised, because he said, 'I thought you were just going to try one marathon today.' I looked at my watch. I'd already totted up over a marathon distance. It was a rare and welcome surprise. I must have got used to more miles than a mere marathon; even with a broken leg, it went by in a flash. I exaggerate. It was slow, but importantly it didn't feel it, and the day was now over. After being told to rest for six weeks, I'd now run two marathons in two days, just six days after my hospital visit. I'd even shocked myself.

It was just Andy and me now. What had started as a group of ten of us thirty-three days ago was now just two. Nikki and others would be coming back, and obviously a few were still supporting remotely, but it was alarmingly daunting to have lost, even only temporarily, our safety net, our last line of defence.

Andy hadn't failed to notice either:

With Nikki and Poppy away for a few days, the on-the-road Run Britain team is for the first time reduced to two, the minimum number with which the expedition can function. Any fewer, and either Nick would have nowhere to sleep, or we'd have nobody to do the running bit.

Andy had found a lovely spot to end the day. The van's driver-side wheels were bumped up on to a sloping grass verge next to a small river. The road next to us, a single track, was virtually unused, except for tractors and farm quad bikes. We were in the remote marshland that borders The Wash, idyllically peaceful, with just the soundtrack of birdsong. The peace would be shattered the following day by strong, driving winds, as Andy's diary attests:

Today's flat route, on quiet coastal roads loosely following the ever-present sea wall, should be a runner's dream, but in the event, a fierce wind springs up around the halfway point, turning what should be a comfortable run into a more arduous trudge. This is the strongest wind since Whitstable, and it's the kind of weather that takes its toll on runners, more so even than heavy rain. Nick and I have talked about why running in strong wind is so exhausting, even if it's behind you. We decided it was to do with the sensory information that your brain has to process. The roar of the wind in your ears and the sensation of it hitting your body is a constant information feed that your brain has to cope with, whether you want it to or not, and that burns energy. As I drive through crosswinds along one of Lincoln-shire's causewayed roads, marginally above the level of cauliflower fields, I have to counter-steer slightly to keep the van in a straight line – not great running weather.

Traditional map navigation is made more difficult today by seem-ingly every road being called, perhaps unsurprisingly, 'Marsh Road' or 'Marsh Lane'. In a county made entirely of horizon, it feels like line of sight should be all that's required for Nick to follow me, but despite the lack of contours, we seem to keep managing to put the few topographical features around here, bigger than cauliflowers, between us, and with Nick's phone battery now flat, we become sep-arated. A few miles of backtracking in the van are required to locate Nick and guide him in to our parking spot for the night, an RSPB car park at Frampton Marsh, where I'm gutted to see from the sightings board that I've missed a white-tailed eagle by one day. Still, it's not a bad spot in which to spend the night. You don't really hear much about Lincolnshire, but it's alright. If you like horizons. And cauliflowers.

'It's so bracing' was day 35's catchphrase.

Having been buffeted by the wind all night, with rain sounding like pebbles dashing the south side of the van, I set off at 6.40 a.m. That is forty minutes late, and the second time in as many weeks that I'd breached my strict timings protocol. Tut-tut. A sign of my dwindling energy, I'm sure. This continued in the weeks to come, both my energy and the start time slipping further.

As the saying goes, it was 'raining cats and dogs'. I'd suggest that these were overweight pets too. I went out poleless and crutchless. The last few days of singles had started to feel like they had done the trick, that my injury was healing while I made progress. So today was a chance to fully load my legs, although tentatively, and see how it went. I changed my mind within the first few miles and grabbed the poles again. I was desperate, utterly desperate not to stumble back into another injury or prolonged recovery period. I did the sensible thing, despite my shoulder taking a battering. I was now using one crutch on the side of my broken but healing tibia. Every step I'd lean into the crutch just slightly, to reduce the load a tad. My shoulder, elbow and wrist took the brunt, but it seemed to work.

I reached the marathon mark just past the Skegness welcome sign. The slogan, embossed in old-town-style coloured writing, now faded and dirty, read: 'Welcome to Skegness. It's so Bracing'. And it was. That moment running past the sign, with the wind and rain batter-ing against my now non-waterproof waterproof, with cars and trucks splashing muddy puddles all over me, felt like the most British moment of Run Britain so far. Hello Skegness, thanks for the authentic welcome.

All in all, it was a rather drab day. Nikki and Poppy were gone, we'd woken up to torrential rain and wind that didn't abate for the entire day, I was splashed by numerous puddles, and blisters had started to form under the soles of my feet, thanks to the general sogginess. We did, however, treat ourselves to an actual meal in an actual restaurant. Yes, you read that right. Andy and I went on a post-marathon date. Andy deserved the Ritz or better, perhaps a gourmet meal with a menu of dishes we'd never seen before. After all, he'd spent the past month pandering to me, navigating, feeding me, and had even, on one occa-sion, donned the rubber gloves and handwashed my crusty pants in the sink. What Andy actually got was a full English breakfast in a manky Wetherspoons, complete with sticky carpet and day-drinking regulars. The worryingly cheap food did actually do the trick though, to the point that we both fell asleep in our individual beds back in the van in a small car park nearby.

This was to be the last of my single marathon days and so this food also acted as a mini celebration of being back on my feet. Once again, we made sure not to miss an opportunity to acknowledge all the posi-tive steps in the journey. Shame about the weather, but nonetheless, the pile of greasy food served with a middle-aged, frumpy grimace was a nice way to round off a day.

Some time over the past week we'd made a rough plan to run three single-marathon days, rest and repair in the afternoons and get back to bigger mileage four days after returning from injury. So tomorrow would be yet another pivotal day. My lower body, in case you hadn't noticed, had been rather battered over the past month, but I'd begun to feel that things were balancing out a little. When I started, I was carrying maybe 3 kilos more weight than I usually did, and now a month in I had lost about 6. So I was about 3 kilos lighter than my usual running weight. This made a big difference, of course. My body fat had also dropped from around 11 per cent to about 8 per cent, an indicator of what the remaining challenge might do to my body. A big fry-up post-marathon, ahead of a longer day tomorrow, was a little reminder that regardless of injury, I needed to keep eating like a king, even if I felt like a dirty, frail tramp.

With food in mind, this meal would serve as a bookend to the poor standards of nutrition I'd become accustomed to. From now on, fewer fizzy drinks and less takeaway crap. In an attempt to give my body a fighting chance to avoid sickness, more injuries or potential malnutrition, I wanted to start a little health kick. Andy and I needed to stock the van anyway, and during my last few days limping through marathons I'd been listening to the back catalogue of Rich Roll podcast episodes. Many of them are about health and well-being. So we did what many born-again dieters have done before: we spent hundreds of pounds on healthy food, hoping it would change our lives for ever.

A boring car park on the edge of Skegness was our home for the evening. As car parks go, it actually had the hat-trick of essentials: it was free, there was no noise, and no height barrier. Bingo. It also happened to be only a minute from where I'd stopped my watch, having completed my day's running. The next morning I could step out, walk to my starting point and off I would go. And with a nearby Morrisons being open twenty-four hours, we had a luxury toilet. And by luxury, I mean it was an actual toilet.

Our last thoughts before bed, having checked the map and completed our usual route prep for the following day, were that we were now basically in the north. We'd been so caught up in injury that we were all of a sudden on the straight section of the east coast that shoots up to Scotland. London was well behind us, and although I was still running away from it, the finish line was closer. Shutting my eyes, I was full of food, my leg felt the best it had in days, and I was keen to make tomorrow the beginning of a decisive push towards Scotland and beyond.

5

To the Border

WAREN MILL ■

NORTHUMBERLAND

TYNE & WEAR

Newcastle Upon Tyne ●

● Sunderland

DURHAM

Hartlepool ●

Middlesborough ●

Whitby ●

Scarborough ●

NORTH YORKSHIRE

Bridlington ●

Hull

EAST YORKSHIRE

Grimsby

LINCOLNSHIRE

SKEGNESS ■

Days 36 to 46
Skegness to Waren Mill

Calculations complete, we worked out it could be less than two weeks on the east coast of England before we hit Scotland. Soon we would be closer to Edinburgh than London. The quaint back roads of sleepy Cornwall and the Eden Project seemed like a lifetime ago. Years in the past rather than just thirty-six days.

Day 36, 22 May, also meant that the start of summer was now less than ten days away. Vitamin D, longer days and the positivity of the season would soon be upon us. Passing from season to season is a normal part of life, but often the admin of existence consumes the little things that indicate the changes in the natural world. On an adventure, however, spending so much time outdoors, you notice the land changing.

As flowers blossomed and wilted, as the heavy rains and marshland turned to sunshine and baked earth, the land I was running on step after step, leaving footprints on hundreds of millions of years of history, began to seep through my shoes and into my soul. Shelves of hard granite, softer sandstone, limestone and squishy clay all began to give up their secrets. I noticed the small details that shaped the landscape, influencing the wildlife and the human life that occupied it.

Continuing north, I was aware of things I'd usually pass by, or remain entirely oblivious to. I'd inadvertently taken myself on a nature, history and culture tour of Britain, all at the same time – a guided walk without the umbrella-wielding tourists. Plus I'd like to think I was moving a little faster than a walking tour, covering more ground. Maybe.

I was becoming more aware of wildflowers, asking myself questions about small pink and purple pin cushions of thrift nestled on their thick green matted bases. When was the first thrift found? How did it get its name? Why does it exist? Furry-stemmed cow parsley lining the hedgerows; corncockle, once the weeds of the cornfield, with their tall stems and small magenta flowers; columbines in limestone woodlands; yellow kingcups on marshland and by streams. I was listening, seeing, smelling and feeling my way around Britain, with the breeze on my face on nicer days, with the suncream melting on my back, with the harsher winds removing the gentler sounds of nature as they were whisked past my ears. And as soon as I ventured into Scotland, I'd see more of the larger, fragile-looking harebells, their delicate frames holding the pastel blue bellflowers to the light.

Mile after mile, step after step, and with frequent stumbles over protruding rocks or loose stones, I'd notice more happening in what was so often my window on the day: the 2 feet square of ground in front of me. But if I ever give advice for anyone venturing on a long journey on foot, I say, 'Look up!' Look up and breathe in what's around you, don't get trapped in the tunnel that becomes the treadmill of ground directly in front of you. Raise your head and trust that your feet will find their path. This is of course all very well and good, and easier on gentle flat paths, or tarmac. But add some steps, kerbs, uneven grass and divots and I had no choice but to look down to avoid falling. I learnt to look up as much as possible, but I also learnt to embrace that plot of earth in front of my feet. I noticed the cracks in tarmac, some I'm sure seeming like the Grand Canyon to ants. On early mornings I stepped carefully over migrating snails and slugs, later avoiding dog poo, insects and drain covers with uneven lids. I became fascinated by the weave of tangled weeds and tufts of grass sprouting from crevices in the ground. I traced them along the floor with my eyes as I passed, one tiny green avenue of life defying concrete, stones and tarmac.

What we get out of life so often comes down to how we choose to encounter the world around us. A random walk along your road to the bus stop can be boring, but noticing the small things, learning about what you're looking at, how things have formed and how they have changed over time, will transform a mundane experience into a highly interesting and inspiring one. Your senses are flooded, your brain is stimulated.

I was profoundly grateful for what this challenge was offering me. Mother Nature had thrown a hell of a lot at us, but her beauty was far outshining the temporary misery of those moments.

Noticing these small gems, I started to ponder everything and anything I came across. Silly things like house numbers and names. I passed 'The Bungalow', which was in fact a three-storey terraced house, perhaps occupied by a fan of irony; one semi-detached house I saw had the number 19 painted in black across the entire facade, as if shouting angrily at an unreliable postman. Houses with shy, retiring frontages, hidden behind net curtains, gates and large hedges, contrasted with more showy houses with mosaic driveways, neatly bordered flower beds and concrete statues of lions or eagles atop their gateposts. They teased by offering a glimpse into the homes beyond, and the lives playing out inside.

With the expanse of sea and sky so often available to me on my right, I'd regularly find peace and beauty on one side of my route, and a mismatch of houses, colours, advertising boards and traffic on the other. The frontier between the human and natural worlds.

The coming of summer was a key time stamp, a prompt to shift through the gears and sharpen our focus. I was over a third of the way through the original hundred days, but less than a quarter of the way through the mileage. From Skegness, waving goodbye to day 35 and plodding eagerly into day 36, if I could average over 40 miles a day, it would only take ten days to reach Scotland, which was fast becoming a mammoth psychological milestone for me. Ideally I'd run further, but we'd have to see how things went. It turned out that over that week we did indeed make good progress. The thought of reaching Scotland back when I was slumped in the dark depths of my hallucinations on the south coast had felt utterly ridiculous. It turned out that some buried belief was still burning away inside, powering me on.

Having run past Skegness's shamelessly named 'Fantasy Island', which simply consisted of a cluster of old caravans and a few unused fairground rides, I hit the east coast proper. Over the next day or two I made decent progress. Barring the occasional blips where I accidentally put my phone on flight mode, preventing Andy from being able to see where I was, the miles ticked by and, better still, my legs were

behaving themselves. Sore, and far from easy running, but further
away from agony and A&E. My next obstacle was the mighty Humber Estuary.

As ever, Andy's thoughts were well ahead of mine:

*It's funny how quickly things can change. During the first few days
of the trip, a friend of Nick's provided some useful information that
wasn't available when I was working out logistics for river and estuary crossings: the Humber Bridge had been closed to pedestrians
following a spate of suicides, one of the tragic side effects of the
pandemic. On a smaller river, having to run around wouldn't be a
major issue, but with an estuary of this size and no ferry services,
this was looking like it could be a significant spanner in the works,
with a route around adding an additional 70 miles. During the first
week, I contacted the bridge authority to explain what Nick was
doing and to find out if we had any options, such as a supervised
pedestrian crossing, but as things have turned out, not only has the
bridge footway now reopened (with the additional time it's taken us
to get here due to injuries), but Nick won't actually need to cross the
Humber Estuary at all.*

*After my mileage analysis in Norfolk, one of the things that
occurred to me was that, as Nick is no longer following his original
routes, we need to keep an eye on his cumulative mileage relative to
where he is on the coast. Now that the original hundred-day target
is no longer applicable, the easiest way to do this is to use his original Plot a Route maps as units of 52.5 multiplied by the number
of Plot a Route days, and then compare Nick's actual mileage with
the nearest Plot a Route finish point. From my scribbles, I've calculated that Nick is around 100 miles short of where he should be by
this point in Lincolnshire, largely due to using coast roads rather
than coast paths. On this trajectory, that would mean arriving at the
Eden Project 500 or so miles short of the magic 5,250, meaning a
lot of running laps in Cornwall. It's good that we've spotted this
deficit relatively early, and we're going to need to stay on top of it to
avoid Nick drifting too far below (or above) his cumulative mileage
target and maintain a nice, evenly spread 5,250-mile Strava outline*

around mainland Britain. The quick fix for the current shortfall is
for Nick to run around the Humber Estuary rather than cross the
bridge.

With the various adjustments we'd made to my daily routes to avoid
extreme elevation and horrible terrain both in a failed bid to prevent
injury and then to aid healing, we had taken a slightly more stream-
lined route than originally planned, despite still being right on the
coast. But thanks to Andy's nerdy spreadsheet, we were on top of the
problem. Although obviously the hundred-day target was now out of
the question, and the two-hundred-marathon distance wouldn't be run
as two marathons a day, the overall mileage of 5,240 miles (plus 10 for
ferries) remained the primary target.

We were breaking my days up into multiple sections. By running
around 40-odd miles, I was now only running a single marathon a
day in one go, and therefore I could only count even a 51-mile day as
one marathon plus change: 51 miles wasn't quite two marathons; nor
was 44 miles, 27 miles, etc. This didn't bother me much, to be honest.
My legs were now dictating optimum mileage and I was just happy to
get back to 44- and 45-mile days while recovering from the broken
bones.

About eleven years ago, I started to keep a running diary, capturing
every time I went for a run. Handwritten, it would mainly just say
things like 'shitty run – horrible weather', or 'amazing, saw a tortoise'.
I'd always include my mileage, so I could keep track. I've since also created a digital copy on a spreadsheet which I transpose from my
handwritten notes every few months. It's a nice reminder of both the
footsteps and those I ran with on any given day. All miles count. As
long as it's tracked on the Garmin it goes in the book. At the time of
writing, I'm on 977 marathons. That's 977 times I've run at least 26.2
miles in one go – a thousand isn't far off. As for my overall mileage, all
the little bits soon add up – I'm currently at around 72,000. By the time
you read this, the number will no doubt have edged a little higher.

So it was decided. Running up and back along the Humber Estuary
would serve two purposes. I'd get my mileage back to within 2 per cent
of the original plan (not bad, all things considered), and the route

along the estuary would more or less guarantee a flat, easy-to-navigate path, which would allow my legs to continue to mend.

I ran through the uninspiring seaside resort of Cleethorpes, through the aptly named docks of Grimsby and on into Barton-upon-Humber. Closing off the evening of 24 May – day 38 – I spent some time chatting to my mum on her birthday. We were both happy I was now back to enjoying the miles rather than cursing them.

Although this week was turning into a good push with some great progress, it wasn't without its downers – mainly the weather, which was all over the place. A mixture of heavy rain, sunshine, strong winds, drizzle and sleet. The trio of rivers, the Humber, Trent and Ouse, kept us busy, having to ensure I avoided running up the wrong river, and I encountered a few slight gradients from time to time, but these minor hills were nothing in comparison to what I'd endured a month earlier.

Wrapped up against the wind and rain I was getting through a waterproof every few hours, Andy holding a fresh jacket out of the window as I approached him to remind me to change. Chafing was to be avoided at all costs. Under the arms, the nipples, between my legs, and even the small of my back would frequently start to sting as the top layer of skin was worn away. A dollop of Vaseline and a new dry top would do the trick for a while.

This part of the country consisted of farmland, smallholdings and hamlets nuzzled next to the estuary. Pylons and wind farms rose from the ground like robots, punctuating the wide, dark, menacing skies and somehow enhancing this rural landscape rather than ruining it.

A little incident the following day would have hurt me psychologically had it not been for Andy. We had a rare bout of sunshine, and I'd removed my cotton buff from around my neck and double-twisted it around my left wrist. I can remember vividly the day my mum and dad bought me this buff, when I was fifteen, in a ski hire shop called Twinner in the same village where Nikki and I had since spent those months during lockdown. It was a bright red paisley printed number, colours now faded and the fabric thinned, nearly translucent. Not only had I worn it skiing for years, and carted it around to competitions, but I'd taken it with me when I ran a marathon in every country in the world. It had become a sort of lucky charm, and I'd wear it no matter what the weather, be it on my wrist as a sweatband or over my neck and head to protect me from wind and rain.

Somewhere along the way, I'd dropped it. I stopped as soon as I realized, frantically looking for it behind me on the road and in the verges. Andy happened to drive past at the right moment. Seeing me in distress, he stopped, and said he'd drive back to find it. That buff was precious to me, very precious, and Andy knew that . . . and without thinking, I entrusted him to find it so I could keep going. And he did. It was wafting around in the road as cars drove past it a few miles back. He pulled alongside me wearing it around his neck to see if I'd notice. Without stopping, he stuck his thumb out of the window with a pleased smile on his face – a smile nearly as big as mine. I shouted loudly after him 'Thank you!' and held my hands together in the air, gesturing how grateful I was.

A couple of cosy RSPB nature reserve car parks later and we were back at the Humber Bridge, only now on the other side of it. Looking back over the water to where we had been just a couple of days ago reminded us how far we still had to go. The estuaries and inlets were playing cruel tricks on us. From the Humber Bridge Country Park, continuing to head east after the river detour, Nikki returned and shared a few miles with me, and Poppy too. Andy and Nikki tag-teamed to give me support in the rain – brilliant, as always. It was such a joy to be back running with Poppy again too. Her bounding energy can sometimes be a drain, but right now it was infectious.

During the writing of my first book a couple of years ago we were holed up in a small campervan park down the road from a village called Goonhavern in Cornwall, near a large sand dune area between a golf course and eventually the beach at Perran Sands. This was a little spot that Nikki, Poppy and I fell in love with. We'd run her in the dunes, training her with treats and trying, but generally failing, to use a whistle for recall. It became known as the 'snuffle patch' because she'd smell with her nose pressed to the floor and run in all directions, chasing whatever scent she'd found. We would only let her explore for twenty minutes at first, as we didn't want to damage her legs or hips with too much running (leave that to me). But eventually, as she got older, she'd gallop through the long grass for hours, disappearing and reappearing in unexpected places, her ears flapping in the wind and her mouth wide and panting.

Recalling these days, Nikki and I laughed because that was the best behaved she'd ever been. Nowadays when we have to put her on the lead she just pulls and howls, wanting to run free. We probably shot ourselves in the foot a little, didn't we? That said, running with her is a dream now, as long as there aren't ducks, chickens, cows, sheep, dogs or basically anything that moves in her line of sight. Once she's tired she'll just trot next to me and look up and lick her lips when she needs a drink. Today, we shared about 10 miles together, with Poppy not particularly impressed with us for taking her out in the rain. Nonetheless, it was a mood-boosting afternoon, despite the weather. Some shared miles with my girls was a treat.

With Nikki now back with us, my mood and energy had been ratcheted up, and it was pushed up another notch with the arrival of Amy. The team had doubled to four and, with it, responsibilities effectively halved. Something about having more people around made everything feel extra secure. Andy and I had some back-up, and we were in high spirits that evening:

There's nothing special about the car park itself, but lying more or less in the shadow of the mighty Humber Bridge, it's challenging for the lead on most spectacular view from any of our night spots so far. I like a good bridge, and this is up there with the best of them. Can something be brutal and elegant at the same time? I think so. I vaguely remember a fact I once heard about the tops of the towers being measurably further apart than they are at the bottom due to the curvature of the Earth. I fact-check it to find that it is not only true, but frequently cited as a means of debunking flat Earth nonsense, and I find the irony of the bridge's location on the edge of one of Britain's flattest counties deeply satisfying.

Not a bad day. Sleeping under the Humber Bridge. And Amy's back to cheer us all up. Amy is great company, a calming, reassuring presence for the team, and it'll be good to have her around for a while.

Having crossed into East Yorkshire, county twelve, just a day or two after leaving the Humber, my legs were starting to twinge a little. Old pains were reawakening, one evil eye opening – threatening. Nothing show-stopping, but a reminder that the hours of taping, amateur physio, strapping, stretching and anti-inflammatories must continue and that ice, rest and elevation should not be neglected.

Having had a few late mornings during which Nikki would come and sit at the end of the bed to chat and eat breakfast with me, I had drifted into a habit of not getting out until sometimes two hours later than planned. I decided it was time to have a word with myself and get these starts back towards the self-imposed strict 6 a.m. departure time. We had now fully settled into the trip, and we needed to keep some structure. Like a new house embedding into its foundations, we had finally come to a point where we had full sight of what the rest of the trip would entail. We'd already overcome so much, and still we were marching forward. Andy and I had had many chats about the point we'd reached in the mission and the general feeling was that we'd be looking back on it all with an outpouring of fondness. Fondness and joy sprouting from hardship and pain. It really was turning into a great British adventure. But we were still well short of halfway.

The general routine had become a long first leg in the morning. Anything from 26.2 miles up to about 35 miles worked pretty well. I'd then eat lunch, nap, and get back out for between 10 and 20 miles. We'd caught up the lost miles and with no more diversions up the coast for a while we'd hopefully not have to worry about drifting too far from the mileage target and could push on at a good pace. I was in a good stride, and Andy now had support down to a fine art, perfectly timing an omelette or beans on toast with my arrival at the van for pre-lunch or lunch. Some days, if it was raining or I felt I just needed to keep going, I'd signal to him as I approached before running on, in which case he'd gratefully tuck into the food while I got my head down and clocked the miles.

If you're a runner, you'll know there's always a moment like this in any big race. It's not brutal miles, and it's not coasting along, nor is it injury or energy preservation, it's just a little spell of momentum – momentum you want to retain for as long as you can.

I was trying to bag a few extra miles each morning to make my after-noons less strenuous, and therefore my evenings a little longer. Enough to occasionally eat with the rest of the crew and feel like we were a family again. Good night spots always made a difference, a particularly tranquil one around this time being an RSPB reserve at Spurn Head, lying on the narrow spit of land that forms the outermost tip of the Humber Estuary. Andy had his binoculars glued to his face again and Amy was editing photos, while Nikki made food.

Andy, meanwhile, could sense I was getting back to normal:

We are greeted in the car park by David, who works for the RSPB and is on the lookout for chancers hoping to park overnight. How-ever, he clearly has a good eye for this, and immediately has us pegged as the kind of people who don't leave litter behind, i.e. not bastards. We get chatting, and when we explain what we're up to, he very kindly agrees to let us stay in their staff car park free of charge. An evening stroll reveals RSPB Spurn Head to be an amazing place, and as I walk down the narrow sandbank, the sun cruelly decides to come out after Nick has endured six hours of relentless rain, but there's no feeling of resentment. Despite the grim conditions, today has been, above all else, a good running day. There are different types of good running day, and this has not been an enjoyable one, but one of grit and determination, one that demonstrates Nick's resolve to complete the mission, and one which has left him with the satisfaction of having overcome one of what will no doubt be many hard days to come.

After a couple of wet days, Nikki had also developed an ingen-ious way to dry my soggy clothes. By now I was frequently putting wet clothes on, sometimes dripping wet – not a pleasant way to start the morning. Using the pull-out table in her Palace Van, Nikki draped a series of towels over it, dangling on to the van floor either side, forming a drying enclosure. Under the table is a small vent where the heating pumps out hot air. All my wet gear was then placed under the table hung on coat hangers or spread across the floor. With the heater turned up high, and with the windows of the

van open to stop the thermostat cutting in, the clothes dried remarkably quickly.

Going to bed knowing I'd be in dry clothes the following day was a
luxury I wasn't expecting to crave, but on day 41 I revelled in it. It was
a good day too. The mighty inlet of the Humber had successfully been
rounded and it was starting to feel like Scotland was just up the road.
And it was . . . just a little further than I would have liked. The first,
massive leg of the south and the east coast of England was soon to be
completed. Just days to go. Tantalizingly close. It was also turning
into a proper summer's day and so, after my morning miles, we did
what the rest of the country was doing: we had a classic pub lunch in
a beer garden. This was the highlight of a period during which I'd
averaged 40-plus miles, consistency finally emerging from the wreck-
age. If that wasn't enough, there was even a seabird colony at nearby
Flamborough Head. Andy went to perve on puffins with his binoculars while Amy photographed them with a long lens. It's apparently
one of the most important seabird colonies in Europe, and Andy was
pleased, ticking off a few new birds on his list. Camp was full of smiles
and positive energy and, briefly, the weather was in keeping with the
mood.

Past Scarborough the following day, and then on to Robin Hood's
Bay the next, I picked up an old railway line called the Cinder Track
which links Scarborough with Whitby along the edge of the North
York Moors. It's traffic-free, tree-lined, ideal for shade or sheltering
from the rain and, better yet, I could run Poppy off the lead. A day or
two of flat, easy paths would cement the feeling I had finally found a
rhythm.

I was enjoying the days; something close to balance had been found.
Although I was running about 44 to 46 miles per day, not the originally
planned 52, it didn't matter. It was a more sustainable distance and
gave us about two hours each day to enjoy the evenings and, for me, the
principal benefit of this approach was that I could rest and repair while
making good progress. Close to 50 miles a day I was happy with. I was
no longer running to plan A, but instead had stumbled across plan B,
and preferred it. We could enjoy it, and I could still complete the mission well within an acceptable time. I'd beat the existing record, the

total mileage target would remain at my official Run Britain 5,240, and I just might finish without any more broken bones. I was, however, still a long way from home, so let's not run before we can walk . . . or rather, run further than I can survive.

The remaining days of May saw a continued run of 44-plus-mile days. Having now tried to put my broken bones behind me, I started to maintain a metronomic consistency to running and resting, a steady rhythm that was a key turning point in the journey. This pacing took us from Robin Hood's Bay all the way to Bamburgh and its glorious castle, just 20 miles from Scotland. The three days that took, though, were not without event.

Nikki had been suffering with pain in her lower back, and it had now worsened. She woke one morning unable to move properly without serious pain, and she was visibly breathing very shallowly so as not to make it worse. Not only was this horrible for her, but we weren't entirely sure what had caused it, and she was totally unable to drive. We suspected that the likely culprit was Poppy, constantly pulling and occasionally jerking the lead while Nikki was walking her. Poppy is a hound, and although she's not as big in stature as male vizslas, she makes up for this in strength and energy. At full pull, Nikki struggles to hold her, and when running, Nikki uses a waist harness, similar to those used in Canicross, where dog and human race together along trails. The issue with Nikki's belt was that it meant the effects of Poppy's pulling were concentrated on her lower back, and with Nikki being very slight, I was pretty sure that was the cause of her injury.

At 5.30 a.m., over the usual morning Marmite bagel and cuppa, we all crammed into the Council Van to discuss a plan. Amy would drive Nikki into Middlesbrough (the nearest big town) to find a sports physio or similar to attempt to resolve the problem, while Andy supported me as usual. Amy would then drive Nikki back to the Palace Van and return to Middlesbrough, where I should have finished running some time in the late afternoon. That, however, didn't account for Poppy.

My father is a particular man. He spent most of his life drawing maps for a living, which is possibly how a sense of precision and obsessive detail got engrained in him, and this spills over into his home life too. Among friends and family, he is notorious for overplanning and being overcautious. A good example of this was 'the manual'. During the negotiations to borrow his beloved campervan he wrote, printed and bound a manual for the van, which sort of doubled as a contract. It covered everything from how to replace a gas canister to how to open and close a window. There were a few hard and fast rules. One read 'Under no circumstances can Poppy or any other dog be allowed in the van', which, to be fair, of all the rules, I could understand. She's big, she's bouncy, and although house-trained, she will no doubt leave a smell and dog hair. So that seemed fair, despite my mum and dad also having a dog. It would have been handy to alleviate the relentlessness of Nikki looking after Poppy all the time to occasionally allow her in Andy's van, but we had followed the rules. However, here we were at a juncture. Poppy couldn't go with Amy and Nikki to Middlesbrough because they had no idea how long it would take for Nikki to see a physio, and the dog would need a run, or at least a walk, during that time.

The plan was hatched. Using the approach of asking for forgiveness rather than permission, because frankly we didn't have the energy to ask, we moved Poppy's bed and supplies into the Council Van and agreed that no photos would make it to social media, revealing our crime. It would be a one-off, and we had a good reason. But Andy had me and now a dog to look after. With Poppy sitting comfortably on a blanket in the passenger seat, I'd never seen her look more confused than she did when Nikki disappeared into another car, leaving her sitting alongside Andy, with me appearing at the window every few miles. It was a strange time for her.

Nikki's back did eventually get sorted, although it remained troublesome for a few weeks. We think it was a nerve. She made it back to Redcar on the coast for lunch, having collected the van, thanks to Amy ferrying her around. And as for Poppy, in the end she was happy all day, which had nothing to do with Andy treating her far too much. Did Dad ever find out? Yes, annoyingly he did. Somehow a photo was taken with Andy peering through the windscreen with a grin and a thumbs up, Poppy next to him in the passenger seat with her nose pressed against the glass. They both looked naughty. Naturally, Dad was following me on social media and spotted this photo, before sending me an angry message. I'm glad to say he was eventually understanding once I'd called to explain the situation. We agreed never again. This became known as the Day of the Dog.

That morning I'd shared a few miles with my godparents Laura and Leo around Saltburn. When I was a boy, Leo was the king of the outdoors. For my brother and me, he was the cool adult, the one who went kite-surfing, who would take us on adventures in the mountains, and who had a jet ski and all the latest gadgets. He always had great stories too. I have no doubt that he sowed the seeds of my own love of adventure. We chatted and caught up over a few miles on the way to our midday lunch stop.

It was a weird day really. Nothing was as usual. In addition to Nikki's back trouble and Poppy's displacement, a weird phenomenon called sea fret was smothering the coast. A heavy fog rolled in off the sea. A distinctive line of thick cloud turned a T-shirt-and-suncream day into a bitterly cold jumper-wearing kind of day within minutes. Not long after our sunshine lunch on the sea wall we were cramming into the van and putting the kettle on.

It wasn't long before thoughts turned to where we should spend the night:

With Nick's route looking like it will end somewhere in Middlesbrough's grey expanse of cement works and refineries, Nikki and Amy have gone ahead to try and find an acceptable car park for the night. Nikki heads for our first choice option, which is closed, while Amy goes for the second, which she rates as a shithole – she reports back to Nikki. Amy is from Totnes, and there's some uncertainty over whether it's just her Devonian sensibilities that have been offended, perhaps by the lack of an artisan bakery or yoga studio at the car park. Nikki comes from a place where gravy is considered a delicacy. 'Are you sure it's not just northern?' she asks Amy. But upon inspection, Nikki confirms that the car park is indeed a shithole. Amy's assessment has been calibrated by a northerner. It's a truly damning review for a piece of tarmac.

Having followed the River Tees upstream into and through Mid-dlesbrough, we ended up staying that night near Saltholme Wildlife Reserve, which was catnip for Andy and fortunately slightly nicer than the place Amy had originally found. Andy's list of wildlife (which you can find in the back of this book) now had over 200 entries. He made the most of the parking spot, with a very early start the following morning:

I force myself out of bed at 4.30 to catch the sunrise. The dawn is still, and in the first light of day, the smoking chimneys, pylons, refinery towers and chemical plants take on an ethereal beauty in the morning mist. Greatham Creek is glassy smooth, a mirror for the morning light, the wake of a lone incoming seal breaking the liquid gold of its surface. I'm tired, but it's always good to get a jump on the day, and to catch some of that magic you only see before the rest of the world has risen.

When I woke up in the little car park of this wetland reserve, the days now a little longer, the morning light was illuminating the chimneys of the industrial north as they belched smoke and steam vertically into the sky – a potential sign of a windless day. It was an odd mix of industry – pylons, cranes and structures along the horizon – and nature, with seals in the foreground, around thirty of them, hauled out on the muddy banks.

A fine, low-lying mist turned the morning sunshine to a hazy yellow. It was now day 45, and another 45-mile route was the target, this time continuous and, as it turned out, with new friends. As with the previous few days, it was a welcome interruption to our newfound rhythm.

Andy and I hunched over our phones at breakfast, finalizing the day's route. Me, still perched in bed with legs out straight, now unshaven and haggard-looking, Andy not dissimilar. However, thanks to a couple of headlands over the last couple of days, where I'd run coast roads rather than coast paths, my mileage had drifted to 3 per cent lower than it should be at this point on the map. The bridges across the Tyne are further inland, and we spotted an opportunity to share some miles together, and also to take Poppy off Nikki's hands for the morning.

Rather than dip under the Tyne and appear on the other side, having missed Newcastle, we would run the 15 miles of cycle path up the south side, cross in the city centre using the fancy Millennium Bridge, and back down the other side. Andy could leave the van behind and return to it by ducking under the Tyne, using the tunnel. He'd collect the van and use its mighty horsepower to chase me down. We hadn't planned it, but it seemed like a great way to share a few flat, easy-to-navigate miles. Poppy would have a decent run, and Andy would kindly carry water and snacks in a backpack.

Most mornings I'd have at least one or two runners joining me, with others coming and going throughout the day. Generally, the group would be at its peak around lunchtime. Every day we would take casual bets on how many people would join, and if anyone would run a full first marathon with me, or perhaps go even longer. By now we'd had about twenty-five people do their first marathon with me, and over five hundred run with me or turn up to show support.

I love running with people. Most runners are a little nutty, and always have fun stories to tell. Plus it goes without saying that people are the soul of any adventure. It's the shared experience that makes the days so memorable and unique. The running community are also so often united. We stick together, we support each other. We recognize that running can be a team sport, while still having individual goals, strengths and weaknesses. Besides, most runners continue to run because they have a profound connection to it. It gives us something that nothing else can. It's a highly therapeutic, cleansing and soulful sport. That's if you can push through the period where you feel like you're dying.

That said, and highly dependent on my energy and mood, most mornings I liked to have at least 5 miles to myself. Ideally a few more. I was genuinely half-asleep until about 10 miles in, my legs turning over slowly and my brain not properly picking my feet up, still in a cosy dreamland. That morning, peering out of the gap in the cream window blinds, we spotted a couple in their car next to us. One of them had running gear on and was suncreaming up – the sign of someone who intended to stick around, because it was hours till the sun would be high enough to do any damage.

I'd try to be polite every morning, even if I was in the doldrums, moody and pissed off because I couldn't have some alone time, at peace with the early hours. This, of course, was ridiculous. So many brilliant people took time out of their day to run with me and show solidarity, turning up often in the rain, miles from where they lived. Me, a total stranger, having kind, selfless people help me to achieve my challenge. Runners sticking together.

I could, if I'd wanted to, just have asked people not to come and run with me, but of course I didn't, because that's not what I truly wanted. It's just that I was a grumpy shit in the mornings. Grumpy till my legs became springy and I had some sun on my back. I hated how my heart sank at the sight of runners gathering around the van, as I hid away inside not wanting to face the day. In reality these occasions were very few and far between, and of course once out with them I was happy, grateful and feeling guilty for cursing them minutes earlier. I hope as you read this you'll judge me a little less harshly, realizing I was exhausted, both mentally and physically. Tired of answering the same questions too, such as 'How are you?', which of course is a perfectly normal and pleasant enquiry, but so often my response must have cut the energy of anyone around me in half. Because the fact of the matter was, first thing in the morning, I generally felt terrible. I'd had less sleep than my body needed, I was losing weight, trying to balance the crew's enjoyment levels, I more often than not had a dodgy stomach, and of course my broken leg was still healing. That, and invariably I was stepping out to begin my day in wet or damp clothes, on cold mornings. Not a recipe for a joyful, smiley Nick. As you can see, a journey like this can create a situation where lovely people coming to share their company could turn me into a moody mess. All because I was overtired and mentally under-functioning.

That morning, watching the couple get ready in their car, I wasn't in a foul mood as such, but I did just want some miles on my own. That, however, was now clearly out of the question. They had made the effort to be here at 6 a.m., so I wasn't about to turn them away. No matter how tired, I just couldn't do that. I gripped the sides of the van door and hobbled out, my legs stiff and sleepy. Andy joined me, a bag of supplies on his back, Poppy already pulling on the lead, keen to get going.

We greeted the couple with politeness and smiles, as did Poppy, although she went a bit further. Poppy likes to jump up at the best of times, but when meeting new people she prefers to launch herself at them, going for a sloppy full-face greeting. She's pretty tall at full stretch, so even a 6-foot bloke will get a snog whether he likes it or not.

As it turned out, the chap Poppy snogged was a vet who adored dogs, so we were off on the right foot/paw. And better still, his name was also Andy. His partner, McKenzie, was just dropping him off before a pre-work yoga session in Newcastle. She waved us off as we began the usual meet-and-greet chat. Our pace was pretty steady, although made a little quicker than ideal by Poppy pulling us along.

Skip ahead 45 miles, and about ten hours, and I could now call this new Andy a friend. From here on we decided to refer to this Andy as 'Aussie Andy' to avoid confusion. Not only is it very handy having a vet run with you if you have a dog, but Andy was one of the nicest people I've met. Both he and McKenzie are Aussies, living in Newcastle having moved from London to establish their careers. He was instantly aware that I might or might not want company, and even offered to leave me to it, before insisting on buying me drinks and ice creams en route. By midday, the four of us – Andy, Aussie Andy, me and Poppy – had been joined by about fifteen others, our noses turned back to the coast having finished the out-and-back loop. Poppy rejoined us later, having had a small break for a nap. Poppy is a diva at the best of times, but running, she must be at the front, frequently and adorably checking the whole crew is still together. She'll turn her head to keep an eye if someone drops off the back, and if they have, she'll run back and hurry them along.

Aussie Andy became the first person to run a full day with me. He did so easily and with a smile. Once finished, we parked up on the edge of a place called Cresswell, in Northumberland, in a small car park near some sand dunes. McKenzie joined us, and we all had an indoor BBQ to round off the day. We had stocked up on meat supplies mid-route to have a BBQ once finished, but the wind coming over the dunes was too strong. Still, an evening in the Palace Van with new friends was a great way to end a day. What a contrast to my mood at the start of the day. It was a reminder to me to draw a line under whatever mood

I'd woken up with, and leave it at the van door. Stuffed with BBQ delights, we waved McKenzie and Andy off after a few beers. It was about 8.30 p.m., my bedtime. Another ten hours of running awaited me tomorrow, with Newcastle, Tynemouth, Whitley Bay and Blyth ticked off.

Before going to sleep, we added our day's work to the line on the map at the back of the van. By now we had already run past what we estimated to be four hundred beaches, and past or through a thousand towns, cities, villages and hamlets. The best part was that we were now actually enjoying it. What a day to round off May.

The first of June, day 46, was our final full day in England. Even better, I covered 45 miles in good time. I was running comfortably for the first time since King's Lynn. I had somehow found another gear. I ran through the entire day with only brief ten-minute stops, no lunch break, and made it to just past Bamburgh Castle by 3 p.m. The castle itself is an absolute gem, my favourite in Britain. Crowning nearly 10 acres of the Great Whin Sill, it occupies a spot that has been a defensive stronghold for over 1,500 years and looks out over the North Sea to the lighthouse on the Farne Islands. I'd raced along this section of coast twice in ultra events many years ago, the castle being the start of one, and the finish of the other.

Despite some annoyingly cold morning mist, the sun had broken through, bringing the warmth we'd been missing for the last few days. It was hot. Not warm, but hot. My legs weren't feeling perfect, but having run here before and loved it, I was pacing along, even consistently registering some of my fastest miles of the trip yet.

On all of my running challenges to date there had come a time when the days stopped feeling like a slog and started to feel like something closer to normality. Like going to work for seven hours. My day was a little longer, between nine and twelve hours, but still. I would get up, get dressed, have breakfast, grab my things, and out I went. Rather than a commute to the office and back, I was running.

That last evening of England was magical. We sat with the side doors of the van open, parked near Waren Mill, on a road looking out over the vast beaches around Budle Bay, small tatty boats keeling in the green seaweedy mud at low tide. By now I'd racked up 1,607 miles, nearly a third of the distance I needed. Everything was falling into place and I'd now managed nearly two weeks of back-to-back 44-mile days.

The routine for evenings had become pretty standard by now. If I finished by 4 or 5 p.m., which I often did, we would spend a few hours together, debriefing, eating, chatting and planning the next day or so. Once food was done, we'd retire to our vans, where Andy and I would conduct the usual rituals. We'd briefly tidy the clothes and crockery away so the van could move without things flying all over the place, make sure things like battery packs and phones were either charging or charged, and place my kit for the next day in a suitable heap, usually under my bed. If necessary, I'd fetch a fresh new pair of shoes out from the little storage box at the back of the van. Andy would check the gas levels, empty the rubbish and recycling, while I'd settle down in bed with ice packs or compression gripping my legs. I'd take a couple of painkillers and down half a pint of water, and that was that. Nikki would drop by once I'd messaged her to say I was about ready to sleep, having done her own van stuff, plus taken Poppy for the obligatory evening toilet break.

If we were in a nice spot, and were unlikely to get moved on by the authorities, then I'd opt to sleep in the tent box. I did so that night but struggled to sleep, pondering how Scotland would treat my legs. Over the last few days the elevation had been no more than a steady 2,000 feet per day, give or take a few flat seafront stretches. This had obviously helped the healing process, and I was anxious about my nemeses, hills, returning to haunt me in the most famously mountainous area of Britain.

6

North to John O'Groats

CAITHNESS

JOHN O'GROATS

Wick

SUTHERLAND

Helmsdale

ROSS & CROMARTY

Inverness

Peterhead

INVERNESS-SHIRE

ABERDEENSHIRE

Aberdeen

ANGUS

Dundee

PERTHSHIRE

St Andrews

Falkirk

Edinburgh

Berwick-upon-Tweed

BERWICKSHIRE

WAREN MILL

Day 47 – 45.32 miles – 2,490ft elevation
Waren Mill to Dunbar
Scotland, you're bigger than I imagined

If you can, I'd ask you to open Google Maps (or even an actual map if you have one), and trace your eyes along the coast of Scotland from the border by Berwick-upon-Tweed, all the way around the north of Britain, and back down towards Gretna Green. What you'll notice, even looking at it on the map on your phone, is that it takes quite a long time to follow, even with your eyes, especially on the west coast of the Highlands, where the fiddly, jagged coastline isn't exactly neat. A world away from the simple seafronts of the likes of Brighton and Bournemouth.

The water to my right, as it always was, was a little further away than usual. Although I could see Ross Low, Foulwork Burn and South Low as I passed them, I was following the main road thanks to impassable paths, complicated switchbacks and dead ends, allowing me only occasional glimpses of the sea. This special day of passing into Scotland was a tad dull for the first stretch as I had to run along the A1. This is Britain's east coast equivalent of California's Highway 1 – sort of. At running speed, though, it felt mostly like what it is, a bloody busy stretch of thundering A road. It's this road that took me to the border, via the last few English towns of Buckton, Fenwick, Haggerston, Cheswick, Scremerston and Tweedmouth, all leading to Berwick-upon-Tweed, and the gateway to whisky, bagpipes, golf courses and lochs.

The day's route was roughly half England, half Scotland, around 22 miles to the border and then 23 miles the other side, with our first Scottish parking spot intended to be a place called Whitesands, just south of Dunbar. The highlight of the day was, of course, the border. When flying into Scotland it's just a mundane internal flight. Arrive by road and it's a little more ceremonial. But arrive on foot, and perhaps because of the expectation building for so long, it felt like any marathon finish line.

To the backdrop of nearly fifty days of injuries, suffering and uncertainty, arriving at the border I had goosebumps and the hairs on my neck were standing up. I wasn't exactly expecting to feel so pleased to be there, with so far still to go, but it felt like a real achievement. Perhaps tiredness and over 1,600 miles in my legs were to blame for my emotions.

I'd had a couple of energetic runners with me all morning. They picked me up about 5 miles in and stuck with me all the way into Scotland. Up towards the border we were running, as usual, into the oncoming traffic on the right-hand side of the road. This, as I'm sure you know, is one of the very basics of running or walking on roads. It's best to see the cars and huge, high-sided trucks with big wing mirrors that can potentially kill you rather than have them hurtling past you from behind with no idea if they've seen you or not.

I've been hit and knocked down three times in my life by vehicles. Once in Chad, by a lorry's wing mirror, another time, also in Africa, when I ran across what I thought was an empty road to avoid some rabid dogs, but forgot the traffic was coming from the other side, and was hit, side on, in a more dramatic collision, up and over the bonnet, though fortunately the car was going slow enough to avoid breakages, but not huge bruises and dead legs. The most recent time was in Italy, also a wing mirror, this time on a small white Nissan driven by a guy in his eighties who was hard of hearing, and clearly his eyes weren't too good either.

I can say, with a good degree of certainty, that you don't want to be hit by a car. I sustained fractures from both wing mirror incidents, both vehicles having hit me from behind, and it could have been much worse. I felt like my traffic injury luck was running out and wasn't keen to push it.

I was about 20 miles into the day, just a couple short of the border, when I got one of the many usual update messages from Andy via WhatsApp. This one was to remind me that we would need to be on the northbound side of the dual carriageway because that's obviously where the Welcome to Scotland sign was, and we were keen to get some photos of me passing this milestone. I'd actually been trying to cross over for the past ten minutes. The traffic was fast and relentless – endless speeding metal weapons with few to no gaps between each vehicle. One of the chaps I was running with was Gary. Remember Gary from back in the south? Aka Pop-up Gary? Well, this brilliantly joyful bloke had timed a Scottish trip to see family rather well and had 'popped up' outside the van a few miles in. It was great to see him again. He became an honorary member of the Run Britain crew, and for a guy in his fifties he could run well too. We both helped usher another younger runner who'd joined us across the road after a good fifteen minutes waiting for the perfect moment. Even then, it was a bit of a daredevil dash.

Once on the right side of the road (the left), various flashbacks filled my head. I reminded everyone that we were at risk and would need to shift it to avoid time in the danger zone. On quiet roads with plenty of space for cars to pass there's less danger, but here, it wasn't exactly safe. Had I been on my own I would have felt a little better, but with three of us, I felt triple the responsibility. We wanted to get some news coverage, but not for the wrong reasons.

We still had a good fifteen minutes of running and I was getting nervy. Big lorries, caravans and fuel tankers buffeted us as they sped past. Their closeness was deafening, with the whistling of wind through wheels and over wing mirrors. Dust and grit were being thrown up, hitting the backs of our legs. We were too close to this traffic. If we weren't hurt, we might be the ones to cause others to be. So I made the decision to climb precariously over a barbed-wire fence and into the field that ran alongside the road. We all got a few bits of clothing caught and looked like idiots, plus we were now running on soft, uneven mud tracks with long grass and stinging nettles . . . but at least we weren't about to become a statistic.

Once up by the border, with the others waiting in the noisy lay-by ahead, we reversed the same fence jump with the help of a small stone wall and carefully rejoined the road. With all the worry I'd not been thinking about the feeling of reaching the border for a while. And so, when we arrived and the camera shutters snapped the all-important photos, I felt a real sense that this trip was within reach. No matter what was getting in our way, I could finish this. The border crossing was a strike through any remaining doubt and hesitation. Scotland, we've arrived.

We gathered around the stone border monument with the whole gang, extra runners included, smiling and cheering for the photo. On the scale of big flashy occasions, this doesn't even make the bottom step, but it felt important. I'd run from Cornwall to Scotland, the long way round, via every beach on the south and east coast. Despite what felt like bumps in the road, hardships and struggles, it was likely, as with life in general, that the adventure so far had unfolded as it should. Passing the border that day, I vowed to roll with the punches. To let the misadventures shape the remaining days ahead.

It felt a good time to step up the miles again, from around 44 miles per day to around 46 miles per day. Having reassessed the schedule, and scratched our heads a little, we settled on a new finish date of 20 August and set some mileage targets based on achieving that. This helped to set an underlying push to the finish, and even though we were so far out, it happened to act as a great motivator when feeling like 45 miles might be enough. The spreadsheet said otherwise, so on we'd go.

As Andy's diary captures, this helped to reset our focus:

It's only as I'm writing this late in the evening that it occurs to me that, at the border, none of us looked across to see what the 'Welcome to England' side of the road was like. A good gauge of the attitude and belief of the team. Onwards only – no looking back!

Day 48 – 46.33 miles – 1,392ft elevation
Dunbar to Edinburgh
The Petri van, three-inch heels and the 500-mile shower

Today's near 46-mile route would take me along the majority of the southern side of the Firth of Forth, 'firth' being a cognate of the Norse word *fjord*, meaning a narrow inlet, and 'forth' simply the name of the river. In case you didn't know.

The day was overcast but muggy, going from a morning with just a vest top and sweaty forearms due to the humid air to an afternoon with three layers – a blue lightweight jacket over two thin, silky, breathable short sleeves, with the usual shorts and compression of course. And by now I wasn't strapping my leg at all. Thanks to the continued stretching protocols insisted on by Andy of an evening, my legs were holding up. Perhaps this stretching malarkey was worth all the chat.

From the two hundred-plus photos on my phone from that day, you can see that I was in good spirits. Days with only a handful of pics are usually those when my mind didn't have the energy to bother. I picked up runners at Musselburgh, Leith, a few around Blackness Bay, and more in the city centre. One unfortunate chap found me just as I was in the last 200 metres, trotting along the esplanade at Silverknowes. He was disappointed but understanding and polite.

Running with a newfound bounce from my first step, I looked out over the teeming hedgerows, bees and insects cluttering the air. The North Sea and the Firth of Forth, as well as various impressive islands such as Bass Rock, marked a decidedly Scottish change to the landscape. It was a little grey, but with the help of multiple signposts for various golf courses, and small fishing villages like Port Seton, it was reminiscent of Cornwall.

I flagged Andy down for the usual early-miles toilet stop. Without discussion, he knew by now that if I opened the back doors and got in, wherever he was parked up on the roadside, that meant I needed the loo.

Following my cubicle visit, I took a photo of the footwell of our tiny van latrine. Our living quarters had officially become disgusting. If you've seen *Men Behaving Badly* or any episode of *Black Books*, that's putting it lightly. In order to access the loo I had to first remove four or five 2-litre bottles of piss. To avoid using the chemical toilet and therefore having to find places to empty it, between us Andy and I had hit full capacity on wee storage, having not been able to empty pee bottles in the places where we parked for the night. Now that we'd become properly dirty we'd sort of gone past caring. Unshaven, unshowered, and with crockery and miscellaneous rubbish lying around, we were quickly becoming a roaming Petri dish. I showed the photo to Andy at the driver's-side window, having exited the van. Andy wasn't sure what I was showing him, until I pointed out that we had 8 litres of piss sloshing around in the back. We joked that mine was probably about 6 litres, and Andy's about 2. My bottles were generally orange and would glow in the dark; Andy's were much lighter. We agreed two things: one, I needed to drink more water, and two, we should probably have a bit of a clean-up.

While I'm on the subject of the driver's-side window, it's worth spending just a few moments highlighting the space where Andy operated for most hours of the day for over three months. Come rain or shine, the window would be down, with Andy peering out of it. The door pocket itself had enough room for a few litres of water, some pastries (from whatever deli or discount supermarket we could find), and my electrolyte and carbohydrate drinks. On the dash was a towel, Andy's towel, which was also used to wipe condensation from the windows in the mornings (due to the wet clothes drying overnight), along with a collection of parking tickets, a notepad (I believe for bird watching) and an ever-changing, sometimes hard-to-find packet of crisps. Along with birds, Andy is a keen crisp fan, and will hunt for obscure packets in small convenience stores like Nisa Local and unnamed 'off-licences'. With the door open, the step to get in was big enough to sit on, uncomfortably. I'd sit there for a couple of minutes, scoff down whatever unhealthy snack I could find, swig water and carb drink, and on I went. The footwell near the pedals was the only space in the van that was clear of clutter, just Andy's bare feet and the occasional crisp that had escaped his mouth.

This little portal from Andy's world to mine was also the signal station. Without realizing it, we had come up with some very basic hand gestures that served us rather well. Index and middle finger in the air meant 'I'll see you in two miles'. Sometimes it was one or three, but usually two. The hand to neck signal meant I was done and at the next stop I needed a break. A mimed glass to the lips said I needed to drink, and both arms in the air meant I didn't know where I was going, at which point Andy would use the indicators to tell me. Not rocket science, but effective. Once I'd finished my brief couple of minutes' rest, which I'd have often in an attempt to eat and drink enough, I'd run on ahead, and Andy would tidy bits away and then drive past me with the thumbs-up signal out of the window. I'd reply with either a thumbs up, meaning 'all good, carry on', or I'd put my left arm straight and high in the air. This would mean I needed him to stop, usually because I'd forgotten something.

So that's the inner workings of a one-man support van in a nutshell. Bottles of piss, a few hand signals, rare crisps, and large quantities of unhealthy snacks. You won't read that in *Runner's World*.

Anyway, back to day 48.

Around 10 miles in, another welcome face appeared – a special person called Lynn. Lynn made her presence known by driving past in her white Mini with her arm out of the window, beeping the horn and cheering. Lynn's around fifty, and she greeted me with a warm hug wearing a yellow waterproof, dangly earrings and a classy necklace, her smile and energy noticeable. I met Lynn for the first time as the lift doors opened in a hotel in Athens, where she and a friend, Rowena, had come to support at the finale of my Running the World challenge. Today she'd made the effort to track me down and say hello. It's these seemingly small gestures that speak volumes. And Lynn being Lynn, not wanting to miss out, she ran with me in three-inch heels and her snazzy clothes. Who cares if it was only 15 metres. We got a selfie in the drizzle, FaceTimed Rowena who was locked down in Spain, and on I went with a huge boost to my stride.

The coast had always been just next to me, rarely more than a few hundred yards away, but over the past few days, nature, along with good old-fashioned industry and infrastructure, had kept the water out of sight. Today was a good day because I was back within a couple of metres of it for the duration.

By this point Nikki really needed a break. It was long overdue. She was being consumed by our challenge, by generously supporting me and the team, when I knew she needed time for herself and her business. Realizing an opportunity with the great city of Edinburgh up ahead, and knowing it was roughly where we'd be closing out the day,

I spoke with Andy to formulate a plan. By now, my running miles-to-shower ratio was about 500:1. I'd not washed since Norfolk. Worse, I'd become rather used to it, telling everyone I met that my body 'self-cleans' every 100 miles. I was of course joking . . . but only slightly. But now was a chance to indulge. The plan was set. Andy would run the last half of the day with me, having taken Poppy off Nikki's hands. Nikki and Amy would drive ahead to a glitzy two-star Premier Inn on the outskirts of Edinburgh, where we'd all meet and shower (separately). The following day Nikki would remain dog-free, while Andy trialled an illegal dog swap day – a day where Poppy would co-pilot him for the duration, both running and in the Council Van. This would leave Nikki to work and have some peace away from our travelling circus, and catch us up later. Although this was breaking Council Van rule number one, NO DOG IN THE VAN, we'd broken it before and, to be blunt, Nikki needed the break more than I felt the rules needed to be obeyed.

The day coming to a close and the miles being filled with at least twenty keen runners, the final stretch carried us just north-west of Edinburgh along the esplanade. Only two tasks remained, having made it to the hotel: one, have a shower, which I did, filling the shower tray with black grime, and two, check the nerdsheet, aka the nerdy spreadsheet, to tot up miles and suss out the next few weeks.

I'd now covered nearly 1,700 miles, an average of 35 miles a day, even with broken bones and a few recovery days. It could be worse. We were, however, about 800 miles short of where we were due to be by this date, so we decided to up the daily miles again, just slightly, to 47 or thereabouts. A small change like this would shave off three days from our total. And if we could increase the miles again soon, perhaps edge back to doubles and beyond, we might just bring the finish date closer still. Either way, the 47-mile daily target was agreed.

The glitch in the day's plan was that Premier Inns don't allow dogs and so with the team deserving far more than a Premier Inn bed, I opted to stay in the van with Poppy while the gang enjoyed a good night's sleep and endless hot water on tap. I was glad to take one for the team finally. They had been suffering for me. This was the least I could do. And besides, I had Poppy to cuddle for a change.

Day 49 – 47.22 miles – 1,444ft elevation
Edinburgh to Torry Bay

Wanting to make the most of the Premier Inn, Nick and I devise a slightly complicated start to the day's proceedings, to address the following:

(1) Poppy will be more settled in an unfamiliar van if she's tired, so the earlier and further she runs, the better.

(2) Nick will have to travel back to where he finished running yesterday to start running today, as per standard protocol.

(3) The more driving we have to do between Nick's stints of running, the less time it gives him to actually run.

(4) Nikki and Amy could do with a lie-in.

(5) We all want a fry-up as late as the hotel will serve it.

The solution is for Nick, Poppy and I to drive back to yesterday's end point before breakfast. The three of us will run up and down the esplanade to bag a few miles, then up the River Almond in the direction of today's route, where Pop and I will run to the van and drive back to the hotel, while Nick gets there on foot. It works pretty well, and we all arrive for breakfast bang on 10 a.m.

This master plan got off to a late start as I'd struggled to get to sleep the night before and therefore Andy had trouble waking me up. His banging on the side of the van stirred Poppy, but not me apparently. We were eventually on our feet an hour later than intended, but Andy and I managed to tick off 11 miles in the morning and get back to the hotel before Amy or Nikki had even woken up. Even better, we caught the final twenty minutes of the Premier Inn's finest breakfast service. I had my first of many full Scottish breakfasts.

During those early hours, Andy spoke of the simple luxuries he hadn't realized he'd missed. Things like the feeling of carpet under his toes, and being able to turn a tap on and water come out. Live with me in a van for nearly fifty days and you'll treasure the simple things. We were existing on 5-litre bottles of water due to the pathetically small water tank. The floor, far from carpet, was a mix of laminate, grit and the general grime and mud that was the result of us getting in and out upwards of twenty times a day between us.

With Andy and Poppy in the support van and Nikki staying behind with Amy in Edinburgh to work and revel in the rare dog-less freedom, there was not much left to do but run. Other than a bit of a hill halfway it was 36 miles of pure flatness to the end. Sweeping paths along the water, cycle tracks and bug-filled hedgerows – it was as close to a perfect afternoon as I could wish for. Running through Grangemouth, over the Kincardine Bridge and along towards Rosyth to finish the day's miles at Torry Bay Nature Reserve, a stunning spot, I was lost in my own thoughts and it was bliss. Sun, but not too much, and a gentle breeze from behind. I finished the 47 miles in good time and got to bed early, Poppy and Andy too. This wonderful day had been a treat.

We'd wake up to a milestone day, day 50 – and what a day it would be.

Days 50 to 51
Torry Bay to Ruby Bay

Day 50 began with Nikki and Amy's return, and the usual set-up resumed. We hadn't noticed it was a milestone day until after I'd set off, when Andy happened to realize after punching some numbers into the spreadsheet. He leaned out of the window as I ran and shouted, 'Did you know it's day fifty?' I threw my arms up in the air with both fists clenched and let out a cheer. It gave me an instant boost of energy. This was shortly followed by the realization that fifty days meant halfway in our *original* plan, and I knew from memory that I was supposed to be on the west coast of the Highlands by now. Instead, we hadn't even reached John O'Groats yet. I somehow rationalized it in my head and pressed on. The sun had got the whole team in a buoyant mood, me included. It turned into a scorcher of a day. With little to no breeze, tucked in along the northern side of the Firth of Forth, it was the first proper full day of baking hot weather. As it turned out, even hotter weather, abnormally for Scotland, was on its way.

Nearly back in line with Edinburgh again, having tracked inland along the river, 10 miles in we detoured downhill to the North Queens-ferry lookout. This little hidden gem has views across the Forth and the path passes under the great Forth Bridge, next to the less impressive Forth Road Suspension Bridge. The Forth Bridge, which opened in 1890, is an icon of Scotland, and it's not difficult to see why. It's a thing of majestic beauty, while simultaneously appearing as a beast of mat-ted red steel. It's elegant and yet wonderfully functional. You can't help but see the sweat, blood and tears that went into building it. Including the viaducts leading to it, the bridge spans 2.5 kilometres and consists of nearly 53,000 tonnes of metal. There was a useful plaque at the lookout point. To this day it is recognized as one of the most famous cantilever designs, and was the world's first steel structure on this scale. Andy adapted the route so we'd pass under it without telling me. I'm glad he did. Despite the very steep hill to and from it, it was worth every step. For many miles after I was pondering what the place must have looked like with thousands of workers, for years on end, during its construction. Somehow this channelled energy into me and I upped my game and finished the day strong.

Other than the bridge, which stuck in my mind for miles, the endless coast paths tracking the water's edge were the beginnings of what I hoped the Scottish coast would be like: sun glinting off the water, her-ons and kingfishers darting around in the nearby streams, the roads next to the coast quieter than England's, with small thatched villages nestled between large strips of green.

These green patches, trimmed and tamed, consisted mostly of golf courses. We were soon to approach the world famous St Andrews, which is of course revered not just by Scottish golfists, but the entire world's. Andy and I shared the same view that these neat, tidy places were too pristine for our liking. They seemed devoid of wildlife, unlike the paths and trails next to them. They reminded me of a ridiculous project that the council dreamt up near a childhood friend's place a few years earlier. When I'd asked him why the roads were closed, he told me that the council were removing the hedgerows to plant wild grass and flowers. Obviously this is absurd. Removing wild stuff to replace it with non-wild stuff that's called wild stuff is bonkers. I suspect that just like these golfing gardens, it sadly all came back to money.

Andy was equally unimpressed:

The only blot on this coastal landscape is its increasingly golfy nature. Golf has never really interested or bothered me before, but as Nick has trudged around the coast of Britain, I've been surprised by how many golf courses he has passed, and they have started to wind me up a bit. As he approaches St Andrews, which I understand is sacred to your golfists, the coast becomes increasingly littered with courses. We count eight on this route alone. The problem I have with golf courses is that, for green spaces, they are so sterile, so devoid of interest. The British coastline, considered by some to be the best in the world, can be a place of beauty, ruggedness, even bleakness and heavy industry; a spectacle of nature and human history, packed with wildlife and interesting places. What it should never be is a giant, out-of-stock garden centre with all the character of an East German supermarket. No offence, golfists, I'm just not a fan of where you keep your sandpits.

I was still stopping regularly, at least every 5 miles, generally more frequently. Plenty of water was needed as my suncream sweated off me, leaving tide lines on my shoulders and down my forearms. With more regularly spaced stops, Andy had now adopted a new tactic. He'd pull up, potter around briefly, and then do a few push-ups at the side of the road. I'd often catch him snatching a few reps. He is an ageing man, don't forget, soon to be fifty (in four years), and sitting down for much of the day was taking its toll, and he didn't want his muscle mass to decline to the point where he couldn't push himself off the toilet seat – a point I was rapidly approaching.

Oddly, the day concluded without Andy for the first time in what felt like living memory. A sponsor had mailed a few packages to a hotel in Kirkcaldy for our collection as we passed. Except that we forgot, so during the last hour, Andy made the heroic 50-mile round trip to fetch and return. By the time he got back, Nikki, Poppy and I were making pasta with the side door open, complete with beers, ciders and sunshine.

Our resting place on this milestone day makes it into my top five of the trip, possibly of all time. We were in a campervan-filled gravel car park overlooking Ruby Bay. From our spot with the side door of the Palace Van open and the tent box up in preparation for an early night, we had views of Elie Ness Lighthouse with the sun casting it in a deep orange light, the ocean now darker and turning purple. A few seals ducked and dived off the headland while groups of van lifers readied their tables, stoves and camp chairs ahead of an evening of BBQs and firepits. Not wanting to be left out, we got the blankets out on the grassy bank that led down to the beach. Andy even arrived with enough time to have a dip in the inviting yet freezing North Sea. He didn't stay in long.

The packages turned out to be more glucose sensors from a company called Supersapiens. The company turns normal diabetic glucose monitors into genuinely cutting-edge data for athletes, and I had been using them for the duration of the challenge. A live glucose score was not only visible through Bluetooth on my phone, but was connected to my watch. Put simply, I could keep an eye on my sugar levels, notice when they were spiking, work out how long particular foods took to take effect and know when my glucose reserves were depleted and requiring a top-up. I could use the data to understand what specific foods my body needed, and when.

With the sun slipping behind the horizon, thoughts turned to the following day's route. I'd be picking up the Fife Coastal Path that rounded the forked double headland, leading to St Andrews, Dundee and beyond. Rather than use the Tay Road Bridge into Dundee and then turn right to track the coast, we'd use the River Tay and follow it left inland, towards Perth. We were still keeping an eye on my total mileage and so these inlets were a handy and legitimate way to make small adjustments to keep me right on target.

St Andrews Bay might as well be called Rich Golfer Bay, but I was actually quite taken with the town, with its feel of a Scottish Bristol or Bath. Large cobbled streets with sandstone houses appeared to over-look golf courses in every direction. It was as if the town of St Andrews was built as a giant clubhouse. My day, though, wasn't about golf, thank goodness. It was about old friends. Some time ago I ran a little race in the Sahara called the Marathon des Sables. It's a brutal 250 kilometres in 50°C heat. Of the seven tent mates I bunked with each evening, only one was female, the only one who consistently finished before any of us every day for the duration of the event. That woman is Selina. She never fails to inspire me. She's modest, outrageously smart, and has her family at the heart of her life, despite having a very successful high-flying career. She's incredibly strong-willed when it comes to running, too.

As I'm a fan of Formula 1, we coined today and subsequent days 'a two-stop strategy' – a phrase from racing terminology, meaning to stop and pit twice during a race. I'd been running 46 or 47 miles quite comfortably now and didn't need to stop for long. However, Azerbaijan were hosting the latest round of Formula 1 and I was keen to watch it, so I derived a reward system for myself. If I bagged my first marathon in the morning, I could stop and watch the F1, and then get out and finish the remaining miles after the race. It was a good motivator to push on through the first half of the day.

On day 51 I watched the race while scoffing my face with an almighty Andy-assembled ploughman's lunch, parked up on the side of a road on the south side of the Tay. The ploughman's, however, knocked me out. The heat of the day and the huge quantities of cheese and bread put me into a food coma and I fell asleep with over half the race still left to run.

I realized this, with sleepy crosshatch lines on my face from the van's cushions, when Selina knocked on the side of the van. I woke up in a dizzy confusion, not knowing what was going on. I'd actually forgotten not only where I was, but the fact I still had at least 20 miles left to run. As you can imagine, it wasn't the best of feelings.

Everything changed when I saw Selina's face peering through the window. Selina doesn't mess around, and she had turned up to run with me. I immediately gave myself a talking-to. After some intros I pulled Andy to the side to quietly ask him how far I was running. I'd totally forgotten the mile count from the morning, which of course he found funny, if a little alarming. He said softly, 'Twenty-one will take you to what we've mapped.' Anything that starts with a two is a good number, so off we went.

Selina has a magical way of looking like she's just out for a gentle stroll in the park, her legs not turning over much at all, but her actual speed is quite literally breathtaking. I was in the habit of running gentle nine-minute miles at best, and with stops, drinks and junctions, usually no faster than eleven. We were sub-eight-minute mileing for some time and I embarrassingly had to ask her to slow down. Reined in to run at my pace, Selina kindly stuck around for the rest of the afternoon chatting as the sun fell behind the trees, both of us sweating and panting as we paced up the hills. It was wonderful to be running with her again.

Days 52 to 61
Newburgh to Ousdale
The windy north, dolphins, puffins and Irn-Bru

Approaching eight weeks on the road, although it felt like eighty, we were only days away from John O'Groats, the summit of Britain. The only problem with these days turned out to be the wind. It hit me and continued to hit me every day for at least a week. If anything, it got worse each day. We looped around the Cairngorms from Dundee, via Aberdeen, all the way around to the southern bank of the Moray Firth and the northern tip of Loch Ness, by which point it felt like we'd been heading inland for ages, such is the shape of the Scottish coast.

All that time I battled the unrelenting winds coming off the North Sea. The wind was so intense here, so utterly unremitting, that it caused me to lose some of my hearing for a few days. The wind dominated the entire experience, a constant barrage of noise dotted with disjointed memories: an award-winning public toilet, featuring shells and glitter set in resin toilet seats; running with two kilt-wearing women; indulging in the drink of the Scots. No, not whisky . . . Irn-Bru. The drink of the diabetic gods.

It's starting to feel like we're somewhere different now, and at a café
on day 53 we go full native, with cans of Irn-Bru and packets of

shortbread, because that's what English people think Scottish people eat and drink all the time. The place names around here are interesting, with signs seemingly pointing to various blokes – we passed through Errol yesterday, while today will take us through Barry, Elliot and Angus. There are also place names that sound like status reports on various saints: St Michael's Inn (but he's off out later), St Ninian's Well (thanks for asking).

Poppy is in a boisterous mood, and needs a long run to blow off some steam, so I get my running kit on, and we join Nick along a lovely coast path. It's warm and after a few miles we stop for a break, delving into my improvised support pack consisting of a bottle of water and two Belgian buns in a bag. After a few miles, we stop for a break, and get through the water in no time. With the bag shaking up and down, the melted icing has all been jostled down from the top bun on to the lower one, which I reluctantly give to Nick. We're soon out of water, so a little further on, Nick goes door to door with the empty water bottle and a kindly local fills it up for us. This is enough to keep us going until we get close to Poppy's collection point, where Nikki shuttles me back to the Council Van.

Andy ran with me several times during this period, his bag acting as a roaming bakery-cum-pharmacy. I changed my shoes for the sixth time as I approached 2,000 miles, which helped the general hygiene levels in the van, and I attempted to pimp up a pizza, but succeeded in dropping anchovies and their not-so-subtle smell on the floor of the van, having tripped up the back step, which most definitely did not. Amy returned home after a good stretch as our photographer, which I think was unrelated to our degree of sanitation. All in all, it was a pretty standard week or so on the Run Britain adventure. Beyond that, I kept up my run streak of 47-plus-mile days, inching closer to the finish, even if I was actually still running away from it.

Only a week after crossing the border everything had started to feel more, well, Scottish. Not only did we pass a sign welcoming us to the Highlands just as bagpipes could be heard playing in the distance, but the scenery began to show glimpses of what Scotland is so celebrated for. The ocean was no longer a murky green, but shades of indigo and bright purple. The coniferous trees seemed more vivid and dramatic, with light green and yellow ferns waving in the wind on the verges. The stone walls, small villages and quaint signposts all helped to create an atmosphere that was non-English, and we were enjoying it.

The ocean wasn't just gifting us colour and the beauty of infinite ripples of light, we were also spoilt by a large pod of dolphins showing us their skills off the coast of industrial Aberdeen. Nikki was out one day snapping away at some puffins on a cliff edge just an hour down the road from Aberdeen when she got chatting to a friendly Scot who recommended a spot just up the coast where it was possible, on a good day, to see dolphins flanking the ships as they came and went.

After a routine McDonald's stop, Andy met me at the spot Nikki had sent us via a location pin on WhatsApp, care of the friendly Scot. Andy pulled in and I ran along the small path leading to a car park at the end of the headland. We weren't sure if we were in the right place because there wasn't much around, just a few cars, a railing and some tatty fishing nets next to some locked-up storage buildings. The view was a mesh of cranes in the port of Aberdeen and mismatched houses of various shapes and sizes, with smaller boats and cargo vessels coming and going. We heard Nikki before we saw her. She rocked up in a jubilant mood with music blaring out of the windows, singing along. She wasn't expectant, but curious as to whether we'd seen any dolphins. We hadn't. She pulled up and parked.

At that very instant two dolphins leapt from the water just outside the harbour. What followed was a magical, seemingly perfectly choreographed display of dolphin acrobatics. A pod of five showed off their skills in circles in the middle of the shipping lane. We all looked at each other in amazement. I sat and gorged on a greasy burger and chips as we watched on in awe. They stuck around for about ten minutes before diving and disappearing out of sight.

I finished that day's miles with a broad grin on my face, while Andy was having fun on the Scottish roads:

Last night's finishing point was on a straight road with no distinguishing features and, with no phone signal, I can't rely on the WhatsApp pin I dropped to mark the spot. Fortunately, some thoughtful soul has chucked a copy of the Screwfix catalogue into the bushes on the verge. This faded tome, lying under a distinctive branch of gorse, makes it easy to find the spot where Nick stopped yesterday, so I don't have to worry about accidentally leaving a little gap in his Strava line.

With each stop throughout the day, it feels increasingly like we are finally running out of British Isles. The landscape takes on a more remote feel, and there are clues here and there to indicate that we're getting further and further from the standard hustle and bustle of towns and cities. As I pootle along an undulating road, Sunday driving on a Thursday, I'm overtaken by a steeplejack, who tears past me in his van – rush hour has a very different feel around here. I'm not sure if I've ever even seen a steeplejack before, and I wonder if he can really be in as much of a hurry as he seems. It's not a profession I'd associate with a sense of urgency, but you can't make assumptions like that. I once met a piano tuner in Bristol who told me that the main thing he didn't like about his line of work was the politics.

The wind was a struggle to start with. As the week progressed, I was getting more fatigued by it as it got stronger. I had some weird notion in the back of my head that Mother Nature was rapping me on the knuckles for mocking the Scottish accent one too many times. Whatever I'd done, she was not happy.

I've run in sandstorms, hurricanes, tropical lightning and golfball-sized hail, but the Scottish wind was a whole different battle. The news updates on my phone read: 'UK records best day for wind energy in history'. All those turbines I'd been seeing were working wonders for our country's renewable energy quotas, but that also of course meant we were experiencing stronger than usual wind conditions, particularly on the coast – aka, my office.

It was annoying at first, then draining, and after a few days it was becoming truly uncomfortable. Stepping forward and making little progress was bad enough, but the noise of it rushing past my ears was unbearable. I wasn't used to having to compartmentalize something so close to my brain . . . the wind felt like it was thundering in one ear, rattling around in my skull and shooting out the other side. Obviously I'd tried everything I could think of. Usually in high winds I would fold my buff over on itself a few times to make it a little tighter around my head. Instead of wearing it around my neck I'd hitch it up to cover just my ears. I ran like this for about a day but the wind was too strong for this thin layer and the din was really making me miserable.

Stepping out into wind and rain is bad enough at the start of a day, but when you've been out in it for so long that the wind is starting to impair your hearing, it feels a step too far. It was something I just hadn't braced myself for. I switched to sound-cancelling headphones, tried the ear plugs Andy wore in bed at night, music, but nothing worked. I even tried my buff over the headphones, but the pressure was too much and after a few hours my head was pounding and painful.

Every day I'd finish expecting that to be the last of it. Thinking I'd wake up and it would be gone. But no, the wind hurled itself at the van most nights, and although occasionally there'd be a break of a couple of hours, it would soon ratchet up again into a whirlwind. It also felt like it was either coming head on at me, making my pace slow, forcing me to be out in it longer, or it would be swirling around me, as if bully-ing me, shoving me in all directions. As for the noise, I'd even attempted to fold and carefully tape wads of kitchen roll to my ears, but that soon started to disintegrate, making the noise worse, and I resorted to just running without anything at all. I was left with no choice but to lean into the pain. If I just accepted it, and even tried to enjoy it, maybe my brain would switch off the frustration. It didn't work. I actually just got angry. I was royally fed up. Worst of all, I could only imagine the remainder of the entire Scottish coast being the same. It freaked me out.

Scotland has more than its fair share of great inventors: James Watt, Alexander Graham Bell and John Logie Baird, to name but a few. Per-haps inspired by them, Andy, unbeknown to me, had put his thinking cap on. One day, after I'd slogged out another 15 or so morning miles in misery, I was downcast and my energy even more so. Where the quiet roads allowed, I'd been sheltering behind the van, switching sides throughout the day to hide from the bullying wind. It was towards the end of this awful stint that Andy handed me some strange red parcels. These were the first off the production line of the newly founded brand

EarPads™, which came with the slogan: 'You may look terrible, but you'll feel great'.

Andy had used his ingenuity and creative skills to produce soft pads about an inch thick that could be held to my ears with a buff or headband and importantly would make an airtight seal around my ears so no bastard wind could get in.

Using two pieces of foam cut from washing-up sponges, Andy had cut wide strips from a rubber physio band to wrap the pads, gluing the outside edges and gaffer-taping the joins for strength. They were remarkably neat. I'm sure he wouldn't mind me saying I was a little dubious at first, but I was out of options and so I became the proud owner of these limited-edition EarPads™. And you know what? They bloody worked, didn't they? Somehow the tacky material of the stretchy exercise band pressed firmly against my ears was enough to form an airtight mould, with my buff around my head so they'd stay in place. In fact they worked too well, because all of a sudden I couldn't hear a thing.

Although stylish, the EarPads™ do have the unfortunate side effect of rendering Nick deaf, making it difficult for him to hear my directions and the approach of oncoming lorries. I imagine these are issues likely to result in a product recall in the future, followed by a series of lawsuits, my eventual bankruptcy and descent into alcoholism. But for now, the EarPads™ are hot property, and most importantly for me, they make Nick look a bit like he's wearing a helmet, which, combined with the rest of his ensemble, makes him look a bit like a Star Wars figure. (From the original Kenner range obviously, before they remade them all muscular.)

This respite from the cacophony of the battering wind was one of the nicest, most relieving feelings I could ask for. Imagine needing a wee for hours, days maybe, but holding it in. While doing that you're unable to think about anything else. The eventual release from that feeling is spectacular. This was similar. My mood instantly lifted, and even though I was still being pushed around, I could run in peace. The EarPads™ were game-changing. I ran for the next day or two

with them strapped to my head, after which the wind finally decided
to let up.

With a wind-fixed grimace on my face, in the early miles of the day
I encountered a rather intrepid gentleman called Dan. In truth, I met
him when I was feeling rather glum, but our paths crossed as Dan was
attempting his own voyage, a figure of eight around Britain by bike,
and I was immediately lifted by his company.

Dan came over the hill towards me in silhouette, a sliver of sun
behind him. And no, he was not on his bike. He'd tracked me down
and abandoned his bike for a day, specifically to come and run with me.
A top human being. We shared a good 24 or 25 miles together, chatting
about adventure and the numerous trips he'd taken on. He had no care
to run a marathon necessarily, and stopped just before – a sign he really
did come out for me, and not himself. We spoke freely about our mutual
love of connecting with people, and with nature, and how adventure
inevitably leads to both. We quickly realized we shared a lot in common and began to plot a challenge we could take on together.

As he was saying his goodbyes, Dan informed me he had no way of
getting back to his bike, which was by now 25 miles in the other direction. His plan was to hitch a lift. Many people would assume that
would be either unsafe, difficult or unsuccessful. But we both knew he
wouldn't have a problem. We took bets on how many cars would pass
before he got picked up. Dan punted for about ten; I halved it and said
no more than five. Either way, we both had enough experience of the
kindness of strangers to know it wouldn't take long. Upon saying
goodbye, with Andy having made the (declined) offer to Dan of a lift,
I plodded on. I'd made it about 15 metres when Dan shouted after me.
I turned to see him beaming as he climbed into a van that had stopped
to pick him up. It was the very first vehicle to pass, and all within ten
seconds. Most people are good people.

Just as we closed out the week, now on the other side of Inverness
and glad that the winds had settled for the time being, an email came
in from the team at Supersapiens. It was my glucose report. Nikki,
Andy and I sat, sheltering from the rain, eating the last of the evening's
food – spag bol actually – as we discussed the two key findings among
a load of data.

The report stated that I was short of calories by about 3,000 a day, and that I was generally hypoglycaemic, meaning I needed more sugar in my diet. As Andy read out the report, my face crumpled into a confusion of doubtful expressions. No way could I be hypo. I must be hyp*er*. I eat so much sugar – more than any runner I know, in fact. My diet was generally appalling. We concluded that it must be in part due to inaccurate data capture. But on review, it seemed as though the data we were providing on my intake was reasonably accurate. My body was burning through so much glucose, I actually needed more. We agreed that if I was to have more, it should probably be from fruit and health foods, not just more Mars bars and pastries. Shame.

By the end of day 58 I'd sustained an average of 45-plus-mile days consecutively for three weeks. I was now extending my longest unbroken streak. I felt fitter than ever. In my head there was no reason I couldn't increase the mileage. With the light failing and the prospect of the first night for a while without wind rocking us to sleep, we shut our eyes and prayed the bad weather had finally run its course. John O'Groats was now just a few days away.

Parked in a pothole-riddled car park on the edge of the A832, we were the only vehicle, the water to one side and the road to the other. Having made it past Inverness, where we'd snatched a glimpse of snow on the hollows of north-facing mountains, I'd run past various forts and bothies on the water's edge. We were well and truly in the depths of Scotland now. We saw fewer and fewer supermarkets, brand-name hotels had disappeared, and the roads had become quieter and quieter. Loch Ness flows into the River Ness and then out towards the Kessock Bridge at Carnarc Point. It was just further north by Munlochy where we'd made camp.

Before bed, the three of us stepped out on to the few metres of patchy, overgrown grass near the water and looked out. On cue, an osprey dived feet first to catch a shallow-swimming fish just a few metres in front of us. Andy gave us a 'twitching' lesson as we watched its repeated returns and attempts, many of them successful. I opened my eyes the following morning to find Andy was already out watching the same osprey. And guess what? The wind had died down, and it was a clear, rainless day. Finally.

I refused to look at the weather app and instructed the others not to tell me the forecast either way. I realized there was no point. I'd be out in it regardless. Of course, Andy was still keeping an eye on, well, everything:

Nick's turning point today is the town of Cromarty, which is like a waiting room for wounded giants. The firth is littered with oil rigs, drilling platforms and various other huge metal structures all towed here for repair or breaking up. It's a strange sight that I hope will take Nick's mind off the afternoon weather forecast.

Day 59 in fact did eventually get a little blustery, but nothing like I'd felt of late. My last text message to Andy as I ran the last 6 miles up the south side of the Cromarty Firth read: 'I feel fine, I could run longer today, what do you think?' Andy probably knew this was coming, but suggested increasing the miles might ultimately set us back rather than forward. He was right of course, and so I called it a day at 48 miles, feeling fresh. Amazingly, I'd completed the 48 miles with 3,213 feet of elevation in eight hours and thirty minutes. Not bad, with over 2,000 miles already in my legs. Andy's diary sums it up:

The last few days have had the feel of steady work shifts rather than feats of endurance, with Nick now taking an almost languid approach to his daily distances, fully relaxed in his running. Despite this, with the lack of elevation on the headland, he's running at a decent pace today, much faster, he tells me, than he feels like he's going. This is telling of the fitness level he's now reaching and how attuned he's become to the daily distance. He's starting to run these days on muscle memory, the sweet spot he was dreaming of during the first few days of the challenge.

Now running over 47-mile days, we made a conscious effort to ensure the revised end date remained possible should we have any mileage slippage later down the line. For now, though, my watch told me I'd burnt close to 7,000 calories today. Time to eat.

The route had been a stunner. If you look on Strava, it's not far off a simple 'S' shape, or perhaps a more messy Zorro sword swipe. The roads were quiet after about 2 p.m.: Scotland were playing the Czech Republic in the Euros, so I had the coast to myself. There was just one more big headland to get around before the final straight up to John O'Groats.

Over days 60 and 61 I clocked up two 47-milers with around 5,000 feet of elevation. We'd now been on the road for two months. Day to day, just like with any habitual routine, it was easy to get bogged down in the repetitive grind and easy to forget the simple privileges we had. Having had weeks and weeks of battling to complete the days in one piece, wishing away the miles, I now had to unlearn that and begin to treasure the hours and minutes. We had a long way to go, a very long way, still about 3,000 miles, but I reminded myself that before long I'd be done, and I'd miss it, so I must enjoy these moments.

With John O'Groats up ahead, just hours away in running terms, I reflected on the miles that were behind me and made a pact with myself that from now on, whatever the north and west coasts of Britain threw at me, I'd remember that the journey was just as important as the destination.

The coast here on the windy firths was gorgeous, quaint and quiet. Mother Nature had turned down the wind and given me a gentle reminder to give thanks not just for the great moments, but the small ones too. Feeling fresh, with legs turning over nicely, I was beginning not just to settle into the miles with ease, I was speeding up, tackling hills more efficiently and generally thinking of each day as part of my basic routine. I was having fun. It was no longer one continuous barrage of physical and mental abuse. Pre-challenge, I'd hoped it would take me about two weeks to get to the comfortable stage. Instead, it had taken eight. Still, eight was better than eighteen.

Once I'd rounded the Cromarty Firth, there was just the Dornoch Firth remaining between me and the road to the top of Scotland. It would then be just a matter of keeping the water on my right, and heading north until the land gave way to sea.

There were subtle changes in the tone of Andy's diary too. We were in high spirits, treasuring the moment, starting to feel at one with life on the road – and wildlife:

_Apparently, it's an open house for breakfast on day 61, and as I
make the tea, a female blackbird hops in through the open door of
the van, clearly used to humans and looking for a quick bite to eat.
I hand her a crust of bread and she makes off without paying. Apol-
ogies to Nick's dad – although the van covenant doesn't specifically
veto avian guests, I suspect they would be frowned upon. In my
defence, she wasn't actually invited in._

The area around Loch Fleet a few miles north of Dornoch was some
of the most beautiful coastline I'd seen since Cornwall. I was willing
my eyes to remember every little detail. For most of this section of
coast I'd been running in the middle of empty single-carriageway
roads, with the tarmac merging into grassy tufts. These became gorse
bushes with their yellow buds overshadowing the green of the bushes
themselves. Behind them was the calm, untouched expanse of water.
My constant companion.

This consistent view would roll through my field of vision as I moved
on. Stone walls drew faint lines across faraway fields, their steepness
revealed only by the lack of trees. The palette to these few days was
faded, overcast mostly, but that didn't spoil the picture. I felt like the
monk in Caspar David Friedrich's famous 1808 painting _The Monk by
the Sea_, which depicts a murky, moody mix of faded hues bleeding
from earth to sea to sky, with a small figure in the foreground. Well,
perhaps the monk bit is a stretch. But I felt similarly engulfed by the
world around me.

The slight sting in the tail came in the form of my longest unbroken
stretch of steep uphill so far. This was a full 7 miles with gradients of
between 8 and 11 per cent for most of the way, climbing from Helmsdale to Ousdale, having dropped down to cross a bridge over the River
Helmsdale. On this last hill to Ousdale, my ears even popped. From
mile 40 at sea level, crossing the bridge, I'd climbed up to over 1,000
feet by mile 48.

These miles would take me to my final rest stop before the push to
John O'Groats. The maths had worked out pretty well. With the various adjustments we'd made to the daily routes, Andy had mapped
exactly 50 miles to reach the top of Britain on day 62, before we'd turn

left and run west, and then turn south towards home. We knew that John O'Groats wasn't quite halfway in terms of distance, but it would act as a mental regrouping spot. And it would eventually work out to be our rough halfway point in terms of days – a good indication that my pace and daily distance had finally become sustainable.

My body was in one piece, but Andy's, not quite. Towards the end of the day he'd shut his thumb in the van door. He didn't dwell on the matter, telling me later, when it was black and blue, that he had another one anyway. All he needed to take the edge off was battered haggis and chips. If a sore thumb doesn't kill you, a heart attack might.

Day 62 – 50.01 miles – 2,706ft elevation
Ousdale to John O'Groats
Reaching the top

The final push northwards was straightforward but not without busy A roads and accompanying traffic. Those who walk, hike or cycle Land's End to John O'Groats usually do so through varying routes that cut through the middle of the country. The approach to John O'Groats can be made on two paths, neither of which I followed, as obviously I was keeping as close to the coast as possible and thus approaching from a different angle. This did mean that I faced a lot more traffic than most people arriving here on foot, forced to follow the road due to the lack of a coast path.

I've run along the central reservations of busy roads in places like Pakistan and Colombia. I've also run through tunnels, and around blind bends in tunnels, some of them at night. They were worse than this last stretch of road, but not by much. The feeling of getting close to 'the top', as I called it, was, however, taking my mind off the danger. It was one of those days when nothing was going to stop me.

I encountered most of the severe elevation in the morning, completing marathon distance along the A99 to the town of Wick. It was then undulating, but with quieter roads. Even if I was still on the A99, not much traffic had the need to venture past the castle of Old Keiss. This was the last but one of a long line of castles jutting out on the east coast, relics of history in a nation that has a proud tradition of repelling invaders.

It was past Wick, as Andy peeled off on a supply run, that the landscape became a hinterland of barren and bleak unknown nothingness. We all knew we were charging towards the edge of a cliff, quite literally, and the surrounding landscape seemed to echo this ominous, eerie feeling. It was like an apocalyptic film where there are scenes of cars abandoned on roads, slaughtered sheep in neighbouring fields, or sounds of wind whistling through burnt-out homes. It was a day of changeable weather too, which made everything feel a little uneasy.

Fortunately Andy had come up trumps on his local supermarket sweep:

Nick takes his usual drink breaks throughout the day, and when we're on roads like this with no grassy verges or walls to perch on, he tends to sit in the van door footwell to take the weight off his feet. As the days have worn on and Nick's weight and body fat have decreased, he's finding this more and more uncomfortable due to his increasingly bony arse. To celebrate reaching John O'Groats, I decide a treat is in order, and stop off at a B&M in Wick to try and get one of those gardener's kneepad things for him to sit on. However, my eye is caught by some charming pink alphabet cushions, so I find an N and a B, one monogrammed cushion for each buttock, and turn the footwell into a luxury sofa. The cushions aren't just practical, they really lend the van a touch of class, and will look and smell great once they've been soaked in two months' worth of Nick's arse sweat.

As I drew closer – just a few hundred yards away, or so I thought – we arrived at the 'Welcome to John O'Groats' sign on the way into the town and stopped for photos. Although John O'Groats is the town which marks the northern extreme of the mainland, the actual spot that is the end of Britain is a place called Duncansby Head. Andy asked me if I was going there. To which I replied, 'Where?' Once he'd explained, the answer had to be yes. We'd come this far. Duncansby Head happens to be up a bloody hill, of course, so it took a little longer to reach the end. Once up there, with various tourists hunting for shots of puffins in the early evening breeze, one chap, having noticed my running clothes, asked me, 'Are you from here? Must be nice to have this as your local spot', assuming, wrongly of course, that I was a local out on a little jolly. Andy and I looked at each other and smiled. That was pretty much the only comment I needed to feel some sense of accomplishment. I replied to the tall bearded American and his wife, 'I live in Cornwall. Near Land's End actually.'

A smattering of cars, campervans and a few tents littered the open green space by the small, white and rather uninteresting Duncansby Head Lighthouse. We marched up and touched the stone bearing the legend 'The most northeasterly point of mainland Britain'. Andy had driven up the winding roads through fields of sheep to meet me, and so as not to waste the tired van's journey we took a few minutes to wander towards the cliff edge. It was a bird-spotting paradise. We stood and stared, as all men should from time to time.

The cliffs were jagged, a sign of the harsh seas of the north. The neatly trimmed grass and carefully erected fences kept idiots like us from getting too close to the edge. We were, though, still able to just about see the ocean crashing on the rocks below. We could even feel its power beneath our feet. In those few minutes on the cliffs, I thanked Andy for everything he'd endured so far. I was serious and sincere, and he got the message. Without him I wouldn't have made it. And we weren't even halfway. In fact we weren't even at John O'Groats yet.

Back down the hill I'd just come up, then down past Puffin Farm, a small farm shop, a fire station and the information centre, and finally down a straight 500-metre stretch of unnamed road to the famous John O'Groats signpost, the one that points in all directions, showing 3,230 miles to New York and 874 miles to Land's End (the quick way), plus many more. This space, at the end of the country, is basically just a car park with a small four- or five-boat harbour taking people the short journey to the Orkney Islands. Andy and I commented on how close they looked. We were both sure the sea would be all we would see. We were wrong.

Still in a focused, semi-rushed headspace we regrouped at the vans, which Andy and Nikki had neatly parked in a quiet corner for the night, and ventured back slowly to the signpost for more photos, taking in the occasion with one eye on tomorrow. We popped a bottle of bubbly, sat on a bench and chatted, discussing the achievement so far as we waited for sunset. It felt like we had summited a mountain to reach the top of the country, but that still meant we had to get back down.

After about an hour, we realized that the sun was still not behind the horizon. The boats and lighthouse were draped in shallow light, the sky was pink, and the sea a deep dark blue, but it wasn't yet dark. We were so far north, and now in mid-June, the sun didn't really set at all. More of a slightly dimmer light for about three hours from midnight to 3 a.m. before the sun started to rise again. With that thought we retreated to huddle in the vans as it had got chilly. Cups of tea replaced the beers Nikki and Andy had finished off, and we ordered pizzas from the nearby overpriced café-cum-restaurant. Pre-bed, we completed a little 'vanmin' – aka van admin – and recalibrated the spreadsheet to check mileage. We were within 0.8 per cent of our desired target. Bingo.

We ended up having a late night, allowing ourselves the luxury of chatting for a little longer than usual, reflecting and joking as though the journey was over. But it wasn't. We got to sleep with just four hours until I needed to be out on my feet again.

I often spent about ten minutes in bed letting my mind wander. That night I shut my eyes and thought of the profound message that the butterfly teaches us. If you help a butterfly out of its chrysalis, by cutting it open for example, the butterfly will simply fall to the floor and die. It's the struggle to break free that builds the strength in their wings and therefore the ability to fly and to thrive. No struggle, no life.

7

A Wedding and a Hamstring

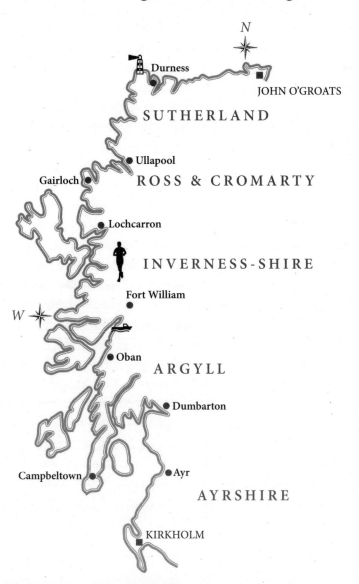

Day 63 – 53.08 miles – 3,051ft elevation
John O'Groats to Armadale Bay

It was a 52.4-mile kinda day. Or at least that was what I felt when I woke from my bed in the sky. The tent box was wind-beaten through the night, but I was cosy and warm. Like most nights, I had fallen asleep with my MyoMaster leg compression sleeves on a forty-minute cycle. After a long day running, this was by far the best post-run ritual I'd come across. If I'd had a dip tank I'd have used that too, but they are a little hard to transport.

Putting them on was like putting on a pair of baggy thigh-high boots that needed zipping up from the toes to the upper leg. Each leg is independent and made of soft silky plastic attached to a pump that inflates the outer shell at a desired rate, designed to compress and release my legs to increasing pressure. The scientific side of this is that they help defy gravity and push the dirty concentration of lactic acid-filled blood from my feet towards my heart. My heart can then pump fresh oxygenated blood to my legs. My red blood cells, and yours too, contain a protein called haemoglobin. It's this that acts as the shuttle bus for oxygen from the lungs. With my legs empty of dirty blood, the fresh oxygenated blood is free to do its thing. My body produces energy from this oxygen and releases the waste product of carbon dioxide. My red blood cells love to multitask, also shuttling this waste carbon dioxide to my lungs for me to exhale. If my body produces energy without this much-needed oxygen, however, which is often the case with high-intensity and prolonged exercise, it secretes a chemical called lactate, or lactic acid. Contrary to popular belief our bodies do need lactic acid, and it's not the lactate that causes soreness in your legs. The soreness comes from an excess or high concentration of it, so helping remove this from my legs should reduce the soreness. Got that?

I'd had a great night's sleep, albeit a short one. And my legs felt good after the overnight therapy. The day was made a little more challenging thanks to the patchy signal, which we knew would be a recurring issue in the coming weeks. Even with a route map saved offline, Andy still needed the internet to track me. On days like this, with no phone signal, we weren't entirely sure of the specifics of our route and it was harder to check in on each other's progress, so it was a case of heading back to a landmark we'd used to mark yesterday's finish point, starting from there and keeping the sea on our right. Fortunately there weren't many roads to get lost down.

Andy tried to persuade me not to run doubles. He didn't put up too much of a fight, but he tried. I had gone to bed knowing I was going to try. I felt good, I was in high spirits after reaching the top, and I knew my body could handle it. And so that was that. I did, however, forget about the hills.

Having set off, I didn't realize that it was to be another milestone day so soon after John O'Groats. Within a few miles I'd pass Dunnet Head. This was our second of the four compass points – the very north. All these different points make everything quite messy, don't they? Just to be clear, Duncansby Head is the most remote point, John O'Groats is the furthest town from Land's End. These points are the limits of the country both longitudinally and laterally – like measuring a TV screen, corner to corner. And finally, Dunnet Head is the most northerly point. Simple, right?

Our previous compass point – east, at Lowestoft – was rather outdone by Dunnet Head. Here there were puffins and gorgeous cliffs; in Lowestoft there was a shopping trolley and some industrial fumes. Each to their own.

After the bleakness of Wick and the last section of the east coast, we were all now falling in love with the beauty of the north coast. Today's route, bar another A road, was mostly along cliff edges filled with puffins, great skuas, razorbills and guillemots. As intended, I completed the magical 52.4 miles plus a little more – the first time I'd completed a double since day 20. Finishing not far from Armadale Bay at around 7.30 p.m., I admit I was tired. The 3,000 feet of climbing hadn't helped, but there was a sense of accomplishment. The trouble was, I didn't much like finishing so late. The happy hours, let's call them, were between about 4 and 9 p.m. Time to wash, eat, stretch or just watch the world go by. If I started early and ran a 48-mile day I'd be done by 5 p.m. If I started late and ran a 52-mile day, I could be finishing as late as 9 p.m. on a bad day. Andy was dubious:

> *Nick clocks the magic number around 7.30 p.m., and we set up camp in a glorified lay-by on the A ... whatever. He's now intending to return to regular double marathons, which concerns me. There is bad weather on the way, and the landscape has become more mountainous. The elevation on the mountain roads is more gradual and predictable than the erratic, uneven ups and downs of coast paths, which is much better for Nick's rhythm and being able to plan effort and judge his pace accordingly, but I still worry that daily 52s will add up to trouble. As England and Scotland play out a tense 0–0 draw in the Euros, I feel like Scotland could prove an equally tough opponent for Nick, with the head-to-head as finely balanced . . .*

It was an uneventful evening because we were all knackered, but we did have ten minutes to look at the map while I devoured two large helpings of Andy's special ravioli with Philadelphia and various canned veg. To my surprise, we were already a long way from John O'Groats. I knew I'd been running away from it all day, but because the top of Britain is so flat we had progressed along it without wasting time finding bridges to cross or skirting around firths and the like. We'd have plenty of that coming up, though. The west coast of Scotland is a mess. Like grabbing a fist full of baguette and ripping it off rather than using a knife. If you know what I mean.

Day 64 – 52.43 miles – 4,243ft elevation
Armadale Bay to Durness

It took me two weeks to run from the border of Scotland on the east up to John O'Groats, but it will take me over a month to run down the

other side back into England. As we contemplated making our way
down the torn baguette coast, we continued with the principle that
our route should hug the coast as much as possible. It was a circumnavigation, after all. The problem comes when you can't access the
land edge because there simply aren't roads or even paths, or the roads
are privately owned, or the path is overgrown, flooded, unmapped, or
leads to nowhere.

Andy and I agreed that if a headland was passable, if we could get
around it, we would try. If a coast road went to a dead end, then we'd
fall back to the next available road nearest the sea. It sounds straightforward, but at the time it seemed so difficult to map it correctly.
Andy had his work cut out adjusting and directing, often while in
signal dead spots. To make sure we stayed on track, we'd occasionally pan out and check my Strava, satisfied that we were maintaining
a nice neat line, hugging the coast, despite the occasional ins and
outs.

Miraculously, I finished another 52 miles despite torrential rain and
the ever-increasing elevation, clocking up 4,243 feet of climb, having
only turned the wrong way four or five times. Pretty good going for me.
We ended up just south of Durness, by a place called Loch Euraboil.
Which I suggested should be Welsh for 'pop the kettle on' – as in
'Euraboil, love, I'm parched.'

I was parched, despite being soaking wet, as Andy's diary recalls:

*Day 64 features some of the heaviest rain Nick has endured on the
trip so far. I stop every mile or so to see if he wants anything, but I
know that in this rain, he'll just keep going. When the weather's like
this, your body is your only heat source, and it will only take a pause
of a few seconds for Nick's wet clothes to wick the heat away from
him. He won't stop now until either the rain does, or he reaches his
full distance. I sit in my dry van and spot a bird I've never seen
before, a great northern diver. I watch this bird, also known as a
loon, as it dives for fish on the loch, completely unaffected by the
rain, while my friend, the solitary loony, runs around the coast of
Britain, absolutely soaked to the skin.*

Day 65 – 53.53 miles – 5,053ft elevation
Durness to Drumbeg
Entering the epic west

If you plan to circumnavigate Britain, by all means look carefully at
the west of Scotland. And if you can, spend longer there than you plan
to. It wasn't without its struggles, but wow was it worth it. You would
not believe how tropical the Scottish coast can look, with crystal-clear
waters and small hidden bays, especially in the freakishly warm weather we had. Inland from the coast is also spectacular, with miles and
miles of rolling hills.

Scotland, especially the far north, has a reputation for bad weather.
I'd been bracing for it for weeks, and we did have some bleak condi-
tions, but I truly feel like I was blessed to experience the best as well,
Scotland treating us to an unusually long and warm spell of weather.
It was not without its incidents though, and Andy did his best to keep
us on the right path:

> With mountains obscuring the sea view, countless sea lochs and
> inlets, and no coast path, it's easy to forget that we're still hugging
> the coastline, to the point where occasionally it becomes hard to tell
> where the sea is, and we have to check the map to make sure we
> haven't actually become disoriented.

It was only just past mid-June, so we hadn't yet reached the peak of
the heat, and in fact on the morning of day 65 it was actually cold. I
headed out with my buff pulled up over my ears and all the way over
my head. I stuffed my cap on top, followed by my trusty rusty beanie
hat – so named because it's orange and old.

The hills of the west coast were beginning to show their true selves.
I'd had a taste of it yesterday, but had even more elevation today, at
5,053 feet. I managed the full double marathon but I could tell Andy
was getting concerned about the risk I was taking in doing this. We did
not want another injury. It would derail our momentum, and with it
our mood. Up here in the deep north, no matter how much I rave

about Scotland, it can be a harsh, unforgiving place, and rather far from medical assistance.

As I ran past one of the many mountain-lined lochs we passed, Loch Laxford, I strayed on to the shingle of the beach running next to and almost on to the road. I immediately heard a loud screeching, which I now recognize as an oystercatcher thanks to my ornithology teacher Andy. In case you're unfamiliar with these stunning but apparently aggressive birds, they're waders, and to me they look like a child's drawing of a bird – black and white, with orange stalky legs and a stout bright orange beak about a quarter of the length of their bodies. Their loud, shrill shriek is unmistakable. I'd disturbed a few nesting pairs that had been hiding among the seaweed and moss near the water's edge, and they were now swooping and complaining as I ran by, dive-bombing me and essentially telling me to eff off. I apologized and got back on course. I could see Andy laughing by the van just up ahead.

I'd veered off course because I was looking down, rummaging in my little pouch to find my phone. I wanted to snap what had looked like a volcano as I ran past. It was a perfect cone-shaped mountain that I was pleased to be running past rather than over, which had been topped by a long dark cloud, making it look just like an erupting volcano.

All day, without really realizing, I'd been heading south. There were still weeks of wiggling around the Highlands ahead, but for now at least it did feel like I was actually, finally, heading for home. The boost this gave me lasted about a week, when I realized the distance that involved. And the hills.

A big hill at around 14 miles ruined my legs. Not to the point of injury, but to the point I could feel the extra fatigue in my whole body. Just drained. I'd charged up and down it without really preserving my legs or any energy. My head was in the clouds and I'd made a mistake. There were eleven hills like this through the double marathon day, yet when Andy suggested shortening my mileage a little, I insisted the double distance would be completed. This was me believing I could edge back to doubles and even beyond doubles consistently. Stopping at less than 52.4 miles today would impact my belief that I could sustain this.

I did finish the miles, and I did get to bed early. Briefly. Parked in a small gravel tuck-in just outside a tiny hamlet of no more than ten houses, we were woken up. We were in the middle of nowhere on the very edge of Scotland and hadn't seen more than about twenty cars or people all day. And yet, an overzealous village warden explained that we couldn't park overnight.

I woke up, unzipped the end of the tent box and stuck my head out to see Nikki speaking with him, trying her best to persuade him to let us stay, keeping her voice down so as not to wake me up. Nikki knew well to try and shield me from this. I am the first one to admit that I don't get on with unnecessary authority. Unnecessary being the key word here – moving two vans intending to stay for one night on a tiny patch of gravel by the side of the road, not interfering with anyone. I couldn't see his point, or understand the issue we were causing. Life is short and we are all here so fleetingly. And, of course, the time I spent calmly asking if we could stay, explaining what we were doing, and how if we upped and left we would have to put the tent box down, put away our beds and dinner plates and drive to an unknown location, only to have to come back in the morning, was time I didn't have to waste. In the end, we relented. I had four hours' sleep that night, once we'd found an alternative spot over 10 miles back down the road I'd just run along.

Day 66 – 46.07 miles – 4,399ft elevation
Loch Poll to Loch Osgaig

Going to bed grumpy is not ideal. Of course, I woke up grumpy too, and a little overtired. However, the majestic landscape pretty quickly washed away my bad mood, with cove after cove of pristine abandoned beaches, fine white sand and water that echoed the turquoise colours of Bali and the tropics.

It was also the longest day of the year, 21 June 2021. Being so northerly, between 58 and 59 degrees latitude, the sun was lingering in the sky over the heavenly beaches of Balchladich and Enard Bay, rising early and falling late. It was one of the most beautiful days so far, if not the best. Until the pains and the rain came.

Pre-run, in my forty minutes between waking and pushing the start button on my watch, the topic over breakfast was a wedding. When planning the journey in late March, I had only one significant immovable calendar event: my best mate Ollie's wedding. It was now less than a week away. With some careful planning I had structured the entire journey so I would not be too far from the venue on the wedding day. So all I would need to do is run my day, quickly change into my wedding get-up and, boom, wedding attended, and back to bed ahead of more marathons the following day. I'd miss the stag do, though. Ollie was of course understanding.

However, the smarter ones among you will have by now realized the issue. I'd made a nice, neat, carefully thought-out plan to be within driving range of the wedding on the right day. It was half the reason I'd decided to follow an anti-clockwise loop rather than the more obvious clockwise direction. But I'd got injured, and the whole schedule had changed, meaning that, with the wedding in Dorset, one of the most southerly English counties, I was now in north Scotland. And I couldn't get much further north if I tried. Bugger. But where there is a will, there is a way. And where the wedding was, I would be. Somehow.

After much discussion over many days, we gradually assembled a plan. First, there was no way around it, I'd have to miss at least a full day of running. Unavoidable. The day before the wedding, I'd run a single marathon day. We'd leave Poppy with Andy, and Nikki would drive us to Inverness Airport for a 4 p.m. flight to Bristol, where my dad would collect us and drive us to Dorset ahead of the wedding the following day. After the ceremony, we'd make an early exit from the reception around 4 p.m., and my mum and dad would then drive in shifts through the night, covering over 1,000 kilometres, up the length of the entire country, and drop us back at the van at Inverness Airport around 4 a.m. Nikki would then drive us back to where I'd last stopped my watch and I would start running at 6 a.m. to complete a double marathon, in order to keep our miles on track. Simple.

Back on day 66, still several days before the wedding, with the sun high in the sky, I completed 36 miles before lunch and stopped to eat, sheltering from the latest drizzly spell. Exhausted and feeling twinges in my Achilles, I decided to run only 10 more miles in the afternoon, instead of 16. Six miles short of a double. I cursed the warden from the

night before, though of course it wasn't really his fault. Andy's persist-
ent and sensible suggestions to 'look at the bigger picture' were right.
Had I attempted another double, even though I felt fine in myself, I
might have caused an injury that would linger and slow me down. Or
worse, force me to stop again. This was not an option. Andy and Nikki
also explained to me that the extra few hours in the evenings to find a
spot to stay, prepare food and be around each other were crucial for my
health, as well as their enjoyment of the experience. I agreed.

Days 67 to 69
Loch Osgaig to south of Lonbain

*With Nick on the throne, I'm at the little sink doing the washing-up
when Nikki drops by for her usual morning visit to see him off. As
she steps in, she greets her boyfriend in a Northern twang. 'Oh my
God, I can smell your shit through the door!' she gasps. This makes
me laugh, which is unfortunate as I'd been holding my breath for the
very same reason. It is clear that their relationship has gone past the
point of subtleties.*

Having listened to the sensible call to preserve my legs and avoid any
fun-sapping heroics, my target for day 67, and now every day after
(barring a few), would be 48 miles.

It's mad how just taking off those 4 or 5 miles changed everything.
The prospect of running 48 miles now felt like someone had asked me
to pass the salt, while 52 miles felt like what it was: running for twelve
hours and losing the entire day. As Andy rightly pointed out, it was the
time off my feet that I needed to think about, not just the time on them.
I was taken aback, because although I knew this to be true, and had
done for a decade or more, I had never felt it so profoundly before.
Ever since then, if I'm planning a challenge, I won't flippantly think of
the 'on' miles, I'll first calculate the 'off' time. This was one of the many
fundamental lessons I learnt on this journey.

In hindsight, day 67 became a pivotal day, because for the first time
since the first injury on day 6 we had a planned path to completion. A

data-led breakdown of the journey to Eden on a specific day, having covered the magic figure of 5,250 miles was now in place. The spreadsheet went from being a guidebook to our bible. I ran the miles the spreadsheet dictated, finishing each day where we'd planned in the morning. I was oblivious to the importance of doing this now and not later. Andy knew, though, that if we didn't think about it now the whole schedule would fall apart. The feeling of having a firm plan, wedding included, was more satisfying and exciting than any of the last two months' milestones. A plan meant there was no more uncertainty. I knew if I stayed healthy, and I could run 48 miles a day, the plan Andy had put together would be right.

The famous North Coast 500 route is a 516-mile scenic road that weaves around the outer edge of the uppermost section of Scotland. We had actually been on this route for about ten days now, without noticing. It had kicked in right back when we passed the northern edge of Loch Ness by Inverness. I only twigged when we started leapfrogging the same campervans time and again, as they'd park up for a few days at a time before driving on and passing us on their way to another beauty spot along the route.

The NC500, as it is known, takes you up and around the best bits of the north Scottish coast. The Northern Highland Initiative launched this tour of Scotland back in 2015 as a tourist drive to support the economy. In its first year it was voted the fifth best coast road in the world and is loved by cyclists and caravanners . . . and at least one runner. We didn't follow it completely, because we were often slightly closer to the coast, taking smaller roads and deviations to stick to our 'as close to the sea' rule whenever we could. Plus, we obviously didn't complete the inland section that closes the loop. But it was on this Scottish equivalent to Route 66 that I surpassed 2,500 miles – a fact we only realized a few days later. I celebrated by grabbing my electric razor and having a shave, using the dirty wing mirror of the van. With no reason to look in a mirror, it was very easy to forget what you looked like. Probably for the best. It was nice to have a shave though, and it did help to transform me from old tramp into slightly younger tramp.

Actually, just the slightest difference to my appearance made me feel stronger, sharper and so much better. Perhaps even faster, too.

South of Ullapool, towards the bottom edge of Little Loch Broom, rain accompanied me on my daily miles and we parked alongside the water and celebrated another day down with a firepit and beers for the others, protein shakes for me. Having missed the mileage clock hit 2,500, I would actually pass a major milestone tomorrow too – the 2,620-mile mark, which of course was halfway. An epic boost for the whole team.

The midges invited themselves to the party, while we invited Jim and Becky, two of the many van-lifer friends we'd met over the last few days. Their grey Staffie Pepper and our bounding Poppy chased each other through the ferns as we talked away the evening, blankets draped on our laps, empty plates resting on the damp evening grass. We had the glow of the van's warm lighting and the gentle crackle of foraged logs burning slowly. It was a reflective evening with friends, food and fire. Enjoyment birthed from balance.

Day 68 was the day we switched from counting up the miles to counting them down. A major shift to the soul of the mission, and I finished another 48-mile day smiling to myself, knowing that not only did it feel like I was falling down the country rather than climbing up it, but I now had fewer miles to complete than I'd already run.

The actual halfway mark passed very unceremoniously in the classic style Andy and I have become accustomed to: Andy gives me a pat on the back, we share a look of accomplishment, and off I run. I was happy to have passed the equivalent distance of a hundred marathons in sixty-eight days, sixty-one of them running days, but I couldn't help but think about what could have been. If I could have stayed injury-free, perhaps by starting elsewhere in the country, or training and stretching a little more, things might have been different. But I didn't. And they weren't. Besides, this was no time for reflecting on the journey: all of a sudden, halfway reminded me that I had to repeat what I'd just done. I think all of us were realizing, more so than ever, that despite being on the home stretch, it was far from over yet.

Day 68 was the most simple, navigationally, that we'd had for weeks. It was one road, no turns, and no junctions – such is the vast unspoilt-ness of the Scottish landscape. I just ran till the miles were done. My reward happened to be the sight of two otters, their paws linked, sharing a freshly caught fish. They were just a few feet away in shallow water, clinging on to each other to remain balanced in a small pool off to the edge of the faster-moving water of the stream. They didn't hang around long – I think something spooked them – but it was another tick on the nature checklist. We were seeing so much more raw nature than I thought we would; Scotland had been bombarding us with such moments.

Just as we'd done on many days of late, we all took a dip in the loch we'd parked up by:

Loch Maree is one of the most perfect night spots we've found so far. The sky is overcast, but the wind has dropped and it's mild and slightly humid, giving the air that soft feel. The low cloud casts the loch in a dramatic light, the surface like black glass, eerily inviting. With pebbles rather than sand underfoot, there's no risk of Nick getting grit stuck in his feet and he decides that the cold water will be perfect for icing his post-run legs, and unable to resist a swim, Nikki and I decide to take the plunge too. Like many Scottish lochs, its sides plummet away steeply to inky depths, and just four or five steps in, we're already out of our depth. The dark water is invigoratingly cold, and it's the perfect way to end the day.

This was Loch Maree, in a small pull-in away from the A832, a nice, quiet spot with signposts leading to the Glas Leitrim Trails, a walking route. The dip, for all of us, was typically short-lived. The water was freezing despite how inviting it looked. Although Andy and Nikki braved it for a few minutes, I retreated and sat on the boulders peppering the shoreline, making a seat for myself with my legs floating out in front of me, my muscles soaking up the benefits of the cold water for recovery. Nature's dip tank.

Despite being careful when returning to the van to dry wet towels and clothes, we may as well not have bothered. The following morning brought torrential windy rain, and by the end of the first 30 miles the van was littered with dripping clothes hanging off every surface available. A small purple circular plastic peg hanger, which I nicknamed the octopus, held most of my clothes, hanging from the ceiling vent. The floor of the van was the usual mix of grit, mud, sweat and water, and the occasional leaf or twig. As it happened, I was running through a place called Torridon at the time, which we all agreed was rather apt.

I'd been leaning into the weather all day, battling strong winds and rain that horizontally assaulted my face, causing me to squint. I hopped in and out of the van every couple of hours, Andy having to endure the regular sight of me peeling off soaking clothes, ringing them out by sticking my arms out of the window, and then donning the driest ones available. Nothing had been washed for a long time and most of my clothing had got to the point where it was clammy with encrusted sweat, even when it was dry. By now Andy and I not only had our little hand signals and gestures, we'd also developed the easy-to-understand phrase 'balls out' as a warning of me imminently getting changed, and giving Andy time to turn away.

I ended day 69 on 40 miles, my first under 48 for weeks. Having stopped for clothes and food at 30 miles, I couldn't decide if it was worth carrying on much more. We were running out of dry clothes, and my feet were showing the early signs of blisters. My very first step out of the van after lunch had been straight into a deep puddle, soaking my right foot up to my ankle. In the absence of anywhere to park for a while, I reluctantly plodded on until we found somewhere that Andy could stop the van and I could safely get in without the possibility of him having to move. We all discussed how mad it was that 40 miles felt like a failed day. Running 40-mile days for some people can feel totally out of reach, but for me, even in the rain, with our target firmly in mind, it felt pathetic. I was past caring, though. The rain sometimes spurs me on, and other times I just fancy a hot chocolate and bed. That's exactly what I did. My lullaby? The sound of the dripping octopus.

Days 70 to 72
South of Lonbain to north of Loch Carron

Day 70 was the first day of Project Wedding. But before we could catch our flight I first had to take on one of the biggest summits of the trip – a child's drawing of a mountain. Look at my Strava and you'll see one big equilateral triangle dominating the elevation chart, from 5 miles to 15, over a sweeping road which would rival many in the Dolomites or Alps. Never had I seen such beauty in such a barren landscape. You'd think a place devoid of trees would be either boring or empty, and yet the low-lying clouds kissed the tops of peaks for miles around, with scruffy, hard-wearing foliage living among the weather-beaten rocks, and the endless sound of water trickling off the hillsides down underground and appearing as small streams. In every direction there was a truly epic vista. A picture postcard. It was just a magical place. As I made my way towards the big climb, the nearby mountain of Beinn Bhàn dominated the view. Skirting around it, my route would take me up and over a smaller peak via Bealach na Bà (Pass of the Cattle). Despite the elevation of over 2,000 feet within just 5 miles, the going wasn't that hard, and nature was distracting me. As gangs of motorbikes roared around the valley, whizzing past me, up and away, the place buried itself in my heart. I couldn't help but stop every once in a while to take in the view. It was a tough run, but the location made it all worthwhile.

By the summit of Creag Gorm, the mountain I was running up and over, the weather had become horrendous. Inhospitable black clouds with big heavy rain and wind, savagely blowing me sideways into the crash barriers on the hairpin bends. Once down the other side, having had a brief cuppa in the van at the summit, enjoying the sound of the wind howling past us, Andy and I debriefed at sea level, looking back up at the spectacular view of where I'd just come from. Mother Nature showing off. Safe in the confines of Loch Kishorn, which even had a little shop, the sky was blue again, there was no wind, and not a drop of rain. It was like two worlds. It got our adrenalin going nicely.

Even though we were enjoying the scenery, we were on a time limit. I had to finish running by 11 a.m. in order to catch our flight from Inverness. The wedding was now less than twenty-four hours away. Having had the earliest start of the trip yet, at around 4 a.m., I completed the single marathon day, as per our plan, in six hours, including the stops for food, changes of clothes, and the 3,052 feet of hill, of course. It was one of those days, despite the weather, and because of the scenery, when I simply didn't want to stop. But we had to. Waving

off Andy and Poppy, Nikki and I made our way to the shabby airport
of Inverness while Andy headed for Loch Ness, where he was going for
a romantic dogsitting break and a trip down memory lane:

> *As Nick and Nikki head north, I head south before turning east and
> I'm soon driving down the western shore of Loch Ness. Poppy has a
> quick dip at Fort Augustus, and then we head back up the eastern
> side, retracing the route of the Loch Ness marathon, which I think
> was my first. It was a long time ago, and I think back to how daunt-
> ing a prospect it seemed to me back then, and how many times I've
> comfortably run marathons with Nick since then, thanks to his utter
> disdain for such a trifling distance.*

The day of the wedding was of course brilliantly emotional, and
worth every inch of the effort. I wouldn't have missed it. A hot air
balloon whisking Ollie and his new wife Rebecca into the sky post-
reception was naturally a highlight. A freshly dry-cleaned suit felt
somewhat strange after months of damp, stale and crusty running
gear, and for the first time in a long time I was wearing shoes that
weren't trainers. And of course Nikki looked effortlessly beautiful, as
she usually does. We had a few moments on our own, sitting in the
sun with the chatter of conversation and clinking of glasses around
us. Neither of us knew what to do with ourselves. Nikki wasn't wres-
tling a dog, driving to find an evening camp or generally keeping the
show on the road, and I wasn't running. I was just sitting in the sun
with glossy polished shoes I could see my face in, looking out on a sea
of people I adored, having just seen my oldest friend get married. It
was a surreal and magical day. We realized afterwards that most weddings go by in a flash and you remember very little. Because neither of
us was drinking, and having come from such an intense few months,
every hour felt like three. We could relish the moments. It felt surreal,
but wonderful.

I did, however, need to run the next day. Because no plan survives
first contact with the enemy – in this case, fun – we left the reception
later than planned. My parents picked us up around 10 p.m. for the
long 600-mile drive up country. Nikki and I quickly fell asleep in the

back like kids who had had too much cake at a party. Which we had. By the time we reunited with Andy, now on day 72, it was 1 p.m. Poppy gave us our usual greeting, which was a bouncing, tongue-heavy mauling, and I changed into the same old damp running gear I'd briefly forgotten all about. Being late back, by about six hours, I decided that, as I'd only be able to run reduced mileage today anyway, sleeping for the remainder of the day would be the best option in the long run. Two days of rest felt like a cop-out, but it just made sense to capitalize on the downtime. A snap decision, but one that felt right. I was in bed by 3 p.m. and fell asleep until the following morning.

As I was dozing off, Andy was checking and double-checking the numbers in his now incredibly complex spreadsheet, running various end-date prediction scenarios, factoring in the last two days. The clever formulas spat out the answer: I'd need at least 47-mile days from tomorrow until the end if we were to hit 20 August. It was doable, and ideally I'd claw back a day or two by bolting on the occasional miles when I could.

Pre-wedding, I'd more or less strung together thirty-plus back-to-back 46-miler days, and these two days out had felt like an interval to grab ice cream before the second half. I was, however, all too aware what two days off could do to the finely tuned rhythm I'd so painstakingly found.

Day 73 – 47.18 miles – 3,439ft elevation
North of Loch Carron to east of Loch Cluanie

Stepping out to resume my briefly paused routine, my legs were creaking and aching as I lowered myself to the floor, my hands gripping tightly on to the doors of the van. We were heading for Loch Cluanie, which is directly east of Fort Augustus, in line with the southern end of Loch Ness. It seemed a lifetime ago I was north of the same loch, beginning my ascent to John O'Groats. And in a way it was.

Unsurprisingly, having had a good rest, I managed the 47 miles in good time: seven hours and forty-eight minutes. I trialled a new snack-and-go approach with Andy, even walking the first mile eating a bowl of Frosties. In fact, the whole morning was a walking buffet. I had two bowls of cereal, a pain au chocolat and two bagels, all on the move. That pretty much sorted me out until halfway, when I opted for a sports doughnut, as Andy called it. It was just a regular doughnut of course, but because we were doing sport the name felt acceptable.

With a big climb towards the end of the day, my Achilles wasn't too happy with me. There is certainly a strong correlation between rest and Achilles pain. When I run, my Achilles stretches and ideally stays supple and strong if I keep running. If I rest, though, it will contract and become shorter. Restarting again is a simple but painful way of restretching it. Once through the initial adjustment it usually settles down. Usually.

Even though I had only stepped away from the landscapes of Scotland for two days, back to the short-term comforts of the village I grew up in for the wedding, returning to this part of Scotland was even better than I remembered. It was sunny too, and better still, our overnight spot was gorgeous. We could easily have been in the Canadian mountains, with a stream and long marshy grassland for Poppy to frolic in until sunset.

At one point, the stream forms a pool just about deep enough to swim in, and I'm surprised to find it's the mildest water I've swum in so far on the trip. Meanwhile Poppy locates the still articulated bones of a red deer's leg, and as she bounds around with the whole assembly in her mouth, the joint hinges back and forth as though the unfortunate animal is having one last majestic gallop through the glen. It's typically thoughtful of Poppy to give it such a fitting and dignified send-off.

Post-swim, Andy inspected the van. He'd noticed a slight bump when it was moving. This turned out to be a small bulge in the front passenger-side tyre. Not something that could be ignored – certainly not for a couple of thousand miles, or even much longer than a few days really. Finding an appointment at a garage for a new tyre was a challenge in these parts and it took most of the evening for us to discover that the van would need to be taken, yet again, back to Inverness, the only place for hundreds of miles around that had the right tyre within a reasonable timeframe. It was a hell of a drive, and not on route, something which needed to be thought about. It was now Monday evening, and the next available slot at the garage was Wednesday, giving us a little time to work out the logistics.

Day 74 – 46.24 miles – 2,255ft elevation
East of Loch Cluanie to Caol/Fort William

I blinded the rare passer-by with the sight of my bright white skin as I ran for the first time in Scotland without a top on. Being outside for such a large chunk of the daylight hours every day for over two months, your exposed areas pick up a pretty solid tan – between the days of rain, hail and sleet that is. Once I was topless I therefore looked like I'd simply swapped my regular blue T-shirt for a white one. My arms and hands, neck and face were very brown by now, but the rest of me was scrawny and hideously pale. As Andy reminds me, this caused other issues too:

> *Nikki, now in charge of photography, tells us that when editing her photos, she has actually had to reduce the colour saturation on some of them due to Nick's extreme knee and hand tan.*

Running comfortably with the sun on my skin and a gentle unScottish breeze soothing my body nicely gave me a hint of what the days ahead could feel like if summer decided to stick around. By the 36-mile mark and having now formed a plan for the pit stop for a new set of slicks in Inverness, Andy made a note to top up on more Deep Heat. My Achilles really wasn't happy about being stretched so much. We'd even resorted to the nuclear option of the special capsicum and Deep Heat combo, and physio tape for good measure. It would have been easy to stop at 36 and not risk the extra miles, but I felt that my legs would actually benefit from more miles, stretching my Achilles to the optimum position and relieving the pain. From miles 36 through to 40 I was steady and cautious, but I picked up during the

last 10 kilometres, running some of my fastest miles of the day. I'd
adjusted my stride to increase my step count, shortening each step.
This classic long-distance running method to preserve your legs is
the bread and butter of super-long runs, but it's easy to forget and
slip out of stride. I fear that's exactly what I did when returning from
the wedding. It was time to switch on again and sort it out. By 47
miles I was more or less comfortable and ready for more, but we
stopped as planned, this time next to a river that seemed to be home
to a biblical number of midges. Andy added mosquito defences to
the shopping list. Tyres, Deep Heat, DEET and, as always, more
water and more sugary snacks.

Days 75 to 81
Caol/Fort William to Crear
Clean clothes, new tyres and no Andy

The aspirationally named Tyre City, who'd promised Andy that his
make and size of tyre would be available on Wednesday morning, were
wrong. Having driven the near 100 miles to Inverness the previous
night, Andy discovered that Tyre City was more of a tyre village, and
that the required tyres would not be arriving until the following afternoon. Not ideal for the mission, and it would of course have been a
show-stopper had Nikki not been around to sub in.

As I pounded the pavement, tracking the coast from loch to loch,
with Nikki doing her job well, Andy was off with little or nothing to
do. We found out later that he was either in the pub or swimming in
Loch Ness, using his one day of quarterly leave as best he could:

*As I'm stuck here for at least the next twenty-four hours, I work out
how I can make use of my time whilst within easy reach of a city. I
stock up on (what always seems to be largely ineffective) insect
repellents and bite relief remedies, dump Nick's foul laundry at a
laundrette and head for a Tesco café with the express intention of
stealing electricity of a greater value than the drinks I will have to*

buy in order to remain there for long enough to do so. I return to the laundrette a few hours later, where I'm relieved to find that the lady who has bravely taken on the service washes is showing no signs of PTSD. Among the bags of washing was the 'bag of no return', which contained seventy-odd days' worth of Nick's fermented, dirty running socks and soiled pants. I make a mental note to find out how to go about nominating someone for a Victoria Cross.

The following morning I wander down through Urquhart Wood to find the surface of Loch Ness without a ripple, the smoothest I've ever seen it, perfect conditions for a swim. Just a few feet from the pebbly shore and I'm already treading water, and it's both discomforting and exciting to think that if I were to swim a little further out, I'd have over 750 feet of black water underneath me.

Having Nikki support me for these two days was a total pleasure. It was nice to just be our little family unit again – Nikki, Poppy and I, the wolf pack reunited. Andy returned to camp at the end of day 76, at which point he presented me with a yellow golf tee. This tee had become a mascot of sorts. Coming from the 'make do' generation, everything my parents have is well looked after, and if something is damaged, it is repaired or bodged to allow its function to continue. This yellow golf tee was mentioned in my dad's heavily detailed user manual for the van. The tee stopped the fridge door swinging open when driving, having replaced the door catch which had long since broken. This golf tee had been lost some weeks ago, and had had to be replaced with one we found lying around near a golf course, but we thought that maybe losing the original might bring bad luck. As Andy was cleaning the van, he'd finally found the lost tee, and he handed it back to me as part of our reunion. This might seem mundane, but it was another small victory to celebrate, and hopefully a symbol of luck being on our side.

Day 77 turned out to be a long and noisy day on busy A roads – an unsettling reintroduction to civilization for the first time in weeks. Having been amid emptiness and alongside serene lochs for so long it took me a while to learn to block out the roar of tyres on tarmac again. It was bland and boring, but progress was made – another 47 miles – it wasn't raining, and my Achilles had calmed down.

Over dinner, we hashed out another little plan that had been bubbling in Andy's brain for a couple of days. Since seeing the sight of Ben Nevis and its summit several times as we skirted around its base near Loch Linnhe yesterday, he was keen to find time to climb it. Or in fact run it. As you'll know, Ben Nevis is the true top of Britain, standing at 1,345 metres (4,412 feet). And so for us runners, it's hard to resist a quick jog up and back.

Andy came up with a plan that had virtually no impact on me or our bigger goal. We were spending the night at Cuil Bay, literally parked with a cluster of other campervans on the shingles of the beach, down a small dead-end road. If Andy left now he could drive to Ben Nevis base camp, stay there overnight, run at first light and get back to us as early as possible in the morning, minimizing disruption. So of course, that's what he did:

At the campsite, I make the most of the electrical hook-up, cutting my hair with clippers before having my first shower since Edinburgh. At first light the following morning, which up here is around 3.45 a.m., I force myself out of bed, put the kettle on and pack a few essentials. I'm away by 4.15 a.m. and although this is plenty early enough to beat the crowds, there are still a few early risers on their way up the track. As I pass the 1,000-metre mark, I enter the low cloud shrouding the top of the mountain, and the temperature drops. Visibility is immediately cut to 50 feet or so, creating a perverse sense of claustrophobia in such an expansive landscape. The cairns have been closely spaced to cope with these conditions, and I use these sentinels, eerie figures which even in the mist stand out starkly against the resilient patches of snow, to make sure I don't drift off track. I reach the summit in a respectable one hour fifty-four, and am rewarded with no views whatsoever.

After a five-minute breather, I set off back down, and as I drop out of the cloud and the view returns, I can see that much further down the trail is already getting busy, and in the last couple of miles the heavy breathing of big groups of walkers has infused the air with the aroma of last night's beers.

I'm back at the campsite by 7.30 a.m. and I set off to catch up with Nick, realizing that, having just run 10 miles with 1,300 metres of ascent, I've done roughly a fifth and a half respectively of what Nick did on any given day during the first week of this expedition. I catch up with him and am pleased to find that I'm just in time for a quick stop next to Castle Stalker, one of the locations used in Monty Python and the Holy Grail. *It's another little pilgrimage for me, and I make a mental note to one day visit the other castle they used in the film, where you can actually hire coconut shells . . .*

I'd begun running at 6.30 a.m., and Andy arrived by the time I'd covered 11 miles, everything having gone to plan. Nikki had subbed in for the early miles but wasn't expecting Andy back till the afternoon. I knew otherwise. Don't tell anyone, but Andy is a much better runner than me, and give him an assault course, I'd put money on him beating most people.

By 15 miles Andy had taken the reins from Nikki once more and was back in the driving seat, quite literally. It was his turn to dry his sweaty clothes on the dangling and now frail octopus. Now all he had to do was drive slowly for eight hours while I finished running. Not easy after a mammoth effort up and down Britain's biggest mountain.

The final miles of the day had us sandwiched between the Oude Dam behind us and Loch Melfort ahead of us. We stayed overnight in the tiny car park of an even smaller chapel near the village of Melfort. Somehow I'd let my right hamstring get a little tender, possibly over-compensating for the injured Achilles. I'd slowed quite a lot by the end of the day, but had made it past 47 miles without needing painkillers. It was something to watch.

With no planned alterations to our tried-and-tested routine, we went to sleep feeling this could be maintained all the way to the finish line, which was now a little over 2,000 miles away. Once again I'd not noticed that in the final mile of the day I'd hit another milestone, the 3,000-mile mark. It would, I'm sure, have been a mental boost, had any of us realized.

Day 79 was split into two halves, thanks to my right hamstring becoming more and more sore. This now left me with just two areas of my legs that hadn't been injured on this trip: my left hamstring and my left knee. The rest had either been strained, torn or broken. I could only hope that they, at least, would cling on.

At marathon distance, as I stopped for an extended break, Andy tried hard to pretend that massaging my thigh was uncomfortable for him. We all know he enjoyed it really! As ever, my legs needed attention. Because I had been running slightly lopsided in an attempt to protect my Achilles, my hamstring had got so tight that I could actually see the difference through my scrawny leg. With me lying face down on the 6-foot bench seat in Nikki's Palace Van, Andy spent about twenty minutes massaging my thighs. His experience of deep-tissue massage, I believe, is not extensive, but with a few YouTube videos assisting, his efforts were helping.

I should probably mention that we didn't have any massage oil – I mean, why would we? I was only running 5,000 miles. So we resorted to cooking oil. While Andy grimaced, running his hands up my inner thighs, Nikki found our ordeal hilarious. But frankly I'd have taken anyone's hands if it meant loosening up my leg, and it seemed to work.

Andy, though, was less impressed:

With the loosest of job titles, the unenviable task of massaging Nick's hamstrings naturally falls to me. After watching a couple of instructional videos on YouTube and taking a deep breath, I attempt to start kneading the back of his scrawny legs, but it soon becomes clear that oil of some description will be required. What follows is harrowing for both of us. Short of draining the engine, the only available oil in the van is a large bottle of cooking oil, and this turns what is already a deeply uncomfortable situation into one which has the potential to cause amnesia. Nikki watches, her laughter punctuated by occasional retching.

Nick sets off again, and although he still feels exhausted, to my horror, the massage seems to have improved the muscle issues in his legs slightly, raising the possibility of him requesting further such treatments.

Another day and another four lochs down, but my hamstring was getting worse, and I decided to pull up short of the usual 47 miles, only managing 42. I felt totally deflated not hitting the miles, but under Andy's guidance we were all very keen to avoid injury stopping play, again. I was worried about it, but judged that if I was delicate enough with my striding, it might improve. Andy went to bed worried this was going to worsen. I could tell by his demeanour that he was not only worried for my sake, but genuinely didn't want to stop the adventure. I was keen to prove I was fine.

The fifth of July, day 80, turned out to be a rather weird day. We were sure we were back in the rhythm of sustainable mileage, but the knock-on effects of taking a couple of days out for the wedding were far greater than expected.

I was 3 miles in and puffing out of my arse. I was panting and bent over like a newbie 5K runner trying to take on an ultra. I really was puffing. I was a little sleep-deprived, after a few late nights and not sleeping as well, and also likely coming down with a cold of some sort. However, Andy was right to put most of my exhaustion down to my leg. I was putting so much energy into moving forward due to my hamstring being more or less out of action. It was an effort to stand, let alone move forward. Sitting on the bed in the back of the van, it felt like nothing I could do would keep me injury-free. I desperately tried to keep my head up and be grateful for what we were doing. I just wanted to sleep and pretend time wasn't ticking. But it was, and I couldn't.

This was a stark reminder of the dangers of messing with the formula. The two-day break had interrupted what had become a very finely balanced routine, so much so that any small adjustment to it posed the risk of causing another show-stopping injury.

Swapping my shoes for the eighth time due to holes in the soles, I slipped a new pair on with a view to getting back out after my first horrible 10 miles to give it another go. That was when Andy interrupted proceedings with some news. About 100 miles back, while he'd been off sorting tyres, we had accidentally run the wrong route and missed a key milestone: the most westerly point of Britain.

Andy wasn't too bothered. I think looking after me was more of a priority. But it really mattered to me. There wasn't a chance I was going to run around the country without actually running around the country. We'd done east and north, so west couldn't be missed. We had to do this properly. All the compass points must be met. And so, in the face of protests, I insisted that we drive back the three hours to Salen on the shores of Loch Sunart, where I'd run from the junction where we missed the turning and complete the lost miles. The bit I'd missed happened to be just over a marathon distance. In my current state this turned out to be a blessing in disguise.

Day 80 was simply abandoned. There wasn't enough time to run the rest of today's miles because of the drive time to get to the junction point. Plus the drive would be crucial time for me to sleep and try to regain some energy. And that was that. We headed for Ardnamurchan with the plan to park up overnight, run the 28 missed miles the next day, and then drive back to where I'd stopped my watch today after a mere 10 miles.

The blessing came in the form of rest. While Andy drove I lay in the back of the van fast asleep. As soon as he turned the key and drove away from the small patch of gravel at the side of the road, I was out. I woke up at a little car park just off the junction we'd missed, feeling very confused. It wasn't just the normal hazy head after a deep sleep. Andy had to recap what we were doing. I was out of it. Knackered, sore, and not really functioning.

I felt terrible for Andy, because initially he hadn't really wanted to go. The road we'd missed was a tiny track only just wide enough for the van. Bar a few villages on the way, it led to only one place, a little lighthouse on a hill. This was Ardnamurchan Point, the most westerly bit of mainland Britain. We'd not gone down it originally because it was a dead end on a small headland. It was an easy mistake to make.

Fortunately, Andy had slowly come round to the idea:

Initially, this detour felt like an absurd and unnecessary complication to me, but the more I think about it as I drive, the more it actually feels like a good idea. At the moment, the last thing Nick needs is anything that will make him feel dejected, and that alone is

Above left: This photo illustrates perfectly the unglamorous side of van living. Andy sorting out my cold compression, and me trying hard to eat before I fall asleep.

Above right: A perfectly captured moment of exhaustion amid the small space we lived in for four months.

Below: Andy reminding me how far I've come, as I rest my legs while lying on the ground.

Above: My shoes mounting up. All of them worn with holes, ready to be retired.

Right: Jotting down my mileage plan for the day before the morning briefing with the team.

Below: All too often I was forced on to main roads to avoid collapsed coastal paths.

Above left: Breathtaking views.

Above right: Wearing the EarPads™ Andy made from washing-up sponges and exercise bands to block the wind noise. I was largely deaf for a few weeks on the east coast.

Below: In the middle of three weeks of horrendous weather in Scotland.

Above left: Scotland offering more bad weather, along with stunning views.

Above right: A common sight: the crew getting ready for another day.

Below: Poppy taking in the view.

Above left: Andy keeping a close watch over me as I progress around north-west Scotland.

Above right: A rare moment: Andy and I (and Poppy) running together.

Below: Resting for a moment to contemplate the view and my place in the world.

Above left: The peace of the seaside.

Above right: Nature was never far away.

Left: The crew prepping for the day ahead.

Below: My favourite photo of the entire challenge. Through a window steamed with condensation, Andy and I discuss the route ahead. I appeared at the window and was greeted with Andy's help thousands of times.

Above left: After a hundred or so days I was trying not to take views like this for granted.

Above right: A photo I've since framed. Hugh Hasting of Getty Images took this of me limbering up on a rainy morning in north Devon.

Below: Celebrating at Land's End only days before finishing.

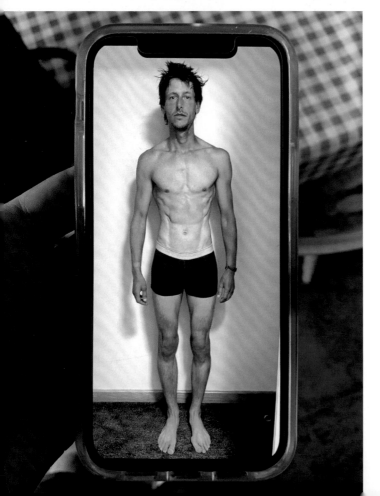

Top: The final day, 200 metres from the finish line on Par Sands Beach.

Above: The finish line gang, along with family and fellow runners.

Left: The day after finishing. I was frail, my body fat reduced from 14 per cent to 3 per cent.

a reason, but there are also other benefits. Nick is asleep within a few minutes of us setting off, so the three-and-a-half-hour journey will be good rest time for him. The route tomorrow will limit him to a marathon, which will be good for his recovery, and although he has aspirations to run more miles tomorrow after the drive back, I know with the time it will take to get back, this won't happen. He'll also be able to sleep all the way back tomorrow. By the time we arrive in Salen and pitch up in a lay-by next to the road heading west, I'm completely at peace with the plan.

In our overnight lay-by, we checked the spreadsheet again before bed. Time was getting very tight. This messy forty-eight hours would put us back, but only by two days. We could live with a new finish line of 22 August, but in order to hit it, after tomorrow, I'd then have to sustain an unbroken run of at least 47 miles every day for forty-seven days. The hundred-day target was now 128 days. A whole month late. If I was looking at this from the outside I would have probably been very blunt about it not having gone to plan at all. And it hadn't. But so far into the challenge, I was loving the misdirection and unexpected twists.

I stepped out of the van to do what became known as the Ardnamurchan Miles, along what turned out to be one of the nicest single-track lanes I have ever, and will ever, run along. Being the height of summer, the trees were in full leaf, the sun lit my way through the gaps between branches, and I was warm but sheltered from the sun and the showers which came sporadically throughout the day. The road out to the lighthouse at the end wasn't without hills, but it was stunning, bordered by flowers, ferns and lush moss-ridden stumps emerging from the woods on either side of the track. The landscape was sensational. Thick forests in a kaleidoscope of green framed barren, windswept hills, massive out-of-place rock formations to rival the blue mountains, and glens and streams teeming with wildlife. To top it off, as we made it to the lighthouse, Andy hopped out of the van and we spent ten minutes watching a pod of minke whales surfacing just off the headland. A special sight.

And what about the hamstring? I hear you ask. Well, it had been

holding the headlines for the past few days but, miraculously, and after
a big dollop of rest, I was now feeling more comfortable. I was running
balanced and even. It still felt tight but runnable. When we returned to
Nikki ahead of what would hopefully be a normal day of 47 miles, we
both looked and felt like we'd been at a spa day. Perhaps that's an exaggeration. But I was fresh despite the earlier injuries and our mood was
bright. Everything was happening as it should.

Days 82 to 90
Crear to Kirkholm

Now, I'm not sure how to say this, but there's a big section of Scotland
that looks like a cock and balls. As such, the following days proceeded
with lots of jokes which I won't repeat here. Nikki and Andy were just
as bad as each other. Me? Innocent, of course. The area I'm referring
to is, of course, the Mull of Kintyre, aka the cock of Kintyre, the Isle
of Arran unfortunately placed to look like the side profile of a pair of
testicles. If you're unfamiliar with this phallic section of the Scottish
coast, allow me to direct you. Search for Glasgow on Google Maps
and look to the west coast, zoom out a bit, and *voilà*. You're welcome.
Sorry, people of Kintyre.

It was on the left side of said penis that we spent the best part of day
82, 7 July, going down. (Perhaps I should rephrase that . . . I do apologize.) Once your mind is out of the gutter, the Mull of Kintyre is
beautiful. Running down the western edge from Kilberry to Kilmi-
chael, the A83 wasn't anywhere near as deadly as it looked on maps.
Lately we'd taken to using Google Earth to zoom in on sections during
our morning bagels to check safety, having had some tough and busy
stretches to contend with. Now, the cleansing silence and the endless
water constantly lapping at my right-hand side was bliss. The frequency
of incredibly handy pull-ins and lay-bys every mile or so meant I was
never far from Andy either. As I appeared at the window for a drink or
some food, he would be wearing a similar smile to mine. The whole
landscape was treating us. I'm really not exaggerating.

With our heads in the clouds and having fallen in love with

Scotland's west coast, my mind turned to leaving it. The laptop said this would be in two weeks' time – we would have run out of Scotland, literally. I was of course pleased we were getting ever closer to finishing, but desperate not to leave this beautiful, boundless landscape. Still, there was only one thing to do. Right foot, left foot, right foot, left foot, sleep, repeat.

Between days 83 and 90 the unspoilt beauty of the lochs and glens continued, but there were small, noticeable changes that hinted at civilization returning. Things like metal pylons appearing when for so long they'd been wooden, slightly rickety, with moss crawling up them. More buildings began to pop up too, and it wasn't long before we stopped seeing quaint local shops, instead rounding corners to see superstores and petrol stations. And people.

It felt like a gear change. Andy had noticed too, though as usual he was more concerned about the changes in me:

The morning of day 85 is warm and we're close to running out of water, which with Nick's required fluid intake would be a serious problem. This hasn't yet happened on the trip, and I don't intend to let it, but there seems to be a shortage of bottled water in this part of Scotland, and I've now tried four or five shops over the last couple of days, with no joy. I eventually get lucky in one of the many shops we've come across around here that also doubles as a post office, souvenir shop, tea room and café – typical of these remoter areas.

Day 86, and Nick is sighing more these mornings. It's less to do with physical exhaustion and more the daunting prospect of the many long days that still lie ahead and the mental toll it's taking on him. The mental side I'm not as concerned about, because there are various ways we can manage this to break up the monotony. Physical degradation is harder to manage.

Even if he can remain injury-free, Nick's now at the point where body depletion and exhaustion are catching up with him. He can't maintain the body mass and health to do this indefinitely, and I'm very aware that the closer he gets to the finish, the weaker and more susceptible to breakdown his body will become. So essentially, we need to make it sustainable for at least the next forty days, and, as such, his diet could do with a few adjustments. If you want to get a snapshot of Nick's average daily intake of 'sports nutrition', go to any seven-year-old's birthday party and look at the food table. There's no doubt that he does need a lot of processed sugar to keep him going, but he could really do with some vegetables to keep his underlying nutrition levels in better balance.

As well as food, we also need to think about kit. With only a couple of days until we are properly back in civilization, it's a good opportunity to get a few essentials ordered. Nick only has a few days of usable life left in his last pair of running shoes, and although he has spares, they're a different brand, and any slight change to his footfall at this stage is exactly the kind of thing that could lead to another stress injury.

Andy was right, of course. As the days continued, and my body suffered through the hardships you've already read about, my food intake was certainly too low. My body fat was now down to under 5 per cent. Upset stomachs and substantial diarrhoea weren't helping my weight either. Photos of me towards the end of the trip standing naked against the plain white background of a hotel room make me look like a prisoner of war. I wanted before-and-after shots of me to see what had changed. Basically, I found my skeleton again.

So, as Andy had suggested, we restocked at the first chance we got, and I resumed taking my 'daily pill packets'. This was a tactic I devised years ago when Running the World. Originally, the bag of supplements was put together to bolster my nutrition in countries where I wasn't able to access enough of the right foods. Now, stupidly, I'd just been eating all the wrong foods by choice, and so was now reacting to preserve what was left of me. This situation was made worse by the fact that I often opted to sleep rather than eat, not really consciously aware that I was missing food.

Andy pushed the idea of trying a thing called vegetables. Which it turns out are quite good for you. I joke of course, but despite actually loving vegetables, life on the road didn't lend itself well to storing perishable foods easily. And so these little pill packets were a good boost to my nutrients. I started to have a bag a day. The tablets included a multi-vitamin, cod liver oil, vitamin D, potassium, iron, spirulina, green tea, a probiotic, two salt tablets and turmeric, plus a few electro-lyte tablets in some water. This wasn't going to fix much, but it would help with energy levels, bone health and gut health, and the turmeric acted to reduce inflammation. Of which I had plenty.

By day 90 we were well and truly back in the territory of human beings rather than sheep, cows and ospreys. The greens of nature were still there, but more often hidden by the grey of concrete and industry. There were a few memorable moments as we edged slowly down towards the border with England, including Andy and the van being pelted by a swarm of giant flies as he waited for me at the side of the road:

As I wait for Nick at the final stop, I hop out of the van for a breather, and within seconds, what looks like an oversized hornet lands on the bonnet of the van with a small metallic 'dink'. On closer inspection, I'm staggered to discover that it's a fly, a full three centimetres long. As I'm photographing it, several more suddenly appear and begin swarming menacingly. The one on the van has some fierce-looking mouthparts, and they look like horseflies, so I beat a hasty retreat and close all windows. As the flies ping against the side of the van, like something out of a budget horror film, I google them, to discover they are the UK's (and Europe's) largest fly: the Dark Giant Horse-fly. Now that is a sinister name. And they're capable of administering a nasty bite. I'm perfectly happy with bees and wasps landing on me, but horseflies seem to bite me for fun and there is no way I'm getting out of the van. As Nick approaches, I open the back window a crack and tell him to just keep running.

We also got into the frustrating habit of not being able to find any-where to park. As we moved into more built-up areas, everything seemed to get a little sparse. Plenty of roads and junctions, just nowhere we could park overnight. This led to a fraught beginning and end of each day. Once I'd notched up the necessary 47 miles, I'd usually stop my watch and stumble into the van. But for a number of days we were then forced to waste a good hour or so driving around to find places to

park. Small roadside lay-bys, old abandoned petrol stations, or just
fields that had open gates – basically anything we could find. The luxury we had enjoyed of Scotland's open roads was not lost on us,
particularly Andy:

*Back in more urban areas, it generally becomes more difficult to
stop the van at even intervals, and I often have to go slightly further
than is ideal for Nick between drinks and snacks. But often, on days
like today, when he's running well, I'll often drive an extra third to
half a mile without telling him, which throughout the day will add
up to two or three fewer stops, the idea being that it gives him the
small psychological boost of feeling like he's getting through the
day a bit faster.*

*One of the benefits of being back in 'civilization' is the availabil-
ity and relative luxury of cheap hotels, and in Dumbarton, at the
end of day 87, we treated ourselves to a rare night indoors. This will
be Nick's sixth shower of the trip, which means he's now averaging
one shower every 550 miles. This isn't far off the service interval for
a high-maintenance car and, remarkably, means that a shower lasts
Nick longer than a pair of running shoes. It's a disgusting statistic,
and one that Nick is very proud of. In the warm weather, the smell
in our van can only get worse.*

There's just one more significant person to mention from this last
week in Scotland, in the form of a chap named Ju.

Ju is a Korean guy who made the special effort to come and run with
me on day 88. We met along the banks of the River Clyde, which flows
through Glasgow. It was a warm day and I was very much in my
rhythm, trudging up one of the many hills alongside the water. Ju
sidled up to me and introduced himself in a soft voice, asking if he
could run for a while. After 10 miles I'd learnt that his family were in
Korea still, but he had been given the chance to study in Glasgow to
become an anaesthetist. That was exactly what he had done. He made
a comment that he loves to run because he can chat with people and
make friends. In his work, it's important that people aren't talking. If
they are talking, he's not doing his job properly. Ju was initially quite

quiet and shy almost, but I soon discovered he is extremely smart, and emotionally aware too, which I find is a rare combo.

Andy could always tell if I was enjoying the company of the people I chatted with. I'd been fortunate to be joined most days by people of all personality types, all running abilities and all energy levels, and of course they were exceptionally kind and giving. By now I'd had over two thousand people come out and run with me, although over the past weeks in remoter areas the numbers had fallen. Some days I saw only a handful of cars, let alone runners. Ju was one of the first new people I'd chatted to in days.

By now, without us really noticing, the whole daily routine has become as second nature as breathing. The cramped interior of the van is a mess, but I know where everything is and can lay my hands on any given item in seconds. Nick and I can tell, by looking at the soles of his running shoes, exactly how many days he has left in them. I know what Nick will want for breakfast, lunch and dinner before he does. From 50 metres away, just from watching his narrow silhouette approaching in the wing mirror, I can tell from his gait how Nick is feeling, how well he's running, and from his body language whether or not he's in the mood to have other runners with him. Today, in a pretty rural spot not far from Glasgow, he is clearly enjoying the company of a runner who's just joined him, happily expending a few extra calories in animated conversation. Once I meet this runner, I'm hardly surprised. He's an absolute gent.

I have to admit that I wasn't in much of a mood to chat when Ju arrived. My manager Yas had unexpectedly left the team, having been offered a job elsewhere, with less stress and decent pay. Who'd blame her? Fortunately Danny, who had already been working hard to support us remotely from his home in Ireland, agreed to take on the role, and I had just spent hours chatting with him on the phone as I ran, to fill him in on bits and pieces. I was content with finally having some silence in order to soak in the day. As was usual, though, having a good-hearted stranger alongside lifted my mood instantly.

Aside from stimulating conversation about everything from cheese to politics, wealth and religion, Ju oozed warmth and friendliness. Andy picked up on it too during one of the many window stops when he'd hand us various snacks from the van. Goodness knows how many times items were passed in and out of that little portal to Andy's right. Every day, runners would leave bags in the van for Andy to transport until they were done with however far they were running. Ju had the awareness that he was drinking our water and that it needed replacing. This was something many runners didn't fully appreciate. I was getting through at least 5 litres a day, sometimes much more on hotter days. If we had a group of ten all having a bottle of water, we would sometimes be filling up every day. An unavoidable but frustrating addition to the daily admin.

Ju and I bonded and truly became friends over the course of the run. He left us about 20 miles in. His feet were sore and his toenails were hurting him. He was a great runner and some of the nicest company I had. All of us that evening spoke of the calming, supportive energy he exuded.

Forty-eight hours later, Ju appeared again. We were coming up to the site of the Electric Brae in south Ayrshire, a strange stretch of road with an optical illusion that makes you feel like you're rolling against the incline. It was as I was approaching a small lay-by just next to this weird phenomenon that Ju wound down the window of his car and said hello, in his typically polite and calm way.

He pulled over and opened the boot. Nikki was running with me and Andy was waiting for me in the lay-by so we could 'have a go' on the illusion road. They were equally happy to see Ju. Smiling, he hauled two huge bags of shopping out of his boot. He had used some of our water during the run a couple of days ago and felt bad about it. Ju repaid us with fresh fruit, veg, loads of water, meal deals, cookies and, better still, a collection of delights from Korea that his family had sent over for him. I don't think I really need to say how grateful, appreciative and touched we all were. It's these small gestures that make all the difference. And it didn't stop there. Over a month later, when I was coming to my final day of the challenge, he called me to say that he was planning to be there at the finish – a mammoth effort for someone with his schedule, let alone the fact that he lived in Glasgow. Sadly, even though the train and hotel were booked, there had been a shift mix-up and in the end he was unable to make it. Rather than just not be there, he wanted to give his hotel room to anyone that needed it. As it happened, I'd just got off the phone to my brother who was asking where he could stay. To all of us, Ju was an angel, symbolizing everything that is great about the world. We have kept in touch.

The bags and countless bottles of water were loaded up, with Andy already having taken the opportunity to try out the illusion in the van:

I make sure I coincide a drinks stop with the Electric Brae, one of Scotland's more unusual visitor attractions, a stretch of coast on a slight incline, with a topographical optical illusion that makes you feel like you're travelling uphill while going downhill and vice versa. Luckily, I arrive at the spot with no traffic behind me and, sure enough, when I stop on what I'm convinced is a slight downhill and let the brakes off, the van begins to roll slowly backwards, apparently uphill. It's genuinely unsettling. I park up in the Electric Brae lay-by. The runners approach and watch other people come and go, conducting their own experiments with various non-vehicular items, including a flask and a tennis ball. Poppy, registered owner of all balls worldwide, is baffled as to how these strangers can have possibly come into possession of one of her collection, and immediately tries to reclaim it.

The Electric Brae, and Ju's gifts to us, lightened the mood and we enjoyed the brief weird bit of fun rolling things up and down the hill. It was a turning point, like a signpost to a new chapter. Waving goodbye to the empty beauty of the Highlands, and hello to the reintroduction of people, a new dimension of buildings and humans – and a new kind of energy. The pace of our life shifted, with England just around the corner.

And with more people came more bloody golf courses, which really got Andy going:

Being back in more densely inhabited areas means the return of those strange little settlements you tend to find around the coast. Driving out of the town of Maidens I enter a straight stretch of road lined with large, identical, sterile-looking white houses, devoid of character and set on wide and overmanicured lawns. It's like driving through Stepford, and this soulless, uniform façade can only mean one thing: golf. Sure enough, as I pass the manned guardhouse next to the barrier (presumably there to keep people with imagination out), I see huge letters on the perimeter wall spelling out the name: 'Trump Turnberry'. Trump – remember him? No, nobody wants to.

Not only was England close, but the weather was now showing signs of a summer heatwave. We were beginning a stretch of three or four days with cloudless skies, sweat running down my back rather than rain and drizzle. Fortunately, our return to urban life was also marked by the frequent sight of pubs, many of which were perfectly placed at the end of a hot day. We took to the routine of ordering food, having a quick dip in the sea, changing, and eating and drinking until the sun went down. Me on the water, of course. It was a lovely way to pass the evenings as we meandered down what remained of the Scottish coastline. I actually shed a tear one evening as I got into bed, at the thought of stepping back into England. I was tired and a little emotional, sure, but I was overwhelmingly grateful for the magical moments Scotland had given us. I didn't want to leave. I would be sad to say goodbye to this wonderful country that had given us so much joy. But it wasn't quite over yet.

8

Goodbye Scotland, Hello England – Albeit Briefly

Days 91 to 94
Kirkcolm to Dumfries

Day 91 closed out thirteen weeks on the road. Over three months together. Thirteen weeks of peeing in bottles, bagels for breakfast, meeting and making new friends, soaking in the coastline, and taking on the extremes of British weather. Through it all, we'd kept each other going, we'd formed and reformed routines, and we had of course overcome injuries, route amendments, team changes and extreme pain, sickness, weight loss and exhaustion. The phrase 'what doesn't kill you makes you stronger' comes to mind. And strong is exactly how I felt four days from reaching the border.

Heat was the headline as I rounded the Galloway Forest, from Ayr on the Firth of Clyde all the way to Gretna Green, where we'd pass the 'Welcome to England' sign in a few days. This headland looks out over the Irish Sea to Belfast. We couldn't see it of course, it was just too far away, but we knew it was there. The Isle of Man just south of us too.

It was on the hammerhead-shaped loop at Stranraer that Andy took a rare day off to brave the full distance with me. Only Aussie Andy had taken on the near 50-mile day with me so far. We'd had around thirty first-time marathoners, who I was honoured to have had accompany me, but only Aussie Andy had managed the whole distance from morning to night.

We had been waiting for the perfect day to leave the van in a place we could loop back to. We wanted to avoid a double shuffle of vans, having to get a lift back to a van abandoned 50 miles behind us, because it would eat into our precious downtime. Here was our chance. The Stranraer Hammerhead was about 48 miles, and with Nikki subbing in to Andy's job for the day, we could finally share some longer miles together. It just so happened to be turning into the hottest day of the year so far.

It was a pretty flat day with constant views over the sea, with small lanes and roads that would have been dangerous if there'd been any traffic. The hammerhead was like an island. Although connected to the mainland, there was very little reason for anyone to be here, unless they were local residents. By 7.30 a.m. the sun was already causing us to sweat, and shortly afterwards heat haze could be seen on the tarmac in the distance. The day took us along quiet roads skirting farmland and rolling gentle hills. We could have been in Devon. With Andy for company, the hours flew by. Our lunch break, sitting in the van with Nikki, was spent talking about all the things Andy hadn't yet appreciated. I hadn't been driving at all, and Andy hadn't been running entire days, so our experiences had been similar but still very different. Andy was now closer to the coalface. He was feeling as sore as I was, or thereabouts at least. And he hadn't fully understood the lack of time I had to eat or do anything during the day. Andy's perception of the various stops I was having to snack and drink was that they seemed long, or at least not brief. Now, running an entire 48-mile day with me, he realized that I was stopping for the bare minimum time required to take on fuel. It looked like I was just taking it steady when in reality, on most days, I was fighting to finish the day before dark while consuming the required calories. Time was incredibly short. We had expected simply to have a jolly day in the sun together, but it was so much more than that. We exchanged perspectives, I suppose, and of course we spent hours speaking to each other, which for months hadn't really happened despite the fact we were sleeping a couple of feet away from each other most nights. It was a blessing to have the day to ourselves.

Needless to say, Andy's legs were more sore than mine the following day, but he kept it quiet:

We finish the day just shy of 48 miles, and I'm glad to have stuck it out for the full distance, partly because it's been a really enjoyable day and it's good to know I can still run that far, but mainly to experience firsthand a fraction of the relentless, gruelling punishment Nick is subjecting himself to. For me, the thought of being

*back in the van tomorrow is a huge relief, but Nick will be repeating
exactly what we did today and, barring injury, every day for the
next month or so. Every. Single. Day.*

Having enjoyed those easy miles together, the next morning I felt
like I was hung over. The heat and possibly drinking less than I should
had wiped me out. Although it had been the hottest day of the year so
far, it actually turned out to be the coldest day of the week. Tempera-
tures just kept ticking up as the calendar rolled on.

It was during my morning 'hangover' that Danny called to remind me
I had a Sky News interview later that day. I was in the middle of having
a shave, using the wing mirror to find the bits I'd missed. I looked utterly
terrible. Dehydration, along with lack of sleep and exposure to the sun,
had turned my face from that of a teetotal thirtysomething into that of
a drunken seventy-five-year-old. The wind, sun and grit had had a harsh
effect on my now weathered appearance, lack of sleep contributing to
the heavy black bags under my eyes. My hair was greasy and I looked a
mess, but it went well and provided another boost of support.

For these couple of days I had no idea where I was. The routes were
better suited to Andy giving me junction-to-junction direction, so I
didn't bother looking at the map at all. I kept expecting to hit the border any moment, even though I knew it was still a long way off. Still,
we were making good progress:

*As Nick climbs into the van at his finish point in Wigtown, the evi-
dence of his improved pace can be seen on his chest, which looks like
a car windscreen, covered in dozens of tiny, unfortunate flies that
have perished in his revolting cocktail of suncream and sweat.*

The day before the border, day 94, we could see mountains across
the water. I hadn't really twigged what I was looking at, and neither
had Andy. At least not until he double-checked the map. It was the
peaks of Cumbria. The loop around the headland had taken us to a
spot where we could see across the water to England. This was the
motivator we all needed, and it gave Andy another reason to reach for
his binoculars:

From a stop on a pretty road with a good viewpoint, I'm treated to stunning views of the Isle of Man, looking more Lost World than Manx TT, its hills rising dramatically from a bed of sea mist. As I look south-east, I suddenly realize that the mountainous terrain I can see in the distance is Cumbria. It's great to see somewhere so familiar to me, and an exciting reminder of how close we are to England. I immediately start trying to pick out the fells I know from their distant profiles.

The mood in camp was now one of countdown. England had felt a long time coming. As the crow flies we were so close, not only to England but actually Land's End, which was just 480 miles away in a straight line. But I am not a crow and would be going the long way.

Day 95 – 47.21 miles – 1,266ft elevation
Dumfries to Beaumont (via the all-important Gretna Green)

On Tuesday, 20 July, at around 2 p.m., having covered 35 miles in blazing sunlight, we crossed the border. All of us expected to feel a big sense of achievement, but it turned out we were all just thinking the same thing: let's get to Wales now. Such were the energy levels, in true expedition fashion the next milestone was always more exciting than the one we were passing.

There was less fuss about Gretna than I was expecting, just a few signs, and of course the famous chapel. What did hit me was the thought of thousands of teenagers running away to get married, Gretna of course being famous for elopements. The Lord Hardwicke's Marriage Act came into force in England in 1754, preventing under-twenty-ones getting married without parental consent, and that's when Gretna became synonymous with young, slightly illicit weddings. It was simply the first easy-to-access village with a chapel over the Scottish border. In Scotland at that time a boy as young as fourteen and a girl as young as twelve could legally marry without parental consent. All that was needed was two witnesses, with almost anybody having the authority to conduct the knot-tying, including the 'Anvil Priest', a blacksmith local to Gretna Green named Richard Rennison, who conducted over five thousand ceremonies.

Next to the little pebble-dashed chapel that was more of a register office than anything was a John O'Groats-style signpost with various arrows to far-flung places around the world. It was right next to the main road, and even on a sunny day it was all a bit drab.

With suncream and sweat dripping down my back, I plodded on towards Carlisle, where Nikki made a detour to pick up four more pairs of trainers to see me through to Cornwall. I was now on pair nine, having swapped a couple of pairs early because of the heavy rain or in an attempt to support my hamstring issue a couple of weeks back. None of us had much energy any more and were back to wishing the days away, a habit we knew we needed to kick.

With the sun still warm long into the evening and all of us drained by the fact we'd made it over the metaphorical hump, we were gifted a post-run blessing in the form of a pub. My watch clocked 47 miles, but there was nowhere obvious near my end point to stay, so I sat on the bank of the River Eden, just past the village of Beaumont, while Nikki scouted out a place and sent me the pin. It was only half a mile down the road, so I told Andy and Nikki I'd walk. By the time I got there, not only had Nikki popped the tent box up and prepared my bed, but she'd used her charms to persuade the landlord of a local pub to let us stay in their front field. I was craving a pizza, and by chance they made their own dough and had an outdoor wood-fired oven. Perhaps the world was gifting us all a reward for finally seeing off Scotland.

Day 96 – 47.09 miles – 910ft elevation
Beaumont to Maryport

By now the world of social media was taking more and more notice of what we were up to. One person who'd followed my challenges for a number of years was a lovely woman called Lauren. She was the first person to see me that morning as I stuck my head out of the tent box with my hair looking like a tangled, matted mess, and my eyes only half open. I wish I'd captured those daily first sightings as I emerged from my cocoon on the roof because I'm sure the various outfits and facial expressions would have revealed a hideous descent in terms of my appearance.

Once I'd changed and eaten breakfast, Lauren appeared from the car park just behind us. I'd not seen her as I emerged; like I say, I was rarely awake until 10 miles down the road. She'd seen me though, as I'd stepped out in my dirty clothes, holding a fresh bottle of piss. What a lovely way to start a day together.

It turned out not only was she great company but it was her twenty-sixth birthday. And you know the significance of that number. She'd never run a full marathon distance either, so of course the goal was set, even if she wouldn't confirm it out of fear it might not happen. Her parents had dropped her off in the morning and would be collecting her at the end of the day. Apparently, this was her birthday present to herself. She'd been eyeing the calendar, waiting for me to run through. I was honoured, of course. A day running with me really wasn't very special though. Still, if you want to run your first marathon, then to do it on your twenty-sixth birthday with someone who's knackered is a smart way to ensure the pace stays slow.

According to Strava, this was the neatest, most tightly coastal route I'd run in weeks. It was also surprisingly flat. A real treat. From the pub by the river with the glorious pizzas the night before, a series of single tarmac roads lined with out-of-control midsummer hedgerows took us winding southwards, all the way to Maryport. Barring a few towns, this was it for the whole day. Lauren and I had the roads to ourselves.

I have to say it was one of the nicest, most relaxed runs of the whole journey. The sun was out, and Lauren and I trotted along talking. She was smart, thoughtful and, importantly, aware of the feelings of others around her. And just like Ju, she downplayed her running talents right up to the line. There were a couple of miles of mild suffering on her part with me picking the pace up a little to drag her to a decent finish time, but that was it. A day running in the sun with good company. I almost forgot about the 1,500 miles still ahead of me. Not quite though, as I plodded on until the sun went down. We were further south now, moving towards the end of July, and the evenings were shortening by the day.

Ever since about day 15, the first thing runners would usually say to me when meeting was 'I was expecting you five days ago', or 'What happened, weren't you supposed to be here earlier?' Naturally my responses to these innocent but brutal comments ranged from gritted politeness to short and frustrated snaps. Over the next few days, as I worked my way south, I had more and more people join me, and I tried to respond to such comments with a joke instead of a couple of words beginning with F and O. Thank you, everyone, but I was well aware I was behind schedule.

When not struggling with broken bones or hallucinations, I generally love running with other people and hearing their stories. The running community really is a community. We – Andy, Nikki and me – had been fortunate enough, for a while, to live in our own little bubble, largely free from the usual day-to-day human interactions. For a time we enjoyed a profound sense of freedom, feeling closer to nature and the island we live on, a connection that is so often obscured by human activity. It was a rare opportunity. But we also form so many of our experiences from a direct or indirect interaction with others, and it was great to be surrounded again by a growing number of wonderfully friendly and selfless people who had come to share our journey, giving up their time to help me clock up the miles.

Over the last few miles of the day, I felt like I'd uncovered the secrets to happiness, such was the newfound appreciation of what I was getting from running and chatting with people. And it couldn't have come at a better time. Nearly a hundred days deep, the thousands of great people who had turned out so far had joined together to form a patchwork of understanding for me. I felt blessed. And if you haven't noticed, I fell in love with running all over again.

We made camp in a reflective and appreciative mood, mindful that we needed to soak in every aspect of this experience, with Andy taking every swimming opportunity he could get.

After ruling out a swim a few hours ago due to the sea being further away than I could be bothered to walk, I open the blinds for one last over the Solway Firth at the sun setting over Scotland. I find that it's now high tide and the sea is only a few metres away from the van. I'm already in bed, but generally, if I'm presented with the option of doing something or nothing, I'll always choose something. Otherwise you never know what you might miss out on. The shallow water is balmy, and at gone 10.30 p.m. I have it all to myself, floating on my back as the very last of the red glow disappears behind the Scottish hills.

Days 97 to 99
Maryport to Morecambe
Reaching day 100

I had just 145 miles to run to reach day 100. Having finally completed Scotland, I was in good spirits, but in the midst of a searing heatwave, ongoing dehydration was causing potential concerns. The cumulative effects of daily calorie deficits were also weakening my engine. My body was well and truly degrading. This was now a far greater threat than any one injury.

During this time Andy and I managed to lose each other for about two hours. This was my fault: I'd forgotten to tell him I was in the pub. Mid-run, and with no phone service or 3G, I rerouted myself to the nearest pub for an important phone call that I'd missed once before because of bad signal. I must admit this caused a mild panic for Andy – something which I should have thought about at the time and didn't. We did eventually reunite, although he wasn't too pleased. He'd taken the decision to drive on and wait on the mapped route I was following, driving far enough ahead to a point I couldn't possibly have reached in the time since he left me. It was a smart move, and one that paid off. The slight issue, though, was that Andy was standing outside in the sun on a baking hot day waiting for me. It really was very hot, so hot that the tarmac in the small lay-by had melted and congealed on the bottom of his shoes. I arrived to see Andy sitting on the step of the van in bare feet, scraping chunks of tarmac off the soles with a knife. It was a lost cause – the shoes and the road had become one. Rather fitting, I think.

Regrouped and back on track, I finished the daily miles opposite a small dairy farm. It was an ideal place to stop, giving us a final glimpse of peace and quiet before the inevitable big towns and seaside resorts which were up ahead. There was a tatty sign affixed to an old gate leading to a field. It read simply 'camping see house'. An old boy in classic farming attire, a little hunched and long in the tooth, explained that for £8 we could stay till the morning and if we needed to use the toilets or to have a shower we should walk through the yard and turn left. For those of you reading this freshly washed, you may not fully appreciate the look we gave each other. Did he just say the magic word? Did he just say *shower*? Surely not. True to his word, there were two cubicles past the yard and to the left. We took it in turns to shuffle over from the field, across the narrow lane and into his little farm complex. Other than some menacing barking from an unseen dog, we couldn't have asked for a better spot, and all of us enjoyed the rare treat of a proper wash.

Although a shower was refreshing, it always felt like I was being stripped of my medals. The thick layers of dirt I'd been carrying around with me for months, symbolizing progress and purpose, were gone. I was now just a clean, scrawny human. I had a full shave too. Nice, but we kind of missed being dirty. With our bodies clean, Nikki suggested we keep our insides clean too. A healthy meal? What was this nonsense?

With Scafell Pike, England's highest mountain, now very close by, Andy couldn't resist the next of the Three Peaks. He set off while it was still dark for another epic early morning, made even better by the view he was treated to at the top. Once Scafell Pike was summited, the door was open to complete a very slow Three Peaks challenge, the last of the giants being Snowdon, Wales's highest mountain.

I'm up at 4 a.m. to drive the forty-five minutes to Wasdale Head, for the second leg of my one-at-a-time Three Peaks challenge. It's a beautiful, still morning, and as I approach Wast Water, England's deepest lake, wispy mist hangs low over the fields. As the Google Maps background flicks from night to day, marking official sunrise, I'm alongside the lake, where the sun won't rise above its mountainous surroundings for a while yet.

I'm up at the top of Scafell Pike in a little over an hour, where there is nobody else about apart from two ravens perched on the summit's cairn waiting to pick at my corpse. After a five-minute rest to take in the utterly breathtaking views I missed out on at Ben Nevis, I apologize to the ravens for denying them their breakfast and get back to the car park. As I drive back alongside the crystal-clear Wast Water, I can't resist a quick swim. The water is perfect. I could stay here all week, and it's so hard to tear myself away, but there's work to be done, and I'm back with the others by 8.45, to find Nick already feeling the effects of the heat.

By now, I'd accrued a 50-mile buffer to the required mileage. This didn't mean I'd run too much, and it certainly didn't mean I could take a day off. It simply meant that I had run 50 miles more than our new plan stated, based on where we were. It basically meant we had 50 miles in the bank if our route diverted or changed from here to the finish. This wasn't much, but it gave us the confidence to be able to simplify the route if necessary.

As it happened, the routes around Lancashire were unlikely to need changing for a while, as we were now back in the land of seafront promenades and esplanades. The first big seaside resort was More-cambe, where we bedded down for night number ninety-nine. Morecambe Bay, like many of the seafronts around the west coast, has the feel of being a little down on its luck, with the obligatory arcade with broken neon lights sitting next to closed business fronts and a cluster of kebab shops all claiming to be both the cheapest and the best.

The shabby, semi-rusty, semi-crumbly buildings had been eaten up by the annual dose of sea salt. Copper oxidized to green, and white-wash flaked to mouldy grey. Beyond the hefty sea wall, the beach was just a bed of seaweed stretching to trawlers and a murky horizon. These towns had character, and I did enjoy running along these fronts, but there was a faded grandeur to them that made it feel like their best days were in the past.

The A road that tracks Morecambe Bay was our spot for the night.

We even ventured into town to find fish and chips and ate them sitting on the sea wall.

Day 100 – 47.36 miles – 1,169ft elevation
Morecambe to Fleetwood
Not the finish line

Day 100 – the final day! Assuming Nick can cover the remaining 1,300 miles by midnight. The original end date is a bittersweet mile-stone. To be this far north when Nick should be rolling into the Eden Project is obviously disappointing, but the fact that he's still going and on target to achieve the complete circumnavigation in what's still an astonishing time, despite the injuries he's sustained, is remark-able and genuinely uplifting.

Waking up on day 100, we celebrated with an extra cup of tea and double bagel. Jam and peanut butter. I'd expected to feel quite deflated when day 100 finally came around, for obvious reasons. But there was no point focusing on the negatives, and we had twenty-eight more days to enjoy before reaching Eden. Exactly four weeks of coastline to explore.

First things first, though. The reward for reaching the hundred-day mark was a dead arm. We'd been in Scotland for so long that this was now our first opportunity to have our Covid jabs. Naturally we were concerned about side effects impacting the now comfortable routine, but it would simply have been irresponsible of us not to have them as soon as we could. Getting jabbed was a no-brainer. It was, however, rather inconvenient.

For the first 13 miles under blue skies, the sun drowning me in white light, I quite literally ran to get my jab. Around the Heysham headland, looping back north following the River Lune upstream into Lancaster, I had everything crossed that there would be no queue so I could walk straight in. By now we'd been away from Eng-land for long enough for the walk-in venues to have opened. We'd checked online most evenings in the lead-up to the border and worked out this was one of only a handful of places within a mile or so of the coastal route that I could run to. It would have been possible to finish early and drive somewhere, but that would have meant driving back and generally wasting time. This would, if all went to plan, have little or no impact on the day and therefore the rhythm of the final weeks.

In Lancaster Town Hall, to our surprise, we were able to complete the various checks, navigate the flow of procedures, receive our arm-numbing dose and get out the other side within twenty minutes. Having turned up in running gear, only stopping and saving my watch data as I entered the building, I was sweaty and very obviously a runner who had just been running. Sitting on the little plastic seat with my sleeve rolled up, answering their general questions, the lovely ladies who jabbed me asked where I'd run from. I told them Cornwall. They laughed and looked at me, not sure if I was mental, probably assuming I was joking. I corrected my answer, saying, 'Nah, I've only done thirteen miles from around the corner this morning.' They gave me the same look and replied, 'Thirteen miles? Wow, that's a half marathon, isn't it? Do you run a lot?' I nodded and said, 'Yeah, a bit, when I'm next to the coast.' And that was that. Jab done. And absolutely no side effects. Andy was fine too, Nikki a little sore-armed, but all in all an alarmingly easy process. We were all expecting to feel the effects, but they never came. I finished the day feeling as I had for the past few weeks, tired but physically fine, my heart rate not reaching much above a hundred.

The 35 miles in the afternoon were a series of complicated back roads with junctions every few hundred metres. A pain for Andy as we'd got into the habit of a simple system where he would stop at every junction that required action. If I came to a junction and Andy wasn't around, I knew to go straight on. Simple as that. It was a hot afternoon too, the forecast predicting 32°C in the not-too-distant future. But thankfully the going was rather flat as we passed through Fleetwood, our last town of the day, having crossed the River Wyre 10 miles from the end.

Day 101 – 47.24 miles – 640ft elevation
Fleetwood to Southport

Compared to the unspoilt Scottish countryside, these few days were an assault on the senses. All those times we'd wished for a supermarket, café or petrol station when we were in the middle of nowhere had come back to haunt us in the form of urban jungles of concrete, plastic and diesel fumes, and candy-floss seaside resorts.

Ten miles south of Fleetwood, having trotted the distance on the flat promenades largely without noticing, we'd suddenly found ourselves in a wonderland of brash fakery, neon signs and bright lights. Had we wandered into a child's drawing of Vegas? Just like the feeling you get when you step into a foreign country and don't even recognize the alphabet, I was bewildered and unsettled, but couldn't help but stare. Welcome to Blackpool.

Blinded by the gaudy signage and unsure where to look, I opted to admire the tram lines that crossed the pedestrian walkways and roads. The sky in front of me was actually rather pretty as the tangles of cables dangling overhead swayed with the wind. To my right, the sea looked rather bleak. To my left, it looked like a sculptor had decided to put away the specially designed tools of his trade and instead use his feet and a spoon for this particular creation.

I have to say, I didn't love Blackpool. Andy was at least a little kinder on it:

Big seaside towns mean esplanades, promenades and seafronts, which as far as I can tell are all the same thing. For running, they're perfect, usually flat and smooth, with easy navigation and traffic-free paths. This was how I'd pictured most of Run Britain before we started: Nick keeps the sea on his right, while I drive ahead a few miles and read a book or sunbathe until he arrives. While this was a wildly optimistic view of how the proceeding few months of my life would pan out, when the routes are straightforward we do take advantage of it, and while he hugs the seafront, I drive off to get fuel and a few supplies, safe in the knowledge that Nick can't get lost.

I make my way through another funny little seaside residential suburb, a maze of classic 1960s bungalows, with roads aspirationally named after places they are not, in this case Lake District locations, none of which are even visible across the water. These humble dwellings, many of which have little faux grandiose additions like statues and porticos, have a very certain British charm, and are, if nothing else, optimistic.

As I drive back to the seafront and head south, something tells me I'm on the edge of Blackpool. There are suddenly lots of lights and plastic effigies of children's TV characters. Even Sooty and Sweep are represented – I thought they'd long since retired. It's all slightly unreal and bewildering, like a curry house dessert menu. On my left is a large building, either a hotel or block of flats, a flat-faced 1970s edifice of rendered blockwork, with first-generation PVC glazing. The only real features are protruding corners with slightly higher elevation and a row of crenellations running along the top of the building, in the most rudimentary attempt to make it look like a medieval castle, yet apparently enough to allow it to be named as such. It makes American recreations of medieval England look authentic and historically accurate.

Is Blackpool the seaside-iest of the seaside towns? The whole place feels like it's made of sugar and plastic, and nowhere else on the British coast has Nick looked so incongruous while running. In its desperation to be the British Vegas, but on an NHS budget, the whole place has a whiff of broken dreams about it, and why anyone would come here on purpose is beyond me. But in this town I'm the odd one out. Everyone who's here on holiday enjoying themselves would probably be baffled by my choice of destinations. By the time I pass Nick as we head out of Blackpool, I feel like I'm starting to like the place.

Still wide-eyed with amazement and confusion, we left the big seaside town behind as the coast took us inland towards Preston, where I was joined by more runners. As usual it was good company as we picked our way through the places between places. Having been treated to the best of the British coast, we were all keen to get this urban section done and get away from the hustle and bustle.

The following day started off in much the same vein in the seaside town of Southport and ended in the very different yet similarly veneered towns of Cheshire, Merseyside separating the two. My mum had lived in Ormskirk, her nearest beaches being Formby and Crosby, so as much as these weren't my favourite places of Run Britain I was actually rather fond of them.

We passed various attraction complexes dotted between seemingly normal terraced houses. Today's gated netherworld was named 'Pleasure Land', where I was certain I would have to try harder to find pleasure than I would outside. Andy dryly pointed out that Grimsby, almost exactly due east of here on the opposite coast, isn't the most grim after all, just the most honest.

Andy's route planning had been immaculate, but even the best of us make mistakes. Our route had us going over the River Mersey by bridge. That's what it looked like on the map, but as we got closer it turned out to be a tunnel, and not one I could run through. There were a few ferries taking commuters over, so with Andy having realized the mistake and calling to let me know, I was happy to find myself one as he went through the tunnel to wait for me on the other side.

I made my way through a little maze of terminals and private gated boatways, meandered along the waterside and eventually made it to the ferry. I bought my ticket and was aboard in no time, keen to sit down and scoff the flapjack and hot chocolate I'd hurriedly ordered at a snack kiosk. The weather had changed from sunny to grey and overcast, all within an hour or so. As the ferry's engines rumbled away under us, still moored to the harbour as the final passengers stepped aboard, I called Andy to say I was on the boat and I'd see him in less than ten minutes. It wasn't a long crossing, but a bit of faffing to allow people on and off would take time. We were drowned out by the boat's PA system announcing departure. Which is when I realized I seemed to be on a river cruise instead of a ferry: the PA commentary was reeling off historical bits and bobs about the Mersey and the city of Liverpool. We immediately erupted into fits of laughter at another classic Andy and Nick balls-up. We were trying to make efficient decisions for the daily mileage and I'd booked a pleasure cruise on the Mersey. Typical.

I later found out, having hounded the staff in an effort to under-stand what the hell was going on, that due to Covid the cruise and commuter boats had kind of merged to allow social distancing across a greater number of vessels, each with reduced capacity. The cruise was now the same price as the commuter crossing, but the commuter cross-ing would take a mini tour up and back before dropping people off. Obviously one of those good ideas made around a boardroom table that in practice is terrible.

Refuelled and informed, I disembarked to friendly greetings from a merry bunch of very soggy runners. Finally out of the industrial maze of Merseyside and into the suburbs of the Wirral, I made good use of the long, flat promenades. I felt like Pac-Man eating up the never-ending miles of these stretches.

It wasn't long before signs telling us we were entering Cheshire started to appear, and as such I knew my day's running was nearly over.

Day 103 – 47.36 miles – 1,404ft elevation
Heswall to Colwyn Bay
Leaving England, entering Wales

Wales just kind of appeared. We had become so used to the twisty-turny coast of Scotland and spending weeks trudging down and around numerous headlands that Wales seemed to come suddenly, the smoother coastlines of the north-west working in our favour, even if I did berate them for their Vegas-style beachfronts.

It took 103 days, but we also found the best runner of the challenge so far. Having had thousands join me, and although it wasn't a compe-tition, Heidi knocked Aussie Andy into a close second.

Unable to find a spot to park up near where I'd finished the day before, on the morning of day 103 we drove back to pick up from where we left off. As always, this was the exact place where I'd stopped my watch the day before; in fact it's usually 10 metres or so further back to provide a little safety overlap. Doing stuff to provide proof for various records in the past has taught me well, and for my own sake I wanted to know without a doubt that I hadn't missed any bit of the country. I was going to make sure my end of the deal held up. I might have been injured and had to slow down, but I would complete what I'd set out to complete, and I would have the proof.

We found the starting point, rejoining the Wirral Way just north of a little inlet of the River Dee, near the village of Heswall. Pulling up, Andy chucked the van on to the left-hand side of the single-track road. There wasn't much room for another car to get past, in fact probably not enough for a motorbike, so Andy tried to usher me out quickly so as not to hold up any potential traffic.

No cars turned up, but neither of us had noticed there was already someone waiting for me by a little bridge over the old railway line. Exactly where I'd stopped the day before. I'd more or less fallen out of the back of the van with my hands still covered in sanitizer and my shorts not really pulled up properly when I came face to face with this poor unwitting runner looking rather timid. It dawned on me then that she would have certainly been within earshot of me chatting and joking with Andy while I was getting ready. I wasn't sure what I'd said, but our conversations were not usually for the rest of the world to hear.

This now rather scared-looking runner introduced herself as Heidi, a veterinary nurse who had lived on the Wirral all her life. Five foot three and petite with blonde hair in two pigtails, she was keen to share some miles together, and her running bag gave me a clue that she knew what she was doing. She'd run a marathon before – only once, she said – and was keen to run another today. And she managed it with ease. The first 26.2 miles of the day went by at a decent pace, the result of the flat Wirral Way cycle path and us chatting away the miles. By this point Heidi was showing me up. She hardly broke a sweat.

We were getting on really well, enjoying the day. The weather was frankly annoying, neither sunny nor dry for long periods, but several miles in we realized we'd passed into Wales and must have missed the 'Welcome to Wales' sign. I hadn't even remembered it was coming up. I'd come off the fast, horrible A road to avoid the lorries, choosing a footpath through the woods, and missed the all-important 'Croeso i

Gymru' sign. The first I knew about it was Andy saying, 'Well done mate, you're in Wales.' It didn't matter, I was elated we were now on the penultimate phase of the trip. England phase one was the big leg up to Scotland, the second was Scotland itself, then briefly back in England, and now Wales. Finish Wales and we would nearly have finished the journey. In my head I had somehow forgotten quite how much jagged coastline there is in Cornwall. For now at least.

Once Heidi and I had completed marathon distance, the plan was to look for a train station so she could get back to her car. But with no station immediately available, she ran on a little further. It didn't take long for me to persuade her to go to 50 kilometres, a milestone she'd not reached before, and a nice round number. The miles ticked on. We passed Flint Castle, the towns and villages of Bagillt, Greenfield and Rhewl, the beaches of Talacre and Prestatyn, and made our way through Rhyl all the way to Abergele.

Despite the headwinds and a huge thunder and lightning storm coming in off the sea for the final miles, Heidi had casually run 47.36 miles in a time of eight hours and twenty minutes – very impressive for a first-timer. A long way from home and now soaked and cold, we swapped some clothes over and packed Heidi off to the station with some snacks before finding a spot for us to stay. It turned out Nikki had found a suitable place just up the road, which overlooked Colwyn Bay.

Having said goodbye to Heidi, we kept in touch, as I did with a good number of the runners who came out to join me. Spending nearly 50 miles with someone, or even just 15 miles for that matter, is a sure-fire way of getting to know them. Rarely in normal life do you meet people and bond so quickly, but suffering together does this and you get to see the grit and passion in people. Heidi has heaps of it.

We pulled up in Colwyn Bay just as Nikki's parents arrived. With the rain still intermittent we opted to avoid sitting on the windy sea-front where fog had now started to descend, and instead bundled into the Palace Van, Poppy barking and jumping as usual.

While tucking into our food and catching up, we also had a surprise visitor. Dan. Remember Dan, who was doing the figure of eight around the country on his bike? Well, he was cycling past, having covered many more miles than me by now. Being the brilliantly kind chap he is, he had been following my tracker and knew we'd stopped up ahead. He appeared with three or four big bars of Galaxy for me and the team, our knight in shining armour on his pedal-powered horse.

9

A Fortnight in Wales

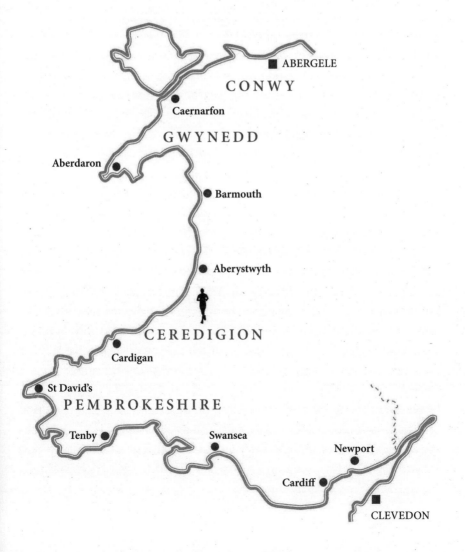

Day 104 – 47.24 miles – 3,577ft elevation
Colwyn Bay to Caernarfon

Starting into a hard headwind sweeping up into Llandudno and around the stunning Great Orme headland road, the views were spectacular. Exposed as I was, right on the edge overlooking choppy waves, the howling wind and stair-rod rain battered me and the coast. But I seemed to have energy to enjoy the weather rather than cower from it. Having had a few weeks of hot sun, this bad spell was bearable for now. Although it gave me shivers of memories from the east coast of Scotland where my hearing was affected by intense winds, I embraced it, but prayed it wouldn't continue for long.

The first 20 miles of day 104 were spent with Dan on his bike, and another kind-hearted soul who was on foot, all of us battling the elements. Running around the windy headland and past Conwy Castle were the main highlights; sadly we missed a chance to join Andy's short diversion to see the Menai Bridge, the world's first iron suspension bridge built back in 1826 by Thomas Telford. Dan, being very used to navigating while cycling, got the route from Andy and subbed in to take the reins. The roads were busy but we had semi-usable paths, which passed under the busy roads from time to time, so Andy would have found it hard to stay close to me anyway.

We spent the night on a little patch of wasteland attached to a 'tyre service centre' that Nikki had found close to our stopping point. Nothing special, but another day down and closer still to returning to where I'd started. The following day Andy completed his hat trick, summiting Snowdon in the early hours:

I'm up at 4 a.m. for the short drive to start the last leg of my disjointed Three Peaks. With the van too long for the (now pre-booking only) car park at the start of the Pyg Track, the classic Three Peaks route, I opt for Llanberis, and park up in foul weather. Snowdon is entirely obscured by dark grey clouds and heavy rain, and the thought of running up a mountain I can't even see is not an appealing one, but I feel like I have to tick it off to complete the trio. At least on this route I can get a little speed up to keep me warm as I'm lashed by horizontal rain and buffeted by the wind. The path is certainly not busy and I make steady if unpleasant progress to the summit. It's not a day for hanging around on mountaintops, so a quick slap of the trig point and I'm on my way back down, now facing into the weather, with sleety rain stinging my face. The good thing about the Llanberis path is that, for the most part, it's not steep, so I can hammer the descent, and I'm back at the car park just inside two hours. My Three Peaks is complete, and although my running times have been OK, the month or so of driving in between means that my overall time won't be troubling the incredible Joss Naylor's long-standing record.

My leg soreness had returned and we realized I'd been letting my recovery routines slip a little. Not a lot but enough to notice it. A gentle reminder that post-run stretching, icing and compression were still needed. If only we could find a place to park.

Our enforced four-week extension to the finish date meant that we'd now be travelling through some of the most notoriously busy spots for British holidaymakers in peak holiday season, the centre of the country generally emptying and everyone flocking to the coast during August. Our entire route to Eden was now littered with hundreds of thousands of extra people. We, of course, counted as tourists too. After a good day's run we eventually found a deserted parking spot by an old radar station at the end of a winding track at the top of a hill. The narrow track had tarmac older than me, faded grey and crumbling, which turned into a grassy patch of rocky wasteland with windswept stone walls leaning as a result of the strong winds. We had a feeling we probably wouldn't be allowed to park there, which was immediately confirmed when Nikki pointed out the massive No Parking sign, but we ignored it, the 360-degree views far too appealing to miss.

We stood gazing out over the cliff edge to the frothy ocean being whipped up by the wind. White prancing horses peaked the blue waves, the wind visible thanks to dense rain showing its movements in the sky. The tent box felt like a risk but we were encouraged by the fact that a cyclist had arrived and was pitching his tent right on the edge of the cliff, using a mossy stone wall for shelter. He was still there in the morning, and of course the tent box was absolutely fine. My view looking out in the morning, as I unzipped the side, was the kind you would paint. The sky was still stormy but the morning stillness gave an impression of calm amid the chaos. Weather was still very much a key part of our days, the ocean becoming a close friend, the sun an absent one of late.

Driving back down the road that morning to begin another day, sheep rose from their cocooned positions having been sheltering from the wind like us. They stood gracefully as we approached, the engine waking them. They had nowhere to be and so at their leisure moved slowly aside. For the first time in a long while I spent most of the day on my own with no extra runners, barring a few miles in the middle. I put in some longer stretches without breaks or food and just got my head down.

I really felt I was on the home stretch, running home rather than just ticking off the miles. It was a weird feeling. I'd not thought about actually running to a place for so long that it gave me a mammoth boost. I was running with good cadence and good balance, my arms low by my sides, and faster-paced than usual. For one period of about four hours it felt like I was floating through the miles, my head clearly dreaming about the finish. Perhaps a dangerous thought so far from the end. I was, however, now less than 1,000 miles away from it, counting down in triple figures.

Meanwhile, Andy was watching the birds again:

Red kites circle like vultures as Nick plods through his last few miles around the headland between estuaries. They're in for a disappointing feed if he does keel over – there's hardly any meat left on him.

Day 108 – 47.39 miles – 3,407ft elevation
Aberdovey to Aberaeron

Still steadily working my way down the Welsh coast, we encountered a couple of hilly days where I was between a rock and a hard place. Or should I say a bloody noisy main road and steep, endless hills. I opted for the hills, knowing that I couldn't stand the noise and danger of hurtling traffic, with wing mirrors whistling by inches from my head, for the entire day. Either route nicely tracked the coast closely anyway, running all the way down past Aberystwyth, with Cardigan Bay off to my right.

A couple of days of dips in the sea, along with double helpings of fajitas, and we were making good progress. Andy enjoyed the sight of me having to scamper back to the van every time I dipped my legs in the sea. While he was swimming comfortably, enjoying the cold water, I'd taken to wearing three layers and a puffa jacket on my top half while standing up to my waist, freezing my legs in an attempt to combine my leisure time with icing therapy. Even with the layers on top I was always out of the water before Andy.

Tomorrow we'd hit the Pembrokeshire coast. The few days we spent skirting around that national park would be filled with new running companions and the sound of chatter filling the warm summer air, helping to make the now increasing elevation feel flatter.

Day 109 – 47.25 miles – 5,825ft elevation
Aberaeron to Newport

By the end of day 109 I'd run over 4,400 miles, so when I unexpectedly got a call from my mate Nick to say it looked like we would probably finish not far from his house near Fishguard, and Nikki having taken some time off to visit friends, Andy and I jumped at the chance to spend the night at his – some rare time in an actual building. It was the second and final time I would spend a night in a proper home, and more than three months since the first, at my brother's place in Bournemouth.

Andy also had his mind on the topography of the days to come:

There are big hills on today's route, and we discuss remapping certain sections before deciding that at this stage it's best for Nick to embrace the gradients and see it as training for Devon and Cornwall, although we'll be keeping a close eye on any developing niggles that may threaten his progress. Although the elevation is much smoother than the rough terrain of the coast paths he endured in the first week, he has a lot less muscle in his legs than he did then. Any sign of impending injury and we'll have a rethink.

Wales had been treating us to the best of its coastline of late, with small fishing villages, quaint coves and narrow roads dipping down into harbours and then back out again to take in the grander views. I'd gone from dodging traffic and expecting to have a wing mirror clip my shoulder or the back of my head to expecting to see dolphins and seals breaching the surface of the early-morning glassy water. The landscape was becoming more dramatic once again, including some tough elevation – and there'd be more to come.

My watch clocked the magic number to signify the end of the day, and by some good fortune we were within a mile of Nick's house. In fact it was Nick's mum's house. He had been visiting for a few weeks – a stroke of lucky timing, considering he's usually out of the country managing his business.

Nick runs the Impact Marathon Series, a charitable race series with events all over the world, new ones popping up most years. We first met in Guatemala where we ran, got chatting, and made friends. It was Nick who helped me set up my charity, the 196 Foundation. Without him I would likely not have got it off the ground, and he now serves as its chairman.

Nick came to meet us and we drove in convoy the short distance back to his mum's house. Their garden has gorgeous views over the water, high up among the greenness of the Welsh countryside. Nick and I ordered curry and chatted for a while as Andy spent the last of the evening light organizing the van, which he'd parked on the driveway. But what Andy didn't know was that the house had motion detection CCTV, which was linked to Nick's mum's phone. At this point in the evening she was yet to return to the house, having been out most of the day. Upon checking her phone she had an alert highlighting the fact that motion had been detected outside her garage.

The image the system sent her, which we now have as a memento of the occasion, was a screenshot of Andy, in just his grubby van shorts, using the wing mirror to shave. It was obviously an interesting sight for Nick's mum, seeing what looked like a homeless man performing his ablutions on her driveway, made worse by the fact that Andy's topless half was the only piece of him in shot, so he looked not just homeless but naked. The text Nick's mum sent to him was one of alarm and bewilderment. We shared many laughs about it over the curry.

What was more weird for Andy and me that night was how odd it felt to be in a home. Specifically a home, not just a budget hotel or building. The homely feeling of chatting in a kitchen, lounging around with dogs at our feet in a living room with a TV, pictures on the walls, a normal-sized fridge and, to my amazement, hot water on tap. Being in a domestic setting with all its familiar comforts was refreshing, but it also reminded us that we were on an adventure. Our on-the-road set-up had become pretty normalized for us. God forbid the thought of waking up and not pissing in a bottle while in a box on the roof of a van parked in a lay-by. It was utterly wonderful to have the time with Nick and his mum, but I speak for Andy, Nick and myself when I say we are all big fans of adventure for that very reason. For having the abnormal begin to feel normal. For beginning to feel, well, intrepid.

After dinner, I did another crazy thing: I treated myself to a shower. A luxury once more.

Days 110 to 117
Newport to Haroldston West (via St David's)

Welsh signposts with random letters joined together pretending to be
words were becoming more common as we followed the national acorn
symbol marking the miles and miles of the Pembrokeshire coast path.

Nick was first up, prepping some breakfast as we gathered in his
conservatory, all of us blurry-eyed and under-slept, thanks to many
drinks and a later than usual bedtime. I believe we had about five
hours' sleep.

The Pembrokeshire coast gifted us a gorgeous blue-sky day and
good friends. Nick started the day with us, as did a handful of other
lovely people and old friends who had been tracking us and came out
for a run. We chatted, we reminisced, we had ice creams (Twisters all
round) and we basked in the glow of a Welsh summer, heat haze shim-
mering on the horizon, buoyed by the occasional random cheer from a
passing car, noticing that we were clearly on a mission. Even with these
last days of Wales totalling around 4,000 feet of elevation per day, the
warm weather and the smiles of good people made the miles pass
unnoticed.

Towards the end of the first week of August we trudged, and the
elevation continued as we navigated our way around the complex and
fiddly web of waterways, river systems and estuaries of the Pembrokeshire headland. Having ticked off one of my favourite cities in Wales,
St David's, we rounded St Bride's Bay and then headed on up the Bristol Channel.

Over those Pembroke hills, Andy and I had another few evenings on
our own, for both of which we treated ourselves to luxury accommodation, paying about £10 a night to park in a field with views overlooking
clusters of multicoloured, multi-sized boats floating in distant harbours. Every cove here was littered with either small sailing boats or
fishing boats, the evening sun casting warm orange light on them, with
us perched up high with the van door open, soaking it all in.

Day 111 was another 47 miles with 4,349 feet of elevation from Haroldston West to Angle via lots of wiggly bits around Milford Haven

and Pembroke Dock. Heavy rain drummed on the roof, drowning out the sound of the kettle as we went about our morning bagel and tea routine. It was hard to step out from the cosy confines of the van that morning, with the outside world gloomy and grey. Having so recently had luxuries like a shower, ice creams and days of sunny miles with friends, it was a morning I was keen to pretend didn't exist.

Squeezing one last day out of my old pair of trainers to avoid the new pair being ruined immediately by the downpour, I ran thinly soled and could feel it in my feet. By now, with my body fat so low, the natural cushioning I once had from a small layer of fat and muscle under the bones in my feet was gone. It felt like bone on tarmac. Barring the thin sole of my now very worn shoes, it was.

My body was now very weak, my weight too low and my bones frail within my skin. I knew that if I allowed mental exhaustion to overwhelm me too, there would be dark miles ahead – reminiscent of my times in the desert where I could see the finish line 10 miles away and yet it took what felt like days to reach it. I knew I must stay focused on each individual day and avoid looking too far ahead. The miles would be covered as they had been so far, by keeping the physical and mental elements separate.

An afternoon of rainy, colder miles saw me picking my way through a harbour complex, where it became hard for both Andy and me to keep a handle on which direction we were facing. The waterways, inlets and estuaries merged with the sea, sometimes making it feel like I was running back up the Welsh coast in the wrong direction. Our mapped route was more or less followed but it was hard to stay on track. I just hoped we weren't adding any unnecessary extra miles.

Andy was just happy with the simple wins, such as finishing up at the perfect overnight spot:

Following a brief bright spell that allowed Nick to dry out a bit, the sky over the last few miles turns gunmetal grey, the perfect backdrop for the massive Pembrokeshire oil refinery. For the second day running, 47 miles brings Nick to a stop right outside a camping field. This one's attached to a farm, and we phone the number on the gate. The chap on the other end of the phone tells us to park anywhere we like and he'll pop by later to collect the money. That is exactly how camping should be, rather than having to provide the exact dimensions of your massive tent in order to secure a minimum two-night booking, four months in advance.

Stepping outside to brush our teeth that evening, we saw stars, the first I'd seen since before my injury on day 6. Progressing north as summer continued I'd been in bed before it was properly dark, or we'd been in light-polluted areas. It was a calming sight. The rain passed and clear skies now opened up to the cosmos. It reminded us about the relative nature of time and distance. From our perspective on the ground, 5,250 miles was a mammoth distance. But for the universe and what lies beyond, it's obviously nothing. And on the concept of time, we both agreed we were spending it wisely.

Having spent about an hour pondering the cosmos and our place in it, still with our toothbrushes in our hands, leaning against a fencepost looking out over the sea and up at the stars, we headed in for one last cuppa before bed.

The following morning, several tents pitched neatly next to us the night before had been demolished by the wind. We woke to chatter and the frantic collection of belongings amid the wind and rain. Despite the clear skies last night, the weather had become grumpy, and it was another marathon of rain before it cleared. Not a single item of dry clothing remained. The van now looked like a cluttered laundry room, without any laundry actually having been done.

As we plodded through the day, Andy in the mobile anti-laundrette, he pondered the unspoken rules of the road:

Narrow, hedge-lined lanes make up most of the afternoon route. It's these lanes that I dread in the van, having to negotiate my way past cars in the tightest of passing places with the van planted in the hedge, or having to reverse back to gateways with the prospect of a tractor appearing behind me. On my first pass of the day, I go out of my way to pull in to a wide spot on a bend, giving the other driver more room than he really needs. I prepare my acknowledgement wave, a finger or two raised from my hand in the twelve o'clock

position on the steering wheel – the standard 'you're welcome' to the
generous thank you wave I'm expecting.

The thank you wave given in these situations can take one of
several forms. There's the standard raised hand, polite, reliable,
unambiguous. Then there's the thumbs up, with its more friendly
feel, a common language among van drivers. There's 'the cowboy',
favoured by lorry drivers, a slowly raised pointed finger, accom-
panied by a faraway look that says 'I'm a knight of the road, and
I've seen a few things' and in a similar manner to 'the biker', a slow
two-fingered doff of the crash helmet. Finally, there's 'the coach
driver', delivered with the same languid speed as 'the cowboy', but
the whole arm is raised to an angle of around 45 degrees, possibly
due to the massive steering wheel and longer distance from the wind-
screen. You've got to be careful with this one, because to the
untrained eye it can be mistaken for a Nazi salute.

I wait to see what sort of wave I'll get from my passee, and I wait.
Nothing. Not even a finger. As I look over, I see a scowl so deeply
etched on the man's face it has calcified and become permanent.
This chap hasn't smiled since the eighties.

Having trotted through Tenby, feeling rather claustrophobic due to
a brief spell of being around lots of people and cars all of a sudden, we
escaped, finishing day 112 on a no-man's-land piece of coast between
Pendine and Laugharne. Another 47 miles down, new shoes run in
nicely with no issues, and a bonus of stopping my watch for the day
right outside a sports nutrition store near Pendine called the chip shop.
Sports chips are much healthier, folks, but it's still a good idea to add
plenty of salt to stop the cramping.

Now tantalizingly close to concluding our Welsh leg of the journey,
we had just a few more days to go. The weather stayed intermittently
bad, but the mood was lifted by a brief visit from Chris and Carol,
Andy's delightful mum and dad. They'd timed a visit to the Gower perfectly in order to pop by and say hello as we passed through. Not only
that, but as both of our sets of parents tended to do, they came armed
with a care package consisting of chocolate, fruit and extra items like
T-shirts and luxury socks. Luxury socks were what we called any

non-running sock that I'd don of an evening to treat my worn-out feet. Reviewing all these special items felt like we were in prison, receiving supplies on visiting day – the goods that would make all the difference to our survival. The gifts were welcomed with open arms and stored in a 'for special occasions' cupboard. Clean clothes must at no point be contaminated by the rest of the van.

At the end of my 47 miles, in a bland car park on the edge of Llanelli, we scrunched ourselves into the Council Van and ate Chinese food together until it sent me to sleep, while Andy overthought the food.

Strangely, in addition to the complimentary prawn crackers, the Chinese takeaway comes with poppadoms, and I wonder if this is a Welsh thing, like rice and chips. It's interesting that many of the little things we consider peculiar to our 'national cuisine' stem from the multicultural roots of what we now think of as British food. Ironically, our habit of appropriating world foods is, in and of itself, a very British thing.

The main talking point over dinner was the rather strange leg sensation I'd been having over the previous three days. We thought it was something to do with a nerve or similar. Every so often, maybe twice a day, my right leg would just give way in an instant. It was never for long enough to cause me to fall and have to crawl, but it was enough to make me stumble. I'd simultaneously get numb toes on the same leg. Having come to the conclusion that it was possibly nerve-related, we all agreed it could be something terrible or equally something not terrible, so we ignored it and pressed on. I've never had the leg thing again since. We coined it narcolepsy of the leg.

Besides leg talk, we all shared stories of our favourite beaches. Rhossili Bay, which Andy's folks had visited earlier that day, was the catalyst of the conversation, with them having fallen in love with it. My favourite beach will always be Fistral in Newquay, where I now live. But Rhossili is up there with the likes of the Gold Coast in Australia or the beaches of Mexico or the sweeping expanse of sand that is the Californian coast. In fact, from the lookout point it is similar to the view facing north when you look out from the lighthouse at Nazaré in Portugal. Rhossili has 3 miles of green cliffs, yellow sand and shallow waves. The only downside is that everyone knows about it.

Having rounded Mumbles headland, I was reunited with Nikki and Poppy. It was perfect timing to have a new boost and her recharged energy – by this point I needed all the support I could get:

Although in good spirits, buoyed by the return of Nikki and Pop, Nick is already very weak and getting weaker by the day. This close to the end, it's easy to forget how much running he still has to do, and how close his body is to the point where it could fail him without warning, in any of a variety of ways. Food is now key, and I'm trying to encourage him to eat more substantially during breaks. Luckily we're well stocked with the parental Red Cross delivery and, of course, cold Chinese takeaway.

Beside the rather grim and out-of-place steelworks at Port Talbot, I helped Andy map the remaining days. What had started as a job I thought would be long and dull after another 47 miles turned out to be really very exciting. Having had dinner and now with our laptops resting on our legs, both of us in our single beds, the van clutter around us, we plotted our path to Eden and the finish line. Working out what was coming in terms of elevation and terrain was daunting, but overall it got me excited. Obviously my excitement was a little premature. When I got my head back in the room, the details started to slowly sink in. Although the finish line looked close on the map, the Cornish hills would undoubtedly throw a few more punches. And Port Talbot felt about as far away from Cornwall as it was possible to feel:

As we pass the industrial dystopia of Port Talbot, the delicate fragrances of the steelworks mingle with the odour of the van to create an aroma quite beyond description, although if it was made into a perfume, I think it would be called Despair, with an advert shot in Cleethorpes.

Our final two days in Wales were sunny. The country had offered up a nice send-off with plenty of runners joining too. With my top off and feeling fresh-legged as I ran towards Ogmore Castle near Porthcawl, the Footpath route we'd mapped the night before took me to what we assumed was a bridge over a river that crossed the tiny back lanes and narrow footpaths that made up the route. So, reaching the river, I was confused to see only water with a row of stepping stones, many of them submerged by the river. It turns out that for Wales, stepping stones and bridges are much the same thing.

Now, a few stepping stones, or even no stepping stones at all, wouldn't usually bother me. But having come so far and having had my fair share of injuries I was keen to avoid a slip or fall that could lead to a sprained ankle or worse. There were only 600 miles still to run, after all, and I'd done a stint on crutches already.

Andy was already on the other side, having managed to get the van there down narrow hedge-lined single-track roads. We looked across this obstacle at one another with a smile of misadventure.

In normal times this would have been a non-event, but I just couldn't risk dashing across the slippery rocks. Flip-flops were the solution. My trainers, leg compressions and favourite running shorts needed to stay dry, as they were the items I only had one of, and wore every day. And I couldn't go barefoot because of the risk of cutting my feet. So Andy waded across in his flip-flops while I removed my shoes and socks before donning Andy's flip-flops, and with a few tourists watching, wondering if I was going to fall on my face and drown in front of them, I made my way slowly across the stepping stones, clutching my running shoes, while Andy waded back in bare feet. The big non-event was over, and I felt rather stupid. The law of sod, however, guarantees that, had I not been so cautious, I would have fallen and injured myself.

A stay on another classically windy Welsh cliff top gave us views all the way to the lights marking the seafront of Minehead. Minehead, of course, marks the starting point of the South West Coast Path, the very same path that ruined my legs in the first week. And the path I'd be rejoining sections of in order to reach Eden. The twinkling lights remained in my mind until my eyes closed and my brief slumber began.

Day 116 was my final full day in Wales. I ran along the road skirting the edge of Cardiff airport and on to Barry Island, which by the way isn't an island at all, just like the handful of other places around the country that call themselves islands, even though they aren't. No idea why.

Having more sunshine and more smiley runners join me for my now daily ice cream was a great start to the day, made better still by meeting two little girls no older than five who had come out with their mum to support me. I crouched down to their level and we spoke for a while. Or I spoke and they giggled and pretended to be shy.

After Cardiff and Barry, the sweeping shadows of wind turbines whipped at my feet as a gaggle of lovely women with their Welsh accents joined me for the final miles. The sound of Welsh voices I knew I would miss – so endearing, and endlessly amusing to me. The phraseology and the little clusters of idiolects are fascinating.

The city of Newport was the nearest big place to the day's end and we approached the 47-mile mark right opposite a plaque with information about the 1607 flood. The waterline marker standing tall next to it indicated that we, the van and many of the nearby trees would have been underwater. I learnt that the surrounding area was devastated by this deluge, particularly on the Welsh side, all the way to above Carmarthenshire. Over two thousand people lost their lives.

While we were deep in thought pondering what the area would have been like after the flood, we were briefly joined by Ellie, an old work colleague of Andy's and mine and a very keen cyclist and artist too. She'd left her paints behind but had cycled the forty minutes to find us. Ellie, like so many people in this book, is a brilliant soul. A gentle, talented, modest person, someone who would help anyone. She was introduced to Poppy and received the usual tongue assault.

Andy amused us all with his latest animal sighting as I iced my legs and elevated them with a pillow under my calves, my head and back resting on the bench seat, while I drained my blood from my feet. He had witnessed the strange sight of a stray dog and a guinea fowl casually walking down the street together, the dog stopping occasionally to allow the bird to catch up. These animals represented our current relationship: two dirty beings, with an abnormal relationship, one patiently waiting for and guiding the other.

Bristol, where Andy and I first met, was just ahead, home to many mutual friends. Ellie got top marks for being the first of what would be a few familiar local faces to come out and show their support.

On day 117 the Welsh accents began to make way for West Country ones, the 'characters' of both equally quirky in their own way. The Severn Bridge would cut the cord with Wales and usher in one last push over the next ten days to the finish line. All of a sudden it began to feel like we might make it.

Reaching the old Severn Bridge first, Andy drove over and went ahead to meet our mutual friend Patch (Patrick), who'd come to welcome us back into England. Of all the border crossings, this was by far the least glamorous. Wales became England as I crossed over the brown River Severn, running along the east path of the passenger footway of the M4 motorway.

I ran on the eastern side so that I didn't miss the 'Welcome to England' sign. Patch, however, followed the complicated network of pavements and pedestrian bridges back from the Severn View services to take the footway on the other side, thinking that was where I'd be. Patch is a tall, broad-shouldered man, and hard to miss. And yet we ended up rather comically shouting to each other across six lanes of speeding vehicles on the bridge. With the deafening traffic, we resorted to speaking on the phone, only seeing each other's lips moving as lorries thundered past, with the bridge shaking beneath our feet. The wind whistling between the suspension cables added to the hectic noise. We arranged to meet back at the main service station which was, remarkably, my first motorway service station of the entire trip. A luxury, eh? Our impossible conversation was relayed to Andy once we'd all met up. We agreed it pretty much summed up the entire journey – chaos emerging from the simplest of tasks.

We were soon joined by Gary and Adam, also buddies from the old days. Of all the people in the world, I've run the most miles with Gary, regularly training with him during early mornings. We'd mark up lampposts with electrical tape around the streets of Bristol and use them for interval training, me struggling to keep up with Gary's impressive pace. He's a runner who could podium across many events if he bothered to train properly. Instead he usually finishes top twenty, which, without training, is even more impressive. He and Adam ran me to the day's finish marker just outside Bristol – sunny miles, chatting freely. Naturally I quickened the pace a little because I was excited to see them. As usual, good company took my mind off my exhaustion levels and the mental stress of being so near, yet still so far, from the finish.

With the latest food stock-up of various essentials, we noticed that for the first time we were buying bread, milk and of course bagels that wouldn't go out of date until after we'd crossed the finish line on 22 August. We really were getting close.

10

Heading for Land's End

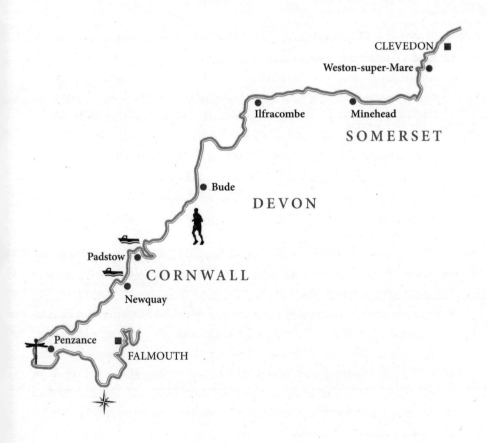

Day 118 – 47.15 miles – 1,295ft elevation
Bristol to Cannington
One week to Land's End

> *Nick has now racked up an incredible unbroken month of back-to-back 47-mile runs, and is somehow keeping his body going, running on empty, pretty much at the limit of what's humanly possible. It's now difficult not to visualize the end, but with hundreds of miles still to run, the closer he gets to the final day, the further away it feels. His legs are operating on autopilot and muscle memory, and his exhaustion is taking a real mental toll. Tempers are fraying more frequently as we all feel the stresses of four months on the road. I sense that Nick is also quietly bracing himself for the sting in the tail: the return of the fierce elevation that will make a few of the final days even more cruel.*

For some reason, on my first night back in England I slept terribly. Possibly the worst night's sleep I'd had for the entire journey. I can only assume that my mind was jumping ahead to the Cornish coast that was fast approaching. I was suffering from a little PTSD after the hills at the beginning, I think. That, and I'd eaten a lot of pizza at a late hour.

The subsequent effect of this was a grumpy Nick. I was in a foul mood again, yawning and stretching out my soreness as I got ready in the van. I used to change after breakfast and then get back into bed to be driven to our starting point, but of late I'd just stayed in bed and got changed at the last minute.

I remembered that today I was running with an old friend, Annabelle, and another acquaintance, Fabian. Our morning together flipped my mood on its head. We chatted as we weaved through the streets of Clevedon, where most roads are just one row of houses back from the water, pensioner-style bungalows and generic cookie-cutter-style estates in the sleepy suburbs and beyond, which didn't do much for my alertness. I even had a couple of close calls with traffic. Old people reversing cars out of drives, not looking. Fortunately I was running slowly enough not to be killed, my stopping speed immediate.

From here it was out on to the Somerset Levels. This would now be the last of the flat for today and some of tomorrow, before hills all the way to the finish. I tried to treasure these moments, but remained sluggish all day. My mood lifted, but I couldn't shake off the tiredness of my body. It was a long twelve-hour slog, similar to that of the early days. We considered stopping early too, but pushed on to keep the consecutive streak of 47-plus-mile days going.

Annabelle and Fabian dropped off about midday with various childcare commitments to attend to. Something which cemented my already concrete certainty that I was on the right path in life was when Fabian had to attend a work meeting by dialling into a video call, having stayed out for longer than planned. It highlighted how much I wasn't missing my old life. I had got lost myself down the rabbit hole of vacuous spreadsheet-focused days, staring at screens that might as well have been turned off for all the good I was doing. I believe it was this little reminder coming at the right time that made me finish the 47-mile day. Not necessarily out of enthusiasm, more for fear that somehow I might end up back in that life if the miles weren't adhered to.

Crossing the small estuary of the River Parrett as the English coastline straightened out west towards the north Devon coast, I closed out the miles, dragging my feet, scuffing my shoes, my head low. I'd been given the boost I needed, but it was running out. I could see Andy was a little worried that our end date might be in jeopardy if I developed another injury, or perhaps my body just shut down. I'd lost a lot of weight. My wrists were noticeably thinner, and I'd tightened my watch more and more as the weeks passed; my skull was also more visible through my skin, the rings loose on my fingers. I was knackered. And what Andy didn't know was that I was concerned too. I can battle through pain, but lacking energy is a different matter. We stayed just south of Cannington, west of Bridgwater. A 7,000-calorie day. I needed more food.

Day 119 – 47.14 miles – 4,421ft elevation
Cannington to Lynton

By now I'd run through twenty-three English counties, thirteen in Wales and twenty in Scotland. (I'll caveat these numbers by saying it's rather difficult to get it exact, as Britain has a very vague and ambiguous classification method, but it's there or thereabouts.) We'd only missed a handful of counties, the ones in the middle of the country – Oxfordshire, Leicestershire, etc. Today we would cross into Devon. With Somerset finally ticked off, it was only a couple more days until we'd be in Cornwall.

From here, the elevation chart started to look angry. After days of running 1,000-plus feet, it would now be 4,000- or 5,000-plus feet. A fourfold increase on heavy legs and a frail, weak body was always going to make the days long. As we were now getting to the point where we had to keep a very close eye on my mileage versus remaining routes, Andy and I spent a few minutes first thing getting all my outstanding Garmin and Strava data into his spreadsheet. Sitting among the piles of grimy, musty clothing, Andy balanced the laptop on his legs, both of us sitting in our boxers, sleepy-eyed, cups of tea going cold as we focused on the numbers.

I'd been recording my mileages each day of course, using my watch, and saving all the data, but we hadn't, for the last few weeks, captured all the exact mileages, including decimal places, on Andy's spreadsheet. We'd tended to just round down to 47 miles, but now we needed to be precise. Once the calibrated watch times had been put in, it was actually good news: we had about 15 fewer miles to cover than we thought, which, when added to the small mileage cushion I still had, would help with the negative mileage difference we knew was coming through avoiding the worst of the footpaths in Devon and Cornwall and instead hugging the coast on smaller roads.

With some very strenuous days of running to come, this perked me up. Within seconds, and without moving, I'd magically clocked off 15 miles. Happy days. My remaining daily average required to complete the 5,250 miles by 22 August would be a little lower than 47 miles, with the option to spread the surplus as I wished. I was, however, keen, for neatness more than anything, to keep my streak of 47-plus-mile days going until I hit the forty-straight-days mark – which I felt would be a good mental boost, and a nice accomplishment to have. These were the little things that might not have mattered much but felt important.

Before I could get carried away, there was Exmoor, looming in the distance behind some hazy low-lying fog. Whichever route we took would involve a massive climb up on to Exmoor, a place I've run before when I set a benchmark distance running from sunrise to sunset some years ago, during the summer solstice.

And before that, there were some very frustrating miles through the Quantock Hills that got me angry. Whichever way I tried to run, I either ended up on the coast path that had been closed due to cliff collapse, or on the A39, which is horrendous to run on in the good places and absolutely lethal to run on in the bad spots.

The national speed limits combined with narrow blind bends tightly hemmed in by tall hedges on either side, with nowhere to jump into, made it the most dangerous bit of road I'd run along on the whole trip. It would only take a lorry to be rounding one of those blind bends at the wrong moment and I would be a goner. No question. Run Britain would end, just days from finishing. It did cross my mind that we might get some headlines and therefore charity donations, but I didn't really fancy dying.

The only other option was to weave frustratingly from coast path to residential back roads, repeating the process over and over until I gradually worked my way along. For some sections I'd run miles along beaches where paths used to be higher up on the cliffs, but then reach dead ends and have to double back or hike up steep hills. This wasn't ideal, and it took me ages to get through the first half of the day. But I did, eventually. It was likely to be one of many such situations we'd encounter over the next few days. Not great for my morale.

At Minehead I stopped for some disappointing chips and a photo of the monument marking the start of the South West Coast Path – a place I'd been before, having run it during the time before lockdown, just as Covid was hitting. I knew what the path was like from here, much of it unrunnable in places. But no matter which way I went, the undulation would become hills, and the hills, as I got tired, would feel like mountains.

At mid-afternoon I arrived in Porlock, and more significantly at the bottom of the famous Porlock Hill, the steepest section of A road in Britain. There are two options here: either straight up the ridiculously steep hill, or avoid it via one of the scenic toll roads with a gentler climb to the top. I think you can guess which route I took. I needed to preserve my legs so I opted for the longest of the toll roads, which had a lesser gradient and was actually runnable, while Andy took the plucky Council Van up Porlock Hill in second gear. I think Andy was rather proud of the old girl.

With Andy already at the top, I gave myself a mental boost by running the hill without breaks and at a decent pace. It was a heavenly section of switchbacks looping up and up under the cover of green and yellow leaves from majestic old trees towering over me. Only one car passed me so I pretty much had the place to myself. A sliver of bliss. My reward was shared with Andy: stunning views across Exmoor and out over the Bristol Channel from some of the highest sea cliffs in the country. It was then on across the moor to begin the descent into Lynmouth.

With 47 miles clocked and my watch stopped, I hopped into the van, and we drove up the hill into Lynton to find a café for dinner, where we were joined once again by 'the other Andy', last seen at Sidmouth, whom I'd met in Niger while Running the World and who had become a dear friend. Andy had taken time out of his very busy and successful life to drive down from London to spend the evening here and run with me tomorrow. His lodgings for the night would be the tent box, in one of the most idyllic little spots we'd found on the trip, the stunning Valley of Rocks. We were parked among sheep, pooing and chewing their way around the field, short tufts of grass all that remained. This car park-cum-sheep grazing area sat just a minute's walk from the steep, majestic cliffs looking out over the water.

Under a sparkly blanket of stars with faint moonlight on the rocks and glimmering water, I let Poppy out for a midnight wee and took a moment to breathe in the journey so far, trying desperately – more so every day – to be grateful, calm and present. With the van door quietly shut and the dog re-curled on my chest with Nikki next to me, I shut my eyes.

We woke on day 120 with wind and rain smothering us. The windows were transparent no more. The other Andy manoeuvred his tall, strong frame out of the small tent box opening and down into the van, to join us for the pre-run rituals. We were all damning the weather, not just because Andy had made the effort to join us, and not just because I'd had enough of rain, but because the route would have been spectacular with clear skies.

Mother Nature, however, was just playing games with us. The rain lessened a few hours in, the wind died down, and grey skies became blue. Our mutual Bristolian mate Gary, who'd run with me just a few days earlier and decided he wanted more, drove down early doors to meet us a few miles in. An hour's drive, a 20-mile run, a 20-mile cycle back to his car, and then an hour's drive back home. Good going. Not a bad way to spend what turned out (in the end) to be one of the most summery days of the trip. His support as always did not go unnoticed.

The gradients became ear-popping and the views breathtaking. We all stripped down to minimal layers and began to take on more fluids. With the sun on our backs and the Valley of Rocks behind us, we were treated to a special appearance from the other Andy's niece, Katie, and her friend Maria. Together, we had a spectacularly uplifting morning. It was as if all the worries and doubts that were grumbling away within me, not to mention the physical ailments, were simply lifted off and chucked aside.

In Croyde we were joined by Maddie, who is without a doubt one of my favourite people I've shared time with. Maddie is a small, gentle soul with almighty abilities. And she's just twelve years old. An already successful competition-winning gymnast, her running abilities are phenomenal. Her teacher Luke, a gentle guy himself, and now someone I'd call a friend, accompanied her before Maddie's ever-supportive parents turned up.

The last miles of the day as the sun sank lower in the sky followed the vast expanse of dunes and sweeping beach of Saunton Sands. We decided to run across the beach and around the sandy headland instead of taking the uneven coast path. Maddie met her parents at Braunton, but ran on further with her dad in tow. We hugged and said goodbye before original Andy joined the rest of us for the last few miles.

Although we'd had huge groups of runners before, we had never had a solid chunk of them sustain long miles. Usually I'd had anywhere from one to fifteen people throughout the day for a few miles spread out over the whole distance. We later calculated it was probably the highest cumulative mileage for a group on any given day of the trip. Andy (the other Andy) ran the whole 47-mile day, Gary did his 20, Katie and Maria managed 32 each. I of course did my 47, Luke ran 14 miles, and Maddie, although she was only going to run 3 miles when she turned up, also finished the day on 14 miles. It was the furthest she'd run, and her first continuous half marathon. I'm sure it goes without saying she did so without sweating. No complaining of pain, no slowing down, and no encouragement needed from us. I am sure we will hear more of this young Devonshire girl when the next few Olympics come around after Paris 2024. We were all blown away.

The weather, the people, and also the route, were spot on. Narrow carless tracks and lanes. Coast paths tracking headlands overlooking calm blue seas, and the sun scorching our skin. Which is uncomfortable for some, but I couldn't get enough of it. From Lynton through Ilfracombe to Croyde, and ending not far from Maddie's school in Barnstaple – 5,451 feet of elevation, but with little to no suffering thanks to the good company.

Buoyed by the hearts of good people, and sustained by sun and ice cream, we camped in a small field with the other Andy, Maria and Katie. Pizzas eaten, and with the mood still high, darkness signalled bedtime once more. One last flurry of excitement before we rested came in the form of Maria attempting to beat her own speed record for putting up a tent. She spent the first eighteen years of her life in Kenya and so is a hardy, worldly girl. We turned on the van's outside light to illuminate the scene, gathered around its sliding door and peered out, watching Maria impressively put up her tent in under three minutes. She did, however, forget the sheet that covers the tent and got rather soaked during a 2 a.m. rain shower. Nonetheless, putting up a tent in three minutes after 32 miles, she had my full respect.

I was now only eight days away from the Eden Project, our finish line. And yes, it would always be 'our' finish line, never mine alone. This day was a great demonstration of that, as Andy's diary records:

There's been a party atmosphere to today's run, and at the end of a wonderful day, it feels like, finally, today marks the start of the home straight. Buoyed by good friends/runners, good weather and great scenery, it feels like Nick now has just about enough mental strength to carry his flagging body through the remaining few days.

With the other Andy having become the fourth person (including me) to run a full day with Nick, Heidi from Cheshire remains the only non-Andy to have done so.

Day 121 welcomed us back to Cornwall. We passed the sign just 10 miles along the coast path, a tatty old wooden one, wind-whipped and leaning. I was back where it had all started on a bitterly cold frosty morning four months ago. My body tingled with goosebumps all of a sudden. I smiled and trotted on.

I was already in a good mood for the day, having had the joys of running with Maddie again for the first 10 kilometres before she went off to gymnastics. She and her parents had come out again, as she'd promised she would.

It's a few flat miles on the Tarka Trail to start the day, and (of course) Maddie is back for more. She runs the first few miles with Nick and a couple of locals before heading home around Westward Ho!, famously the only place in the UK to have an exclamation mark in its name and, perhaps less famously, the only place to share a battle cry with Lion-O from ThunderCats.

The weather is irritatingly indecisive, causing Nick all manner of clothing changes throughout the morning. With visibility not great, and Nick facing 6 miles on the A39, I drive ahead to assess the danger levels. I deem this stretch of road to be well within his tolerance levels – perhaps Italian on the danger scale, certainly nothing sub-Saharan. Then it's back on to narrow lanes for the rest of the day, and time for the van to endure another fern-whipping. To avoid an unnecessary 7 miles on a road around the valley south of Welcombe,

*I've mapped Nick on to a mile and a half of coast path. It's hilly,
and the steep steps won't do his legs any good, but overall, this short
offroad stretch is worth it to keep him on track.*

It was indeed another steep day with plenty of steps, plus brambles
and branches snagging my legs as I ran along the smaller paths up
towards Bude and the home of the truly James Bond-like GCHQ listening station. I'd never seen so many security cameras in one place.
On the headland looking out to sea, massive golfball-like satellite
receivers and big dish-shaped things are all you can see, surrounded by
barbed-wire topping three layers of fencing and even more double-
looped wire behind that. I would assume they lock their doors at night
too. For miles after I thought about all the things they might be listening to. I started to speak out loud to them as though the bushes were
bugged, hoping some technician would hear my rambling through his
monitoring equipment.

Finishing now in the dusk as the light faded, we stopped the watch
at 47 miles in another car park, not far from Duckpool, the wild coastline demonstrating its usual windy ways as we headed to bed having
successfully completed forty days of 47 miles on the trot. Tomorrow
we would hit 5,000 miles, and I now only needed an average of 40 miles
a day to finish on time and on perfect mileage. That sparked thoughts
of the last few days in more detail – things like parking locations and
ferry times, because let's not forget we were back in Cornwall now, with
headlands, rivers and harbours to navigate. Plus it was now mid-
August, the height of summer holiday season, and we'd be jostling for
position with the tourists.

After the early miles away from Bude to Boscastle, I passed through
Tintagel, Port Isaac, Polzeath and Trebetherick to finish on the Camel
Estuary in Rock. The day, however, wasn't plain sailing. Aside from
the 5,200 feet of elevation with some huge steep climbs, for the first
15 miles of the day I was troubled with rare stabbing stomach cramps.
Every step felt uncomfortable. I guess my body was just telling me it
was still not happy with me, like a whining child. I told it we were
nearly there, and to wait a little longer. Rest was coming. Just not
quite yet.

The special 5,000-mile mark was crossed near Tintagel, the birthplace of King Arthur. It was nice to have a milestone coincide with somewhere interesting. So many to date had been in places of no note whatsoever. It felt fitting.

A slow, sluggish morning, but nonetheless, somewhere around Tintagel, legendary birthplace of King Arthur, Nick ticks past the 5, 000-mile mark, a feat which would surely have earned him a place at the Round Table, until the other knights observed his appalling table manners, at which point he'd have immediately been relegated to the kids' table.

Seriously though, five thousand miles. Just pause and think about that. Five thousand miles. On foot. In four months.

To celebrate hitting 5,000 miles we did what a lot of people do when celebrating. We went out for a meal. Although we were in Cornwall we did it Midlands-style. A curry. The only difference, of course, was that I ran there. We picked the curry up in Wadebridge having clocked 40 miles.

Although it felt like a complete luxury to have extra time at the end of the day, and a curry for good measure, when I stopped my watch it hadn't really sunk in that I wouldn't have to run more than 40 miles a day any more. I was actually quite sad it was nearly over, mentally bracing myself for the loss I'd feel at leaving all this behind. The curry filled us all nicely, and before I could think much more, another day was down. Five thousand was a good number, though. It weighed comfortably in my thoughts as I nodded off to sleep.

Day 123 – 40.17 miles – 4,977ft elevation
Rock to Porthtowan

With Nick having decided to go for 40-milers every day, I map the remaining days down to one decimal place, finding a combination of routes with stopping points at Land's End and Lizard Point totalling a perfect 5,250 at the Eden Project. From the campsite, as the crow flies, it's only around 20 miles to Eden. That's how close Nick

is to finishing, the small matter of the Cornish peninsula notwith-
standing. When we discuss the end point, we've just been referring to
it as 'Eden', which is apt, as it's started to feel like some sort of
promised land, such is our eagerness to hit the finish line.

Having stayed on a campsite to the west of the River Camel last
night, we drive the 15-odd miles back around the estuary to Rock,
where I drop Nick at the start point, before driving all the way back
round to wait for him in Padstow. It's very inefficient, but sometimes
it just works out that way. It's August, yet miraculously I manage to
find the only vacant, free parking space in the whole of Cornwall,
and wander along the harbour towards the ferry slip to watch the
sole passenger cross the river on what should be the final ferry of the
trip, depending on how things look when we get to St Mawes. As I
wait, I watch grey mullet milling around in the shallows, waiting to
become expensive dishes in Padstow's famous seafood restaurants,
for people who haven't yet seen Seaspiracy.

No matter where you go in Cornwall it won't be long before you find
a hill, and most hills in Cornwall, I think it's fair to say, are usually
accompanied by blustery coastal winds. Today was no exception, but it
didn't matter. Day 123 was special for me because we would be running
through Newquay.

Newquay has always felt like a second home to me. It's now my first
home. I do live out of a van, so I guess maybe that doesn't count as a
home, but I'd suggest a home is where your heart is, as the saying goes,
and Newquay will always have my heart. The friends I've made there
and the time I've spent there mean it's like no other place in the world.
I can't run more than a mile in the town without bumping into someone I know. And if you take the clock back, I have spent at least
twenty-five of my thirty-two birthdays in Newquay, not for the bars or
the stag-do nightlife but for Fistral Beach in all its glory. I'm not far off
seeing every beach in Britain, but Fistral will always be my favourite.

As kids, our family would come down in our old Elddis 320 camper
van from Dorset, stay near Goonhavern in a small campsite a few miles
away, and each day journey early to Fistral Beach, parking along
the esplanade. Each morning, while my brother and I slept in the bed

we shared above the cab, my mum still fast asleep in the back, Dad would drive slowly down before sunrise and get a spot. I park in those same spaces now. There's nothing better than sliding the van door open to the sound of the ocean, going for a run in the early morning, and returning as the sun rises. Sitting on the headland with a cup of tea, watching the light hit the water for the first time, the town stirring and the familiar screeching of the gulls overhead, is a wonderfully invigorating start to any day.

With Newquay in the diary for today's blustery run, the sun came out and I cruised down the coast, from Padstow, past Constantine Bay, Porthcothan and Newquay airport, and via Porth before detouring off route a little to run past the local bakery I had been thinking about all morning. I picked up a few iced buns before continuing on past a few cafés and shops where friends work.

I hadn't realized, but this route change was a little spanner in the works for Andy. He'd spent a while making sure each section would end exactly where we needed it to. The original route had us going up and around the Gannel creek to Crantock. Having banked more miles than needed to visit the bakery, we were looking for a shortcut. At low tide I knew that there was a slim chance I could avoid the creek by crossing on the beach and wading across the Gannel. This would mean I could weave through the coastal bits, still right next to the water, but taking my time a little more and staying on track for the right mileage at the right end point. I slowed down a bit, waiting for low tide. It was a place I'd run hundreds of times and I knew if the tide wasn't right I'd need to swim.

Approaching Fistral Beach before attempting to cross the Gannel, I stopped for a few moments to say hello to my friends in the little café on the south side, built into the cliff with views across the beach and ocean.

From there, I continued along the coast to the Pentire headland where I made one final pit stop to see my friend Tara at the Lewinnick Lodge, the best hotel in Newquay by a long shot, tucked away far from the hectic rowdy nights of town. Tara was busy helping guests when I stopped by, so instead I sat for a few minutes on the terrace and finished the rest of the water I'd been carrying, my smile nearly touching my ears.

The final push of the day was to get across the Gannel and then south past Perranporth to Porthtowan. But my cleverly thought-out Gannel crossing didn't exactly go to plan. Up high on the Pentire headland, I pushed my way through thick bushes to reach the rocks leading down to the beach. Pristine yellow sand for a quarter of a mile, and then back up to join the coast path. The only problem was, it wasn't quite low tide, and the Gannel was still very much a river. Andy came down with me equipped for plan B, with flip-flops and spare socks for the wading option. Unfortunately the water was more like nipple-deep instead of ankle-deep. It was only around 15 metres across but enough to soak me to the bones. My back-up plan, formed on the spot, was a bit ridiculous, but it would save us a lot of hassle. Had I turned back and run all the way up the Gannel into town and back along the road, as per the original plan, I would be adding many more unnecessary miles to my day. And because I was running to specific points until we reached Eden, it was much simpler to stay on track.

The saving grace, or should I say Greg, was a lifeguard with a life-saving board. He was doing his duty, keeping watch on swimmers and surfers, but kindly took time out of his day to help me across. He stood waist-deep in the Gannel while I crouched on all fours on his board with him pushing me across. I was convinced I'd end up wet. I didn't. Bone dry. Miraculously, not only did I make it over the Gannel without incident (with Andy doubling back to grab the van), but I arrived at the proposed finish point at exactly the 40-mile distance we had hoped for. Not bad. We had to have a bit of luck, I suppose, and Andy's expert mapping skills.

Towards the end of the day, I drive past a field, where each of three consecutive telegraph poles has a buzzard perched on top of it. This strikes me as unusual, until I realize that they are waiting for the combine harvester working its way up and down the field to flush out field voles and other delicious pre-sliced mammals. It's a reminder of just how long we've been on the road now. When we set off, these fields would have been bare furrows, and now it's harvest season.

Nick ends his run for the day and, remarkably, despite all the deviations and route changes, he hits exactly 40 miles at the exact end point I mapped him to on my route – possibly the first time it's happened that way on the entire trip. Unbelievable. We park in a small National Trust car park, where I rearrange some long grass to hide the 'No Camping' sign.

As I began my 124th day we had just a tad over 200 miles to go. I would be setting out to run to the end of the country. Finally, Land's End was just 40 miles away.

With my legs up, draining away the last of what I still thought of as my overnight stagnant blood, I had my usual bagel and cup of tea. I was more tired than I had been on most mornings of late, and the weather was similarly moody, drizzly and grey. I shut my eyes for just another couple of minutes before having to ready myself, but as my eyelids shut there was a knock at the door. It was a chap by the name of James. We'd not met before but we'd shared a few messages on social media, and I'd been expecting him at some point. I squeezed on yesterday's damp sweaty gear, just like always, and stepped out to meet him. The day began. Off we ran.

James was easy company and a good runner too, training for his first ultra, so we chatted away the rainy miles talking running, adventures and nutrition. James is a nutritionist with a lot of experience, specializing in gut microbes. I discussed my terrible diet with him and offered up the question of what would happen if I did the same journey only eating McDonald's. My diet wasn't far off that, and James seemed to think it would be a bad idea. I agreed enough not to try it.

Each of the coves we passed, each roadside tuft of grass, every drop of rain and every windy gust felt more and more Cornish as we got deeper and deeper into the county. Hayle, St Ives, St Just, Sennen Cove. Cornwall really is a masterpiece of natural beauty. Every inch of it was now crawling with tourists, even in the rain. But we didn't care, we were in our bubble, and I was just days away now.

With low visibility in the dreary weather, we were denied any coastal views, but we'd had a fair few over the last few weeks so I just got my head down, chatting away the rain. Having had yet more kind runners join us, they dropped off after about 10 miles. There was nothing else for us to do but plough on to the end of the country. Eventually, having covered 30 miles, the cloud finally lifted a little. Rounding a bend, up over the brow of a hill, I suddenly had a distant view of Land's End and, very faintly, the Scilly Isles beyond.

After the seemingly endless slog north, John O'Groats had felt like it would never come. Land's End felt like it had arrived too suddenly. By complete chance, it had taken us sixty-two days to get to John O'Groats, and it had taken us exactly sixty-two days to get from there to Land's End too. Spooky. And we hadn't even planned it that way, much. The journey back down had been dealt with more swiftly than the injury-stricken trek up to John O'Groats, despite the mileage for the second leg being higher. It somehow just didn't feel like we'd had to do enough to reach the lower extremity, maybe because there'd been so many distractions as we'd got into a rhythm, and we'd obviously institutionalized ourselves to the grind of big mileage.

With the weather becoming almost pleasant, we delayed and enjoyed the final miles to the signpost – the same signpost that the one in John O'Groats had been pointing to all those days ago. This one was pointing back north, to a place I had no intention of visiting again soon. James and I ran along the A30, hugging the side of the road, expecting cars to come flying over the brow of the hill at any moment.

The country road turned into a large car park, with fluorescent jacket-wearing attendants. Had someone told me the place had been designed by children as part of a school project, I'd have believed them. It could have very easily been left alone, but instead it was a commercialized mess. Hot dog stands, burger hatches and doughnut sellers made the already fake courtyard area feel like a cross between a theme park and an elaborate Methodist chapel. It could have been a simple gem of a spot, but reaching Land's End was a little disappointing. However, once we'd sat down on a rickety bench with a bottle of Nosecco (the non-boozy stuff) and some disappointing hot dogs, we soon had smiles on our faces. James had only joined us for the day, but he did well, and was still fresh at the end, great company too. I think he got a good taste of a day in the life of Run Britain, bar the Nosecco. We don't have that every day.

While the others sat and chatted, James and I, still sweaty and getting a little cold, walked a few hundred metres back to the van through the car park, past gangs of tourists, to retrieve jackets as the evening turned to dusk.

Having tried a few hours earlier to grab a photo of the Land's End signpost but given up thanks to a long queue of people, we got our shots in the end, some of which are my favourites from the trip. I was draped in the Union flag with my scruffy gear on and my now longish hair stuck to my forehead with sweat (and possibly Nosecco after the obligatory shake-and-spray celebration at having reached this far). The photos weren't good, I look terrible actually, but that was kind of the point.

We had one last conundrum to solve before disappearing to our beds. James had been a brilliant running partner for the day, but he was now 40 miles from his car with no way to get back. He knew the deal. He knew we weren't taking him because we still had to prioritize sleep. And so I suggested hitch-hiking, explaining the tale of Dan being picked up by the first van that came past. With that, James stood up from the bench, a little achy and wrapped in a spare puffa, turned around and asked the nearest person to him for a lift. Initially the chap looked at us with some concern, wondering if we were a bunch of youths having him on. We politely explained what we were doing and his uneasy face turned to a smile – he was heading James's way. With that, he paused and went to speak to his wife. Ten minutes later he reappeared and said yes. James wasn't murdered by them, and got back safely.

Having found a little campsite down the road from the Land's End monstrosity, we woke on time on day 125 with another milestone ahead of us: Lizard Point, the southernmost point of mainland Britain. Lizard Point looks out over hundreds of shipwrecks, all buried beneath the waters of the busiest shipping lane in the world. If you're lucky, you may see a dolphin or three. We didn't see ships or dolphins, just ocean and mist. This being Cornwall, rain filled the air as if it was appearing rather than falling. The morning was cold and soggy as I stepped out once again. It was made much less appealing by a fourth month in the same manky clothes. The bonus, though: guess what I had for breakfast? Yes, of course, it was a bagel.

Now that we were so close to the end of this journey we were all starting to think about the things we'd miss and the bits we wouldn't. I think we all agreed that having hot running water, or just running water, would be top of the list of new pleasures, plus a day in one place, where the 'to do' list was blank. Having prolonged this discussion for a while, hoping the mist would bugger off, we realized everything we were experiencing we would probably want back as soon as it was gone. I had a feeling, though, that Andy wouldn't miss washing my pants, or having to drive:

> *On a quiet lane, I encounter some more Cornish traffic, in the form of some geese that seem very reluctant to move. It reminds me of when I lived in the south-west and the traffic reports at the end of the morning news mostly just told you what type of livestock had escaped on to which road.*
>
> *Nick gets on the coast path at Mousehole, and from here he is able to run a fairly straightforward and relatively easy few miles into Penzance, a town which, among all the quintessential Cornishness, looks like it's been lifted and dropped here from somewhere on the east coast. Everywhere there are signs for pirate-related ... everything. After all the small towns, it is a useful place to stop though, and once Nick's had some food and drink, I head for Sainsbury's for what I hope are enough essentials to see us through to the end. After four months, it's a funny feeling knowing we now have enough fuel, food and water to complete the expedition.*

The easy few miles along the coast path were simple with no issues. Mousehole to Penzance and onward. The fine rain was still falling, so I sucked it up and got on with it. I had a compass milestone to tick off. From Penzance to St Michael's Mount I was just hugging the coast as usual, but now running directly east. I was heading straight for the finish line – not for long, but enough to get a whiff.

From there to Porthleven and down to Lizard, the coast path continued. There were fewer and fewer people around, and so I was alone in my head with nobody to distract me. Andy and I had a rare hour apart while Nikki was ahead scouting sleeping spots and snatching some time to walk Poppy. Andy had left me to complete the basic 'no navigation required' coast path, while he went to pick up some essentials from the sports nutrition store (Sainsbury's). As well as human fuel, he popped some in the van too – the last fill before the finish, the last trip to restock bagels, the last few bottles of water. We really were nearly there.

The 40 miles finished, but I wasn't quite where I needed to be. The coast path had caused a slight diversion, or perhaps I took a wrong turn, we never did get to the bottom of it. Andy was expecting me to run past him at the entrance to a small visitors car park for Lizard Point. I'd missed him somehow and was already there waiting. Being in Cornwall, we were back experiencing the signal blackouts of the early days, and so I wandered around till I found him. I covered 43 miles in the end.

Having found Andy, we set off down to the marker stone on the floor just before the cliff slopes away down to the sea. We had now made it to the most southerly point of mainland Britain. What a milestone. About ten people were milling around with us, taking photos. We stood and stared as all men should from time to time, standing together but enjoying our thinking time alone, and we were content to move on, having ticked off the final compass point. After a pat on the back from Andy and a shared expression of respect and thanks, we headed to the van and went in search of pizza. A sports pizza, of course. The foghorn over the shipping lane continued all night – a sign it was likely to be the same weather tomorrow.

Day 126 – just three days to go. Three is the magic number. I woke feeling ready for anything. Well, I woke up tired, and then psyched myself up for it. That's about as enthusiastic as I got now.

My body was looking pretty frail. Standing on the scales, I learnt I'd lost 10 kilos and my body fat had dropped down to 3.5 per cent. Looking at me, I was mostly just skin and bone. Ribs were pushing through my sides and my cheekbones poked against the skin of my face. I didn't quite look dangerously ill, and I didn't feel it, but there was no doubt that I was a lean mean farting machine as I plodded through the morning. Maybe that's where all the weight went.

With the lanes of this remote part of Cornwall even smaller than usual, the van was having trouble fitting down most of them, the ferns slapping its sides, brambles leaving their marks. This was more of a problem when it came to Cornwall's narrow old stone bridges. It was important that I stuck to the route, so while Andy would have to deviate a lot, I'd carry on as mapped. Every few miles I'd stumble across a tiny hamlet by the water's edge, a few streams, about four cottages, and nothing but tiny overgrown roads. Meanwhile, Andy would be busy doing a nine-point turn on a steep hill.

I ran through to Coverack while Andy skirted around to find a suitable spot to pick up my trail again. By the time I got to him, he was well and truly over the Cornish lanes. Hazy memories of days 2 and 3, with Andy dashing around, came flooding back to me. To Andy also. It's beautiful here, but not the place for a big van, and he made the most of having to drive around it.

The remoteness of the smaller Cornish resorts means that the ones I get to early in the day are quiet, and with Nick following a stretch of coast path into Coverack, happy to run unsupported for a few miles, I have the rare luxury of an hour to myself on the edge of a deserted town, with nothing to do but get a coffee, read a book and look at the view. Will this be what it's like when I return to civilian life?

When Nick arrives, he's not feeling great, so as usual we target the prime suspect, low blood sugar, with a can of Coke. For long-term health it's not a great solution, but for the next three days we're both happy to go for any quick fix that will keep him on his feet. Having been anticipating the final stages for so long, psychologically these few days will feel like they'll never end, and I'm relieved that Nick is running shorter distances for this last week, which will take the edge off the mental challenge as well as the physical slog. By the afternoon, he's feeling a lot stronger, which is a good thing, as this close to the finish he has plenty of admin to take care of while running, making it a slow but productive end to his day's running.

For the record, I too wouldn't suggest Coke as the fix for prolonged endurance challenges. That would be mental. But it has its emergency uses when it's required. When I met up with Andy I had the low-blood-sugar shakes, my hands trembling as my brain screamed at me to eat. We deployed the sports cola. Full-fat, red-canned Coca-Cola, the second best black nectar on the planet. First, of course, Marmite.

Andy was right. Having been anticipating the final stages for so long, psychologically these few days felt like they were never-ending. My mind had already calibrated running to the shorter 40-mile distances, and the thought of running more shocked me. No thanks. A sign of how willing my mind was to stop the 47s.

Being in the final days, I attended to masses of social media requirements and finalized the finish line plans, making calls while running throughout a slow but productive day. I'd spent four or five hours on the phone without noticing.

Nikki's overnight parking spot skills are award-winning. We joined her in Falmouth, parked right next to the water on the promenade above a cluster of beach huts on the thin crescent of Castle Beach. The weather hadn't improved. But I now had fewer than 80 miles to run. We were now more or less certain I'd be crossing the line. But none of us said anything out loud. We turned out the light and waited for dawn to ring the bell on the final lap.

11

Closing the Loop

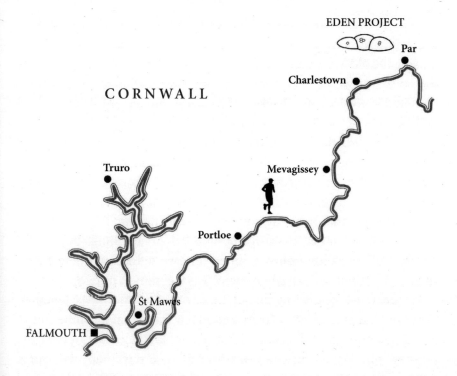

EDEN PROJECT

Par

Charlestown

CORNWALL

Truro

Mevagissey

Portloe

St Mawes

FALMOUTH

Day 127 – 41.12 miles – 4,146ft elevation
Falmouth to St Mawes
The final forty-eight hours

At 6 a.m., my alarm sounded, triggering a feeling of Christmas Eve. Butterflies, eagerness, excitable apprehension. Parked on Cliff Road outside the old Victorian chateau-style Falmouth Hotel, I pushed back the covers, yawning and stretching, my face unshaven with droopy bags under my eyes, my cheeks, wrists, chest and legs all shrunken and skeletal. The kettle started whistling.

I sat up with the duvet over my legs, my feet firmly on the floor, slowly beginning to make myself feel more alive. I had a rare jam bagel for my penultimate day, Andy passing me a tea before opening the window to a cold morning with mist lying flat on the sea. Andy and I went about our habitual morning routine, boxed into our tiny van full of four-month-old mess. It wasn't fly-infested or anything, but it was untidy. Still, as Andy rightly pointed out, we did know where everything was. 'It's in the van somewhere' was a common phrase.

We knew we needed to savour these ordinary moments together. We didn't have many left. I spent a good few miles that morning thinking about how much Nikki and Andy had sacrificed to support the journey, physically and emotionally. All these days had, without a doubt, dented all of us in some way. No matter how much we'd enjoyed it, we were certainly ready for it to be over. We were all running on empty.

Day 127 was one of the most navigationally complicated of the whole trip. From Falmouth, our resting place for the evening needed to be St Mawes, which from where we were as the crow flies was a couple of miles via the ferry crossing. To get the perfect mileage, though, meant going around the massive harbour complex, a decision we'd built into our mapping a few days ago that also removed any possible ferry complications this close to the finish. We didn't want any last-minute changes on the final two days, such as the ferry not operating or ferry times not matching up. And so we'd planned with this in mind. We would run around.

The Carrick Roads is the series of estuaries and waterways that make up Falmouth Harbour, with Pendennis Castle on the headland on the Falmouth side looking across to St Mawes Castle – the gate-keepers to this waterway. We, however, would be crossing the road bridge in Truro, north of the harbour, just over 20 miles into the run.

After 20 miles of country lanes we're on the edge of Truro, the final city of the expedition, which has one last traffic horror for us. In a typically Cornish incident, a lorry has shed its load of giant straw bales on one of the busiest roundabouts in the city, and while Nick is able to keep running as planned, I take a different route to try and get through another way. Fortunately, before I get to the other road I was planning to use, Nick has called to let me know not to even attempt it, as the diverted traffic from the centre has now ground to a complete halt caused by a low bridge, and I'm able to turn off before getting snarled up in a jam that would have cost me at least an hour. It's one of a few occasions we've had on the trip where Nick has been able to direct me on to the best routes, rather than vice versa.

Twenty or so runners had joined and dropped off, as and when they needed to, by about midday. I was chatting as usual but conscious that my phone was beginning to buzz more often. By the end of the day I'd had over three hundred WhatsApp messages, some from friends and family wishing me luck for the final day, most from the extended team of volunteers who had jumped in to help make the finish line as simple as possible. We were keen to have people there of course, but the venue was keen to ensure everyone was in the right place. As much as the Eden Project did a great job of hosting us, I was having to deal with the red tape and logistics of running a large group of people through the already big groups of people at Eden. Finalizing every detail took time.

We also had the little issue of two finish lines. I ran from Eden down to my first section of coast on the first day. And so the loop would technically be completed down at Par Sands Beach, the place where I'd picked up the coast path. It seemed sensible, then, to gather as many supporters as possible on the beach. We'd celebrate the pre-finish line there and, being a public beach, anyone could turn up. From there, runners and supporters would jog the last few miles back up the final hill into Eden and run in together. We agreed that things like access passes would not be needed.

By the end of day 127 all this admin had fried my brain, but I was keen for the last day to be one of jubilation, sort of like a running party all the way to the end. We prayed for good weather.

We nestled down for the night on the headland near St Mawes, just south of where I would set off tomorrow. In another classically Run Britain-style car park, we had one final evening together. On our bit of gravel, off to the side of the road, under the boughs of trees in full summer foliage, we reminisced, and we waited for a special arrival.

About three years earlier, Nikki and I had taken our van on a little Cornish trip to St Ives around New Year time. We arrived late and parked our big van in a very small car park overlooking the water. In the morning, we slid open our door to see another van, its owner getting ready to go for a dip in the sea. We smiled and said the obligatory good mornings. As it happened, he was also called Nick, and he turned out to be a fantastic photographer. If you have a chance to look up a short film called *Dawn Days* by Nick Pumphrey, about sea swimming and finding peace, you'll see what Nick is all about. He's connected to nature and the outdoors in the most authentic way I've ever seen in someone. The sense of being present in any given moment oozes from him. A balanced soul. A few weeks out from Eden I called him and asked if he could be around for the final day. He and his mate James, aka Warby, who is also a great photographer and videographer, would be our honorary camera crew for the finale.

It had grown dark by the time Nick arrived in his blue VW. We had a cuppa and discussed the main feelings I'd like to capture for the final day, ahead of an early night ahead of an early start. Nick was happy with his responsibilities, and Warby would be turning up at about 5 a.m., having made a long drive to be here. Tomorrow, after some early morning photos, I'd run at 6.30 a.m. on the dot, making sure I stuck to the route to hit both finish lines at the arranged times.

As I fell asleep, I couldn't quite believe I only had one day left. The end of the adventure. How did I feel about the experience? Had it been what I'd imagined? My head whirled with thoughts as I drifted off. Little did I know then that I would never again be able to have a conversation involving any beach or stretch of coastline around Britain without waves of goosebumps and floods of memories filling my mind. The emotions ran deep. When speaking about individual moments, or when someone mentions the name of a beach they're going to on holiday, I see the faces of the people who ran with me, I remember the weather, I recall how my toes felt, how I perceived the team to be feeling. Every tiny piece of the puzzle became so mentally engrained that ever since I have been covered with mixed emotions every time I recall any of the Run Britain days.

Andy was in a reflective mood too:

Nick is now on the cusp of completing a truly remarkable endurance feat, and we can finally relax in the knowledge that, for the first time, we know he will make it. For the first time in 127 days, I have no doubts about him being able to reach the finish line. He now has just 30 miles left to run, a distance he can crawl if he has to. Tomorrow, first and foremost, will be a party day.

Day 128 – 37.64 miles – 4,295ft elevation
St Mawes to the Eden Project, St Austell
Reaching Eden

So I started the day with exactly 30 miles left to run. I would then have completed the equivalent distance of two hundred marathons covering an entire lap of the country. A country I'd fallen in love with all over again.

The alarm sounded at 4.30. I was as groggy and sleepy-faced as ever, my limbs feeling just as achy and just as unwilling. I lay in bed for what was supposed to be a thirty-minute snooze to ready myself. It being the last day, my mind had me on my feet in about two minutes. I wanted to run. I actually wanted to run today.

On the same enamel plate, with the same now cracked and stained maroon mug, Andy passed me my bagel and cuppa. We joked about what bagels were going to signify for us once the trip was done. Those last few moments in the van that morning were so precious. We all knew it. We wanted it done, but in achieving the goal the little family we'd formed would be broken up.

I'd only been awake about ten minutes and was sitting in my boxers chomping down on my first bite of bagel when Nick and Warby appeared. We all greeted Warby warmly. For a change we all had smiles on our faces and bubbled with excitable energy. I, of course, looked a state, though. My toes were black and blue with nails missing, and my hair was greasy and matted, sticking up like a trampy peacock. And there was of course the sight of my skeleton appearing to try and escape through my skin. Barring a little muscle around my legs – not much, but a little – I really was just skin and bone. As I pushed my feet into my socks, another piece of flaky foot skin peeled off to join the rest of the mess on the floor. Nick and Warby got a few gritty early morning shots.

At 6.28 a.m., I stepped out of the cramped little van one last time.

I was wearing all the usual faded, torn and tatty clothes (a mix of gifted clothing), my compressions, shoes and socks now with holes in, and had with me my usual earphones which we'd been charging religiously, and my phone of course, for photos. Everything was on its last legs.

As I ran off down the single-track road with Nick and Warby shuttling ahead to get good vantage points, I heard the thud of the van door closing, then the other one, and then, after a few seconds, each tired engine started up, breaking the calmness of the morning. Amazingly, Mother Nature was treating us to a final day of sunshine.

The first couple of miles of the day were the last time during Run Britain that I ran on my own. About twenty minutes of reflection. I had a lump in my throat and a few tears. The overwhelming feeling wasn't one of accomplishment, it was about friendship and gratitude. I felt like the luckiest person alive. Andy and Nikki had actually stuck with me the entire time. We'd made it. I could crawl backwards if I had to from here. We had done it.

My internal meanderings were interrupted by a few cars passing, and then Nick and Warby snapping away. And then shortly after that runners started to appear and a day of chatting, laughter and sunshine began as we weaved our way towards the finish.

From St Mawes to the Eden Project, direct, would only have been about 15 miles, but for me and now a merry bunch of multicoloured smiling runners, sticking to the coast was the name of the game, which meant Andy and I having one last dance of navigation, driving and directions, with WhatsApp messages telling me which tiny back lanes he was unable to get down and where I'd see him next, relayed to Nick and Warby. They of course needed to be ahead in the right spots to get the shots they were after. I wanted the photos to sum up the journey as a whole. To show the admin, the faff with the van, Andy supporting, Nikki and Poppy, the landscapes, the weather, my emotions, and of course all the runners who had taken on these miles with me.

By the time I reached marathon distance they'd captured hundreds of beautiful shots: moments of embrace among friends reuniting, new faces joining us, shared team ice creams, and the now familiar sight of me and Andy discussing the route at the van window, huge smiles on our faces, laughing as we held our phones in front of us looking at the map. Both of us looked a state, but we were happy. It was fitting, too, that we'd actually taken a wrong turn and were trying to get back on track when the photo was taken.

Throughout the day, from as early as 7 a.m., people had been shouting from their doorsteps, cheering me on as I ran past. Runners came out to support in big groups for small sections and dropped off when new groups arrived. Families holidaying in the area beeped their horns as they drove past, either aware of what we were doing or just realizing that we were obviously doing something special. Kids waited patiently at the side of the road with handmade cardboard signs with 'Go Nick' and 'Well done Nick' in big bright lettering. Looking back at the final day's photos, there were so many cheery faces. Heidi, Dan, Dani, Gary and Pop-up Gary, among many others, made the effort to travel from all corners of the country to run the last few miles in with me. These are people who are still friends today. Good people making the effort to support me. I owe them all so much; they made the final miles of my 5,250 so special.

At around 28 miles, parked up at the end of Duporth Road in Charlestown, Nick stops at the van for what will be his final lean on the driver's door for a few swigs of water. While I drive ahead and park up to join him on foot for the last couple of miles, Nick will follow the seafront and beaches all the way to Par, with his group of local runners able to provide directions if needed. Somewhere along this final stretch of coast, Nick will pass the magic number: 5,250 miles. Two hundred marathons. Plus a bit for ferries.

By 32 miles, having now completed the official distance while basking in sunshine and friendly chatter for hours, we had got within a mile of Par Sands Beach, where I'd officially close the loop. We slowed down a little as we neared the beach. I think everyone thought I was mad not to race towards the finish line, but I was keen to get there at the right time so that the arrangements when we got to Eden would all work as planned. And there was a little part of me that simply didn't want it to be over.

For the final stretch to the beach our group of about twenty runners was joined by even more folk from the local running club in St Austell. We all got a photo together by the first St Austell signpost we saw, obviously signalling that the end was near.

Andy had parked up and run back to join us to share the final miles together. He handed me the Run Britain-branded Union flag and came prepared as always with water and a bag of supplies in case I needed anything. We exchanged a brief look of 'This is it, we did it!' and carried on.

Running along the beach to the finish line at Par was as close to a *Chariots of Fire* moment as I could have asked for. Nick and Warby darted around taking photos, while across the 200 metres of sand between me and the finish line I could hear the large gathering of friends, family and runners cheering as we approached.

I ran under the finish line banner with clapping and smiles all round to complete my lap of the British coast. I was standing on sand I'd run through back on that bitterly cold morning in April. Having hugged my parents, my brother, Andy's parents, Nikki, and more people than I can remember, and feeling very emotional, we regrouped and made one last 3-mile push to the final finish line. The real party would begin when we made it to Eden.

Retracing the steps I'd made all those months ago, and with the final hill slowing us down nicely, we hit Eden bang on time. I'd been constantly updating Danny and Nicole of our whereabouts. Andy and everyone in vehicles had gone ahead to park up and line this second, proper finish:

In the complicated fruit-themed car park complex of the Eden Project, I park up and am about to leap out of the van to make sure I get down to the finish line in time when it suddenly occurs to me that this is it – the end of Run Britain for our support. Our little Council Van has been the butt of many jokes, but this plucky little camper has never put a foot wrong, never let us down, and without it the expedition would simply not have been possible. I pause for a few seconds and give the steering wheel an affectionate pat. Nikki, in her infinite patience, thoughtfulness and resourcefulness, has been absolutely indispensable. I've perfected toasting bagels. But the unsung hero of the Run Britain team has been the Council Van. The old girl deserves a medal.

With my Union flag draped over my shoulders and a mass of runners in tow, we turned left into the gates of Eden and down the switchback road into the basin with the huge domes in the background. The walkway was lined with people clapping and the finish area full of cheering, smiling faces.

I crossed the line and immediately hugged Andy and Nikki. A few photos, a few words of thanks to the runners who'd helped me to the line, and without really realizing it I was thrust straight into interviews with various camera crews. With my friend Jeremy playing music and stacks of pizzas arriving for everyone to tuck into, I could hardly believe we had finally done it.

The last hours of the day were a total blur of happy energy. Over an evening meal in the pub I was joined by about fifteen of the closest team, family and friends. The mood was high. I thanked them all again, and tried my best to express my gratitude to Andy and Nikki for their tireless support. I could tell the three of us were thinking the same thing, though. What were we going to do now? We were going to miss it.

After 5,250 miles, after eighteen gruelling, gritty, sweaty, exhausting weeks of slowly drawing an outline around mainland Britain with his feet, this extraordinary, intense, wonderful, brutal, joyous, epic journey is finally over, and the celebrations can begin.

What Nick has achieved is truly astonishing: Run Britain is comfortably the fastest ever on-foot circumnavigation of Britain. Land's End to John O'Groats. Twice. The long way. In 128 days.

It was a seemingly impossible challenge that has relied on the efforts of a great team, but which has, ultimately, only been made possible by the unwavering self-belief of a thin man who dreams big.

The 2003 edition of Lonely Planet Britain *described it as 'quite simply the most beautiful island on earth'. I couldn't agree more.*

This has been the best job I've ever had.

It was late by the time we'd changed, eaten and got back to the little Premier Inn we'd stayed in at the start. The following morning we spent a few hours cleaning the vans and generally feeling weird and unsettled not to be in the routine. The real feelings of joy and accomplishment would, we found out, come later, once we'd had a chance to absorb everything. Because we were still in mission mode. It was hard to turn off after so long.

Most friends and family left by midday, until it was just Andy, Nikki and me. The three of us again. Then Andy was off. He was sharing a lift back and couldn't stick around any longer. I hugged him goodbye. Nikki too. Waving him off felt wrong. My parents later came by to pick up the van and drive it back – the first time Andy wasn't behind the wheel in over four months. It was a surreal feeling. My mind couldn't keep up with the fact that the adventure was over.

Nikki and I drove back that evening to my parents' place to declutter and finally wash, sort and begin prep for our birthday week – mine on 26 August, Nikki's on the 27th and Andy's on the 28th. Andy spent his with loved ones, having not seen them for a long time. Normal life had resumed.

Nikki and I spent our birthdays in Newquay together, treating ourselves to a nice hotel, so I could have baths twice a day and eat myself healthy again. From the moment I stepped out to run on that final day, I was an emotional wreck for about two weeks. I was of course pleased to have finished, who wouldn't have been? But Nikki and I missed Andy, we had to readjust to real life again, and I kept experiencing bouts of gratitude for the boundless help from so many good people, but guilt too, that I'd made people suffer to achieve something I had wanted to accomplish. My mind and body were frail and I needed time to process everything.

Eleven and a half million steps, covering a total of 5,257.71 miles, with over 300,000 feet of elevation, passing through over four thousand towns, villages and cities, past every beach in Britain, through all types of weather imaginable, shared with over six thousand runners and supporters, and all with Andy, Nikki and Poppy by my side. A journey that will bond us for the rest of our lives.

And, of course, we won't be stopping there.

Postscript

Writing these final words, I'm hunched over my laptop in the van. Light low, papers, Post-its, photos and half-finished cold cups of tea lie strewn around. Poppy's patiently waiting for me to be done and to get her exercise routine back. I've neglected her somewhat during these last months writing this book.

The thing about telling stories about real life events is that you're accessing your memory all the time. I have lived this journey all over again, revisiting photos, diary entries, GPS data and phone exchanges. I've felt our struggles, I've laughed over silly things, and I've been moved to tears. I feel grateful, joyful and sad all at once. I'm filled with deep love and a sense of loss for the journey. What the three of us achieved, with the help of many others, will stay with us for ever.

I hope as you read these pages that you gleaned a sense of the intense effort required to continue that same forward motion, day in, day out, for the 128 days we were on the road. And not just by me and my legs, but by those around me. I also hope you'll see what we achieved as a window into how bright, full and magical life can be if you spend just a short time outside the comfort zone, living life differently. We all have a tiny fraction of time on the planet, and it is important to use it wisely. Running around Britain made me feel truly alive.

My friendship with Andy is something that I will never allow myself to take for granted. He gave a chunk of his life to enable me to pursue a goal. Not just a few hours putting up a shelf or driving me to the airport like many good friends do. Andy gave four long intense months. Months where he suffered too. I could never repay him for that kindness. As for Nikki, as I mentioned earlier, she and I went our separate ways a few months after the journey finished. I'm glad to say we are still good friends and can look back on these times fondly. Just as with Andy, I am indebted to her kindness and support for ever. She went above and beyond what most partners would and gave months of her life to help me achieve my goals. The three of us share a special bond. And let's not forget Poppy either.

Our journey around Britain gave me a fresh appreciation for the island I call home. What I'd thought of as 'just Britain' before setting off on this journey couldn't have been further from the truth. Our little island holds treasures that can only be found by looking. The British coastline is packed with rich history, beautiful people and a wonderful array of communities, cultures and local identities, each of them unique and fascinating. Away from the beaten path, this green and pleasant land, though windier and hillier than I would have liked, hosts an astonishing diversity of wildlife. The natural landscape of our little island is truly awe-inspiring. I urge you to explore it.

If Run Britain has confirmed one thing for me, it is the value of stepping into the unknown and basking in the flood of opportunities that can offer. Life is thundering past us right now. It is not a spectator sport. We have to grab on and hold tight. We have to take risks, however daunting and uncomfortable they may seem, in order to grow.

Just like the butterfly and its chrysalis, you must first struggle in order to live.

Acknowledgements

Attempting to acknowledge everyone individually is impossible – there are just too many names to remember – so I'd simply like to whole-heartedly thank all who touched this expedition in any way, big or small. From shouts of encouragement from car windows or doorsteps, and small acts of kindness and generosity, to the selfless support of my team, family and friends, the inner circle of this endeavour.

I am particularly indebted to Andy Swain, Nikki Tombs, Yasmin Li, Danny Ryan, Nicole Hupen-Johnson and Amy Bullock, and to the brands who sponsored the challenge: Bremont, Supersapiens, Oofos, MyoMaster, Freetrain, Pooch and Mutt, Fit Kit, Berczy, Jaybird, Fractel, Gold Standard, Science In Sport, Airofit, Gel-Pak, SunGod, Better You, Compeed and TentBox.

For their beautiful photography, and capturing the reality of the journey on camera, my thanks to Nikki Tombs, Jack Anstey, Sarah Afiqah Rogers and Hugh Hastings.

To all the runners who shared footsteps with me – this journey was transformed by your energy and kindness. I appreciated your time and company more than you will ever know.

And my eternal thanks for the thousands of donations in support of the 196 Foundation.

Run Britain in Numbers

5,257 miles run
300,000 feet of total elevation
1,200 running hours
640,000 calories burnt
760+ litres of water consumed
15 pairs of trainers worn out
2 broken bones
12 kilogrammes of weight lost
9 showers
40 wild toilet stops
1 wedding
61 counties crossed
4,000 hamlets, villages, towns and cities run through
11,000+ support-van miles
3,500+ runners and supporters
4,000+ new donations to the 196 Foundation

Andy's Wildlife Collection

Birds

Arctic skua
Avocet
Barn owl
Barn swallow
Black guillemot
Black swan
Blackbird
Blackcap
Black-headed gull
Black-tailed godwit
Blue tit
Brent goose
Bullfinch
Canada goose
Carrion crow
Cetti's warbler
Chaffinch
Chiffchaff
Chough
Coal tit
Collared dove
Common buzzard
Common gull
Common sandpiper
Common tern
Coot
Cormorant
Corn bunting
Cuckoo
Curlew
Dipper
Dunlin
Dunnock
Egyptian goose
Eider
Feral pigeon
Fulmar
Gadwall
Gannet
Goldcrest
Golden plover
Goldfinch
Goosander
Great black-backed gull
Great crested grebe
Great northern loon
Great skua
Great spotted woodpecker
Great tit
Green sandpiper
Green woodpecker
Greenfinch
Greenshank
Grey partridge
Grey plover
Greylag goose
Guillemot
Herring gull
Hobby
Hooded crow
House martin
House sparrow
Jackdaw
Jay
Kestrel
Kittiwake
Lapwing
Lesser black-backed gull
Linnet
Little egret

Little grebe
Little tern
Long-tailed tit
Magpie
Mallard
Manx shearwater
Marsh harrier
Meadow pipit
Mistle thrush
Moorhen
Mute swan
Osprey
Oystercatcher
Peregrine falcon
Pheasant
Pied wagtail
Pochard
Puffin
Raven
Razorbill
Red kite
Red-breasted
merganser
Redhshank
Redpoll
Reed bunting
Reed warbler
Ringed plover
Robin
Rock dove
Rock pipit
Rook
Sand martin
Sanderling
Sandwich tern
Sedge warbler

Shag
Shelduck
Shoveler
Siskin
Skylark
Snipe
Song thrush
Sparrowhawk
Spoonbill
Spotted flycatcher
Starling
Stock dove
Stonechat
Swift
Tawny owl
Teal
Tree pipit
Tree sparrow
Treecreeper
Tufted duck
Turnstone
Twite
Wheatear
Whinchat
White-tailed eagle
Whooper swan
Willow warbler
Wood pigeon
Wren
Yellow wagtail
Yellowhammer

Mammals
Red deer
Roe deer

Muntjac deer
Red fox
Common shrew
Pygmy shrew
Field vole
House mouse
Brown rat
Wood mouse
Polecat
Pine marten
Stoat
Otter
Harbour seal
Grey seal
Minke whale
Red squirrel
Grey squirrel
Pipistrelle bat
Daubenton's bat
Hedgehog
Rabbit
Brown hare

Amphibians
Common toad
Common frog
Palmate newt
Smooth newt

Reptiles
Adder
Common lizard

ABOUT THE AUTHOR

Nick Butter is an endurance runner, adventurer and motivational speaker. He lives in Newquay.